T0289491

OPTICHANNEL RETAIL. BEYOND THE DIGITAL HYSTERIA

GINO VAN OSSEL

OPTICHANNEL RETAIL

BEYOND THE DIGITAL HYSTERIA

DEVELOP AND IMPLEMENT
A WINNING STRATEGY AS A RETAILER
OR BRAND MANUFACTURER

LANNOO
CAMPUS

This book was originally published as *Retail. De digitale hysterie voorbij*, LannooCampus Publishers, 2018.

D/2019/45/99 – ISBN 978 94 014 5950 1 – NUR 802

Cover design: Gert Degrande | De Witlofcompagnie
Interior design: Wendy De Haes
Translation: Ian Connerty

LannooCampus Publishers is a subsidiary of Lannoo Publishers,
the book and multimedia division of Lannoo Publishers nv.

LannooCampus Publishers
Vaartkom 41   P.O. box 23202
3000 Leuven   1100 DS Amsterdam
Belgium   Netherlands
www.lannoocampus.com

CONTENTS

INTRODUCTION
THE MESSI SYNDROME

'An optimist takes the chance of losing;

a pessimist loses the chance of gaining.'

Hazrat Inayat Khan (Indian musician, writer and philosopher)

'Footballer for FC Barcelona and the Red Devils. And if that's not possible: policeman.' Yes, my youngest son William knows exactly* what he wants to be when he grows up. He is only ten, but I already like his view on life. Dare to dream! Aim for the best you can be and don't let practical objections get in your way! Because in life, you never know what might happen...

While waiting for FC Barcelona to come knocking, he currently plays for Ritterklub, our friendly local football team. But it is clear that several of his teammates also share the same dream. At training, the Barcelona shirt is easily the most popular among the boys – preferably with the name of star player Lionel Messi printed on the back – followed by the Red Devils, the Belgian national team.

As a parent, I try to view reality with a little more level-headedness. In Belgium, roughly 60,000 boys are born each year. From each generation, only five will be good enough to make it into the national team. In other words, one chance in 12,000! And William is lucky that he wasn't born in a bigger and more populous country. With ten times as many births, the chances of a boy to ever play for the German *Mannschaft* are as low as one in 120,000. And for budding Brazilian Neymars, the situation is even worse...

So what about the likelihood of one day being selected for FC Barcelona? To make this particular dream come true, William will be competing with thousands – in fact, tens of thousands – of young footballers from all over the world. With some 75 million boys being born somewhere around the planet each year, he has as much chance of winning the national lottery as he does of ever playing for his favorite team!

---

* In a rapidly changing world, it is perhaps no surprise that my son has now adjusted his ambitions in the weeks between the first and final versions of this manuscript. His Plan B is not longer to be a policeman, but to become a scientist instead.

What Messi, FC Barcelona and the Red Devils are for football, Google, Apple, Facebook and Amazon are for the business world. Entrepreneurs dream that their brainchild will one day develop into an equally successful and highly valued company. Permeated by the spirit of Silicon Valley, start-ups frantically searching for investors are nowadays keen to play the 'profit is highly overrated' card. Their great and most inspirational example is Amazon. In its almost 25 years of existence, the largest webstore in the Western world has made less accumulated profit than Apple in a single quarter. Even so, in 2017 the stock market valued Amazon as being worth roughly 650 billion dollars (give or take a billion or two).[1] This is as much as the combined value of America's five largest retailers.[2] In September 2018, Amazon's market value finally reached a trillion dollars, making it the second company to break through this magical barrier, just a month after Apple. But perhaps Amazon's was the more remarkable achievement. It was made possible thanks to the company's unbelievably high price/earnings ratio of 220 to 1, which is ten times higher than the average of America's five leading retail chains.

THE GREATER FOOL THEORY

The 'greater fool' theory argues that the price of an object is not determined by its intrinsic value, but by the often irrational expectations of buyers. So long as a buyer thinks there is a bigger fool willing to pay an even bigger price for the same object tomorrow, he is prepared to spend an irrationally large sum of money to buy that object today. This theory holds good in particular for real estate, works of art and shares. As a result, this theory accounts for the 'bubbles' that periodically occur – and then burst – in the stock market. Likewise, the valuation of a number of technology companies can only be explained by the theory of the greater fool![3]

Market capitalization of Amazon compared with America's five largest retail chains
(in billions of $). Source: Yahoo Finance

Most dreams turn out to be illusions. The vast majority of digital start-ups
are doomed to failure. Even those who do manage to survive (and perhaps
even thrive) are soon destined to discover that Amazon is playing in a league
of its own. To make matters worse (depending on how you look at it), the five
largest American retailers today all have an average share-price-to-earnings
ratio that is significantly higher than the average technology company quoted
in the American Nasdaq exchange.[4]

The valuation of a company obviously has a lot to do with the future expectations of investors. For traditional retail companies these expectations are highly unfavorable, at least if we can believe what we are told by the media. And there are always new prophets of doom who seem to enjoy adding even more fuel to the fire.

In 2013, for example, Marc Andreessen was already predicting the demise of the brick-and-mortar store.[5] The combination of fixed rental costs and the inefficiency of large stocks of goods would, he contended, prove fatal. Or to use his own words: '*Software eats retail*'.[6] Of course, Marc Andreessen is not just anyone in the business world. As a serial entrepreneur, he was, among other things, one of the co-founders of Netscape. With his investment fund he has backed Twitter, Groupon, Pinterest and Facebook. He also cashed in quite substantially when Microsoft bought Skype for 8.5 billion dollars. Today, he is a member of the board at Facebook, HP and eBay.[7]

In other words, he is someone whose word counts for something. What's more, he didn't just fabricate his predictions out of thin air. There were plenty of indicators. Since 2010, the number of shop closures in the United States has increased dramatically. Sears, once the icon of the American consumer society, has shut down more than half of its stores, before filing for bankruptcy in 2018. J.C. Penney and Macy's have also been badly hit in much the same way. Many of the shopping malls that use these department and general merchandise stores as anchors to attract customers have also been swept away in this tidal wave of closures. It is expected that by 2023 half of today's existing malls will have closed their doors.[8] The website www.deadmalls.com charts this depressing decline in stark detail, by inviting people to share photographs of empty shopping centers.

Moreover, this is not a specifically American phenomenon. There is plenty of bad news in Europe, as well. The number of empty shops in the continent's high streets has reached record proportions. Blokker Holding is selling out, C&A is up for sale and Carrefour is engaged in a worldwide restructuring program...

Given these figures, is it really any surprise that the media is talking about a potential 'retail apocalypse'?[9] Are we indeed heading towards the last days of the physical store?

Of course not! In reality, the doom-and-gloom predictions of the jeremiahs hide a much more nuanced picture:[10]

» A first signal is that in recent years the e-commerce companies have also decided to play at being shopkeepers. How would Marc Andreessen explain that just four years after his gloomy prophecies Amazon has splashed out 13.7 billion dollars to acquire Whole Foods? The Chinese e-commerce giants Alibaba and JD.com are also investing billions in traditional brick-and-mortar stores. In recent times, JD.com has been opening as many as a thousand new neighborhood supermarkets each week. By the end of 2019, they hope to increase that figure to a thousand new stores each day!

   Within the next five years, their ultimate objective is to create a network of a staggering one million stores, mainly in rural areas, where they will be run by franchisees.[11] This reflects an earlier trend already noticeable in the actions of the American online opticians Warby Parker and men's fashion webshop Bonobos, both of whom opened showrooms across the length and breadth of the United States. In the Netherlands, the online consumer electronics retailer Coolblue underlined its belief in physical outlets by opening its XXL stores, which seek to offer customers improved brand and product experiences.

» The glut of vacant shop premises is at its peak in medium-sized towns, where shrinkage in the core shopping area was inevitable. But in the big cities retailers are still queuing up to lease the best premium locations. And while many smaller shopping centers may be closing their doors, crowds in the US are still flocking in droves to the Mall of America.

» Not every sector has been as badly hit by the shift to online. Music, film and gaming have certainly been digitalized (farewell Virgin Megastore and Blockbuster), but builders' merchants and DIY stores have been less affected by the 'irresistible' march of e-commerce: worldwide, only 3% of their turnover has switched to the internet.

» This picture of winners and losers is also reflected in terms of shop size and format. The general warehouses and department stores have lost out heavily to competition from e-commerce. But the discount channel is more than holding its own, as witnessed by the popularity and growth of Lidl, Action and Primark, none of which has a webshop truly worthy of the name. Hypermarkets have been hard hit, but local neighborhood supermarkets have been sprouting up all over the place (also see the box entitled: 'Carrefour: a victim of e-commerce?').

» It is even possible to see winners and losers within a particular format and/or sector. The department stores of De Bijenkorf in the Netherlands are thriving, while the once comparable V&D has gone to the wall. In the United Kingdom, John Lewis continues to win market share, while Debenhams and House of Fraser are struggling desperately to keep their head above water.[12]

» Not every problem is the responsibility of e-commerce. Many retailers are not suffering from online competition, but from the excessively heavy burden of debt they are carrying from the past.[13] As a result, they were already fatally weakened before the online game even started. They didn't (and don't) have the necessary resources to invest in their future. This means that as soon as their turnover is badly under par for two or three consecutive quarters, there is no other real option but to file for bankruptcy. The Dutch Macintosh Retail Group, once the proud owner of Brantano, Scapino, Kwantum and Halfords, was forced to close down simply because it no longer had the money to buy new collections for its stores.

» Last but not least, a number of fundamentally strong retail formats have shown a remarkable resilience to survive and bounce back, even after major restructuring or bankruptcy. The Belgian Brantano and the Dutch Miss Etam have both been successfully reborn under the wings of the FNG fashion group. The Amsterdam-based Hema chain of stores managed to reinvent itself in a manner that has won over the hearts and minds of consumers in many European countries, not just in the shopping streets but also online.

CARREFOUR: A VICTIM OF E-COMMERCE?

As I write these words, the Carrefour group has just announced a major restructuring, which will see the scrapping of thousands of jobs. Social media soon set the general tone for the public response to this announcement: there was a positive deluge of posts blaming e-commerce for the sorry plight of the French distribution giant. 'They'd do better selling out to Amazon' was a comment that appeared more than once in various forms. By extension, this was also taken to mean: the traditional shop is dead.

Is this true? Or is it just another example of digital hysteria?

There is certainly no denying that Carrefour has missed the digital boat. The new CEO Alexandre Bompard has even said as much himself. In fact, Bompard had been brought in nine months earlier specifically in the hope that he could repeat the successful transformation he had implemented at Fnac Darty, the French consumer electronics retailer. In other words, there was already a widespread recognition that a digital overhaul at Carrefour was long overdue.

But the problems go much deeper and are much older than that. The core problem is that Carrefour realizes more than half its turnover from its hypermarkets. Unfortunately, this is a store format that is under severe pressure worldwide. What used to be a customer benefit ('everything under one roof') has now become a liability ('a little bit of everything, but expert in nothing'). Long before the advent of e-commerce, Carrefour was already losing customers hand over fist. People now prefer to buy non-food products – electrical goods, fashion, sports items, etc. – in dedicated specialist stores like MediaMarkt, H&M or Decathlon, which offer a far wider range of choice within their specialization. Similarly, for grocery shopping an increasing number of consumers prefer either the lower prices of the discounters or the convenience of smaller, more local supermarkets – a trend that has been exacerbated by the growth in smaller families and single-person households, who tend to shop more frequently and more impulsively. Why should they make the effort to drive to a hypermarket on the edge of town, when they can find what they want just around the corner and often at an equally low price?

It was partly for these reasons that Carrefour in Belgium carried out a first major reorganization in 2010. Large household appliances and sports equipment were scrapped from the store's product range. Not because of the threat posed by e-commerce, but because of the savage competition experienced from category killers à la MediaMarkt and Decathlon. Back in 2010, there was no e-commerce threat in Belgium. For example, the Dutch bol.com – today the No.2 player in the local e-commerce market – had been launched only months previously and had fewer than 25,000 Belgian customers. Zalando – the current No.3 – only made its entry into the Belgian market a full two years later.[14]

Even so, the reorganization did not achieve its aims. In subsequent years Carrefour in Belgium continued to lose its share of the groceries market to discounters such as Colruyt, Aldi and Lidl. Once again, this evolution had little or nothing to do with the rise of e-commerce, which has remained negligible in the food and drink market. The situation is different in Carrefour's home base in France, where e-groceries now represent 5% of the market, with E. Leclerc as the major winner.

It is true, of course, that in the non-food segment the rapid growth in e-commerce after 2010 has indeed had a serious negative impact on the hypermarkets. Webshops offer more convenience and choice. As a result, consumers are no longer prepared to make the effort to visit distant physical stores that only sell a fraction of the range they can find online. This immediately explains why in Belgium the restructuring of competing hypermarkets like Cora and Makro was inevitable.

Makro, for example, has now closed down its entire multimedia and consumer electronics department, inviting MediaMarkt to open its own stores in Makro premises as a shop-in-a-shop alternative. This underlines how the crisis in Carrefour is not specific to the company in particular, but to the hypermarket model in general.

During the past 20 years, Carrefour has invested heavily to save its hypermarkets. Every so often a new CEO would be appointed and new test stores would be opened, in the hope of finally turning the tide. And when it didn't work, a new CEO and new store concepts would be tried. All these changes created confusion among Carrefour's customers, so that the company's image became less and less clearly defined. By failing to opt for the roll-out of smaller local supermarkets and a properly developed e-commerce platform, the company effectively wasted millions investing in the past rather than in the future.

Is it not correct, then, to talk of digital hysteria when the decline of Carrefour is attributed exclusively to the rise of Amazon and e-commerce? It makes even less sense to see Carrefour's difficulties as a portent for the end of the physical store! A comparison with the American Walmart shows just how ludicrous this proposition really is. Back in 2000, the American distribution giant, which also runs hypermarkets and is more directly exposed to competition from Amazon, was the biggest retailer in the world, with Carrefour then occupying the No.2 spot. Today, Walmart is still the biggest, but Carrefour is now down in seventh position, with a smaller turnover than it had almost two decades ago...

And what of the social media comments with which we started this section? Is it likely that Carrefour will indeed be acquired by Amazon? Almost certainly not. Carrefour is not active in the two countries that currently form Amazon's most important European markets: the UK and Germany. What's more, a chain of hypermarkets – a store format belonging to the past – would represent a burden that Amazon can well do without. I am happy to think that Amazon may have looked at the acquisition option, but suspect that, if so, they quickly came to the logical conclusion: not to touch it with a ten-foot barge pole.

So where does this leave us with the idea that Carrefour is somehow the 'victim' of Amazon and soon to become its prey? The answer, of course, is nowhere. It is pure digital hysteria.

...AND VISIONARIES

So is there really nothing going on? Of course there is! If you want to know what, I suggest you read the fantastic book by my colleague Steven Van Belleghem. In *Customers the Day After Tomorrow* he explains with great insight and precision how artificial intelligence, big data and automation will fundamentally redraw the battle lines to win the hearts and minds of the customers of the future.[15] He also cites numerous examples of less well-known companies whose inspirational example you might be wise to follow.

More specifically in relation to the retail sector, I would also warmly recommend the visionary *The Future of Shopping* – rightly chosen as the 2018 Management Book of the Year in the Netherlands. In its wisdom-packed pages, my good friends Jorg Snoeck and Pauline Neerman do not confine themselves to the digital trends we can expect to wash over us in the years ahead, but also devote their shrewd attention to wider social developments, such as the ageing of the population and increasing urbanization.[16]

But for every Steven, Jorg or Pauline, there are a hundred other digital gurus who can see no further than Amazon, Apple, Facebook and Google as role models for the retail world of tomorrow. Add a dash of Airbnb, Alibaba, Uber, Booking.com, Netflix and Tesla, and you have a predictable cocktail of cases that is repeated in the literature ad infinitum.

Of course, the success of these companies appeals to our imagination. And they do indeed embody how the digital revolution has turned many sectors upside down. But what can you actually do with these examples, impressive though they are? Ricardo Semler, the Brazilian entrepreneur and management thinker, has made the following telling comparison: 'It's like me taking a photo of George Clooney to the barber's and telling him that's the way I want to look when he has finished. It just isn't realistic.'[17]

Today's retailers and brand manufacturers have heard it all before, hundreds of times. They are not just sitting on their hands, waiting for the next wake-up call from the next smart-ass prophet of doom, exhorting them to 'act before it is too late!' They already know that they don't want to end up going the same way as Kodak, Toys"R"Us, Sears or goodness knows how many others (you can fill in your own names).

The last thing they need is another superficial message from the self-absorbed coterie of digital 'evangelists' (the word says it all!), who specialize in proclaiming half-truths based on very little real business knowledge and a very selective choosing of their facts. Their recommendations go no further than the installation of the obligatory digital mirrors in shop fitting rooms! Yesterday, beacons were thought to be the answer to everything. Today, you need to invest in Amazon Echo. Tomorrow, it will no doubt be something else.

BEYOND THE DIGITAL HYSTERIA

This is what I call 'digital hysteria'. I would be the last person to deny that the challenges facing our retailers are huge. But the opportunities available to them are huge as well. If we want to exploit these opportunities effectively, we need to move beyond the current digital hysteria. Hence the purpose – and the title – of this book.

It all starts with the need to properly analyze the changes that are likely to confront us in the years ahead. This means being able to distinguish between real trends and passing hypes. In the following pages you will also read about

Amazon and AI, but they will be viewed in a more critical light and with greater nuance than in many other recent management books.

However, the analysis of these trends is only a means and not an end in itself. You need to go further than where the visionaries stop. As a retailer or brand manufacturer, you need to see how you can turn this analysis into a winning strategy and an effective plan for its implementation.

For me, you can say that you have a winning strategy if you belong to the top 25% of the best-performing companies. But achieving this is much more difficult than it sounds. To begin with, it means that you need to keep 75% of your rivals behind you in the pecking order. But even that is not enough. The number of retail companies currently going to the wall is considerable, and the list looks likely to get even longer in the years to come. If another 20% of today's retailers disappear from the scene, this means that you need to be among the top 25% of the surviving 80%. In other words, you must become a top 20% company!

DARE TO GO FOR GOLD!

Before you start, you need to be fully aware that the digital age will be a golden time for companies that excel, but a nightmare for those that don't. As a result, retail is destined to become a sector of winners and losers. So make sure you go for gold! Discover the positive power of daring to think big. This is the only way that your company can become the new Messi in the retail landscape. And even if you don't reach the giddy heights of the Barcelona wunderkind, you can still significantly increase your chances of enjoying a successful career as a pro footballer. Sometimes in life (and in business) we have to settle for the bronze medal – and that is no mean achievement. But make sure you at least get to the finals and don't get knocked out in the qualification rounds!

HOW DOES THIS BOOK WORK?

In the first part of the book we will analyze why we are currently standing at the end of the beginning of the digital age:

1. How has e-commerce developed so far?
2. How has the retail sector reacted to these developments?
3. What does the second wave of e-commerce hold in store?
4. What are the challenges and opportunities, both today and tomorrow, for retailers and brand manufacturers?

Next, we will identify and discuss the basic ingredients for an optichannel strategy. Based on a clear customer focus, the right degree of competitive strength and the availability of sufficient financial resources, this is the strategy that will separate the winners from the losers.

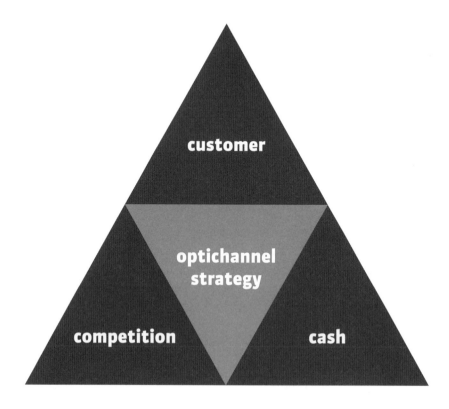

Part 2 will be devoted entirely to the customer, with the retailer and the brand manufacturer in the role of a customer travel agency, whose sole purpose is to provide an excellent customer journey. To do this, we need to address the following questions:

1. What is our target market?
2. What does the ideal customer journey look like?
3. How can we serve our customers like a butler?
4. What does a meaningful optichannel-customer relationship look like?
5. What role does the shop play in the customer relationship?

In part 3 we will examine the new kinds of business model that can make an optichannel-customer relationship both workable and sustainable:

1. What is the new commercial-economic reality?
2. How can we develop sufficient competitive strength?
3. What does our new value chain look like and how can we finance our strategy?

The fourth and final part zooms in on the practical implementation of the optichannel strategy:

1. How can we organize ourselves to make our strategy work?
2. What are the most important steps to make us one of tomorrow's winners?

I wish you a fascinating and successful customer journey!

PART 1

THE END OF THE BEGINNING OF E-COMMERCE

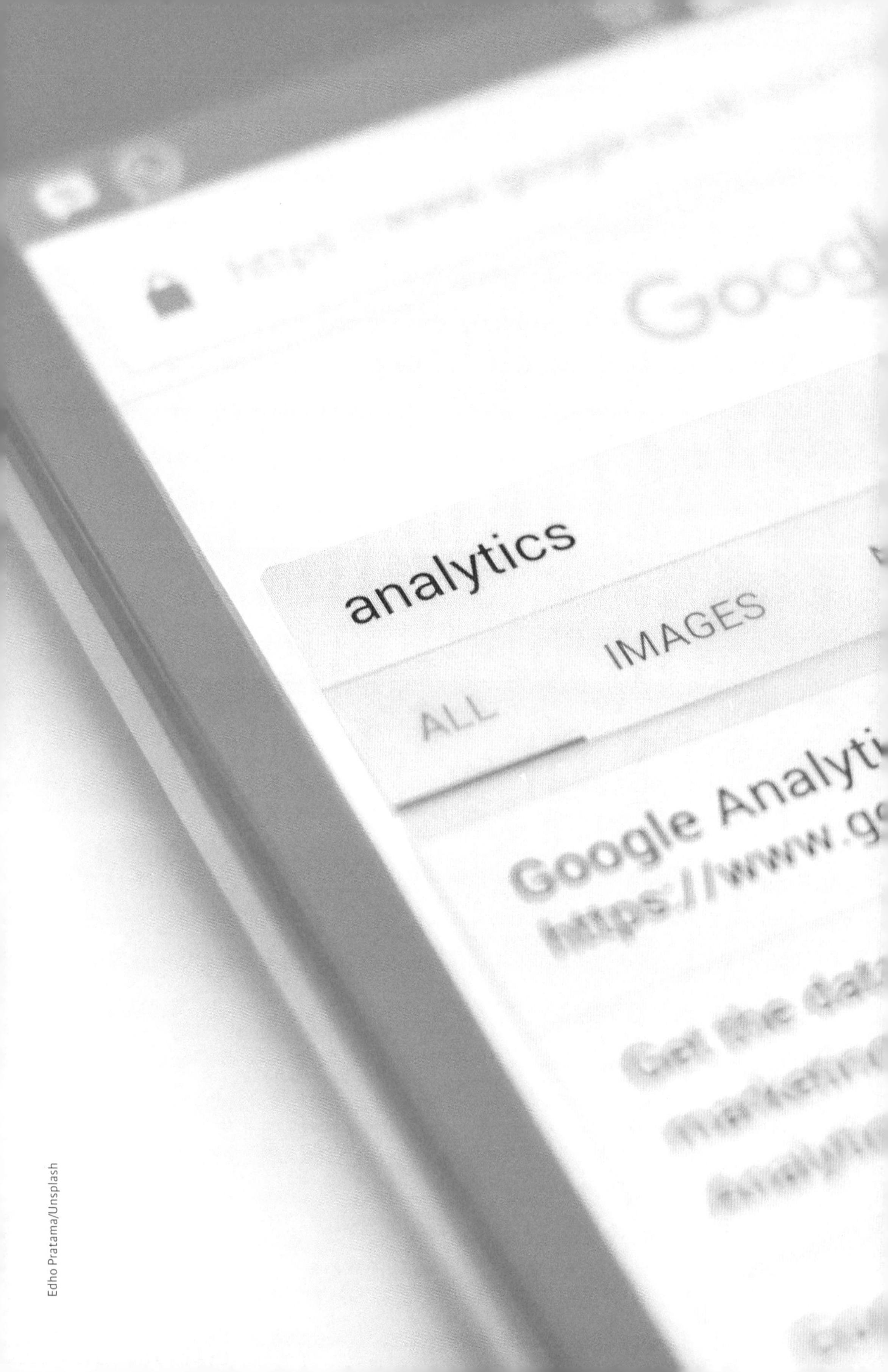

Edho Pratama/Unsplash

CHAPTER 1

THE FIRST WAVE OF E-COMMERCE

'The winner takes it all, the loser's standing small

Beside the victory, that's her destiny.'

ABBA (Swedish pop group)

This year we set a new record in the Van Ossel household: I think at least 90% of all our Christmas presents were bought online. And I suspect we are not alone. Most of you will be familiar with what I mean. Our personal buying behavior merely reflects one of the fastest growing trends in consumer buying behavior in recent years, as described in dozens and dozens of market research reports.

HOMO ECONOMICUS

One of the most characteristic features of the first wave of e-commerce is how rationally we manage the buying process. Once we know what we want to buy – whether it is a computer game, a laptop or a pedal bin – we quickly compare prices on the internet, to make sure we aren't paying over the odds. After that, the rest is child's play. We drop our chosen product into our online shopping basket and confirm the order.

In comparison, how we actually came to choose the product doesn't seem to matter all that much.

Recently, my son Simon asked me to purchase the computer game *Overwatch – the Origin Edition*. His cousin had told him just how great it was and now he wanted it for himself. At the same time, my daughter Jasmine needed a new computer for her schoolwork. For school, a basic laptop was enough: she was more attached to her smartphone for her other social media 'interests' and had no intention of doing anything complex, like editing videos or processing photo montages. The online 'laptop buying guide' of PC World soon directed me to what I needed. While I was busy, my wife asked me to see if I could find that new pedal bin we wanted for the bathroom. We had seen a model we liked while shopping in town, but they didn't have the right color. No problem! Another five minutes searching online and I had found the cheapest price for a Brabantia bin in matt steel, with a promise of next-day home delivery!

Three different purchases and three different ways of selecting the product:

» on the basis of word-of-mouth advertising; in other words, a recommended choice (the computer game);
» via an online help option; in other words, a highly functional choice (the laptop);
» by searching in physical shops; in other words, an emotional/intuitive choice (the pedal bin).

But in all three cases, at the moment of truth I switched into a professional purchasing mode. Like a true homo economicus, I went in search of a webshop that could sell me my chosen products at the most advantageous conditions. In other words, it became a rational and calculated search for certain products on the basis of clear specifications.

So as a vendor in these circumstances, how can you win my custom? The first condition is that you must have the product I want in stock and must be able to deliver it when I need it. If the product is a present for someone's birthday in two weeks' time, a delivery period of five working days is not a problem. But as a general rule, most customers prefer deliveries as quickly as possible. That's why every webshop will tell you that the shorter the delivery time, the higher the conversion rate.

After that, I opt for the cheapest supplier who gives me sufficient confidence about the quality of his service.

SHOPPING!

A second common characteristic shared by all these purchases is that the need for them does not originate in the webshop. It was not the case that during a visit to Amazon's webshop I was suddenly overcome by an irresistible urge to buy a computer game, laptop or pedal bin. No, I already knew that I needed these things and then went in search of the best place to select and buy them.

This is one of the main 'weaknesses' of the first wave of e-commerce: it scores very badly when it comes to convincing shoppers to make impulse purchases. What a difference with the shop floor of physical stores! A visit to a supermarket is a constant test of your willpower. Strategically placed displays repeatedly tempt you to buy a bag of crisps, or try the latest French cheese, or pick up a pack of washing powder at this week's '15% off' price. And even when you finally arrive safely at the check-out, you are hemmed in on both sides by chocolate, chewing gum and sweets!

Ikea is unquestionably one of the champions of this kind of temptation. You arrive looking for a new bed: you leave with two candles, a vase and a photo frame! The people at Ikea call store presentations that are directly in the line of sight of approaching shoppers – for example, at the end of an aisle, where the shopping route turns to the right – 'now or never' moments. These are the places where there is a good chance that customers will notice the products. Consequently, these are the best places to put your most tempting products. This is all part of Ikea's 'open-your-wallet' approach: as soon as you have decided to buy your first product – so that you are going to have to wait at the check-out anyway – your resistance to buying other products is significantly reduced. As a result, Ikea tries to persuade you to make this first purchase as early on in your visit as possible. This explains, for example, why there are large displays of cheap scented candles or cuddly toys as you enter the store...

This tactic doesn't work in the webshops of the first wave of e-commerce. If you are searching for a bed in the virtual world, you are directly routed to the product page with beds, so that you don't first pass scented candles (or anything else) on your way!

If you google 'bed', the search engine will lead you to the Ikea webpage for beds. Even if you surf directly to the Ikea website, you will still be inclined to look for the quickest route from the home page to the product page you need, either via an internal search function or via the menu buttons.

Ikea may still try to tempt you with pop-ups and other attempts at cross-selling, but this is at odds with the consumer's wish in an online environment to find what he is looking for as efficiently as possible. Consequently, he will either fail to notice these attempts, or, if he does notice them, there is a risk they will irritate him so much that he leaves the site. The only thing that sometimes works is the cross-selling of accessories: if you have just bought a digital TV, it is not unreasonable to ask if you might also be interested in buying an HDMI cable.

This explains why the first wave of e-commerce only appeals to the head, and not the heart. Online buying behavior is purely rational!

HOW EASY IS IT TO SHOP FOR GROCERIES ONLINE?

A lot of people don't like to shop for groceries. And who can blame them? You need, perhaps, 25 or so products, but have to find them in a supermarket with a surface area of more than a thousand square meters, containing somewhere between ten and twenty thousand different items. And once you have finally found everything you want, you have to queue at the check-out before you can actually pay for them!

Given this scenario, why is online shopping for groceries so slow to take off? In the United Kingdom, where the large supermarkets have been offering an online service for almost 20 years, the market share is still less than 8%. In continental Europe, France is the only country where e-groceries account for more than 5% of total sales.[18]

One of the main challenges to persuade more consumers to buy their groceries online is the fact that the first time you do it, it takes you more time than you would need for your normal visit to the physical store. You are not generally buying a single product, but a whole basketful of products, each of which must be added to your digital receipt one by one. However, from the second time onwards, everything goes much quicker. The webshop has registered the details of your first purchases, so that if you buy them again – and in supermarkets, between 70 and 80% of purchases are repeat purchases from your previous visit – there is no need to re-register them. This is why supermarkets generally feel that three online visits are necessary before customers become fully convinced of the time-saving benefits of this method of shopping.

The problem for the online supermarket then becomes how to persuade customers to keep on adding new products to their list of purchases. An experienced e-shopper needs an average of three clicks to find a product.[19] He remains on each page for an average of six seconds. This means that he needs 3 x 6 = 18 seconds per product. But it is not always possible to find and choose all products with the same speed: shampoo takes 24 seconds, a banana just eight seconds. Of course, these timings can vary significantly from webshop to webshop: the greater the user-friendliness, the shorter the search time and the higher the conversion rate. For each additional second that a consumer needs to remain on a page, the conversion rate falls by 7%.

This major impact of search time on conversion and therefore on the total number of products sold is linked to the fact that almost no-one buys all their groceries online. If the online search for a product is too long, the consumer will simply opt to buy the difficult-to-find shampoo the next time he is in a physical store.

In addition to improving the user-friendliness of their webshops, the supermarkets are also working hard to try and better predict the purchases of their customers. Whoever buys washing powder this week will be unlikely to buy it again next week. As a result, it will be placed lower down the next week's list of automatically suggested products. Depending on the customer's past frequency of purchase, it will then be moved systematically back up the list as the weeks pass.

Physical supermarkets that also have a webshop, like Tesco, Carrefour and Real, have a major advantage over the online pure players like Ocado, Amazon and Peapod, who do not have brick-

and mortar stores. The loyalty cards of the supermarkets' offline shoppers can be used to automatically create a list of suggested products when those same shoppers first shop online. This obviously increases user-friendliness, which in turn is likely to increase the speed of penetration for the online-offline hybrids.

These hybrids also have a competitive advantage when it comes to subsequent orders. Because only very few consumers buy all their groceries online, the physical stores automatically have more details about the totality of their customers' purchases, both online and offline, so that they are better able than the pure players to develop more made-to-measure shopping lists for each individual customer.

As a side effect, online supermarkets also unintentionally increase brand loyalty. If, for example, a customer purchases a package of Ariel washing powder, this brand will automatically appear on his suggested list of purchases next time he goes e-shopping. This increases the likelihood that he will buy the same brand again. And again. And again. This is not always the way things work in physical supermarkets. Research into offline purchasing behavior may suggest, for example, that Mrs Smith will buy whatever brand is being discounted that week, whereas Mrs Jones will remain true to Ariel, but will time her next pur-chase to coincide with the week when Ariel is being discounted. Even so, this combined information must once again make it possible for the physical supermarkets to offer a more personal-ized – and therefore better – service than the online pure players when their customers do eventually go online.

AND THE WINNER IS...

Because the first wave of e-commerce has already been going on for 20 years, it is becoming increasingly clear who are the winners and who are the losers. The winners can easily be divided along two dimensions:

- » The geographic market: Amazon and ASOS sell on multiple continents, whereas Zalando is only active in Europe. Bol.com confines itself even further to just the Dutch-speaking Benelux (the Netherlands and Flanders), while Coolblue also operates in French-speaking Belgium.
- » The assortment: generalists like Amazon or bol.com offer a broad range of products: in theory, they sell just about everything. In contrast, the specialists only have a narrow range. ASOS and Zalando limit themselves to fashion, whereas Coolblue primarily sells products with a plug.

This distribution allows the development of different product-market combinations, each with its own 'winner takes all' model. It is a typical phenomenon in many countries that the top ten of the top hundred e-commerce companies generate more turnover than the other ninety.[20] What's more, the biggest tend to get bigger, while the rest are left to fight over the few remaining crumbs. Market consolidation is taking place at lightning speed! Viewed worldwide, roughly half of all online orders are placed with fewer than twenty major players.[21]

Amazon, for example, is growing twice as fast as the American e-commerce market in its entirety. And because the company is now clearly the market leader, 70% of every additional dollar the American consumer spends online goes to Amazon.[22] In other words, just a single webshop – Amazon – claims 70% of the growth, while the other 100,000 American webshops are required to fight for a share of the remaining 30%.[23]

A similar situation is developing in the Netherlands. The ranking of the largest webshops is headed by bol.com, with Coolblue in second place. Both these players are growing faster than the market as a whole and are therefore increasing their market share. In this respect, Coolblue (38% growth rate)[24] is doing even better than its rival bol.com (30% growth rate).[25] In other words, in the 'consumer electronics' segment, the generalist bol.com is losing market share to the specialist Coolblue, which is strengthening its position.

But in terms of sheer size, bol.com is increasing its lead over Coolblue, since its current turnover, on which overall growth is based, is much larger.[26] In 2017, bol.com saw its turnover increase by just over 400 million euros to 1.6 billion euros, while Coolblue had to be satisfied with 'just' 300 million euros, taking its total turnover to 1.2 billion.

Once again, the same trend can be seen in the worldwide and European fashion markets, where ASOS and Zalando lead the way with a respective growth of 28% and 23%.[27][28]

How can we explain this increasing consolidation? There are basically four main reasons:

» Force of habit: convenience is the new loyalty.
» The rapid increase in available choice: everything under one roof.
» The declining difference in price.
» Customer loyalty programs.

CONVENIENCE IS THE NEW LOYALTY

A first and very simple explanation is that the consumer, motivated by habit and laziness, develops a preference for certain webshops. Once you have made an account with a particular webshop, and assuming you are satisfied with your previous purchase, there is a strong inclination to place your next order with the same shop.

Amazon focuses heavily on this need for convenience. As early as 1999, it had already patented the so-called '1-click buy': by registering your credit card details with the company, it is possible to make your next order with just a single click of the mouse.[29]

The fact that every webshop is different also plays a role. Once you know how to navigate on a particular site – where is the search function, what do the different menu buttons mean, etc.? – you can find what you want much quicker – so that you are tempted to stay there rather than to look elsewhere!

DOMINO'S ZERO CLICK-APP

For the American pizza company Domino's, digitally made orders are more efficient – and therefore more profitable – than orders made by telephone. What's more, research shows that digital ordering also improves customer satisfaction. When the landmark of 50% of digital orders was passed in 2015, the company's CEO challenged his people to find a solution that would allow customers to order a pizza while waiting at a red traffic light.[30]

The answer was a smart version of Amazon's '1-click buy'. Based on the proven assumption that many customers make the same order time after time, in 2016 Domino's launched its 'zero click' app. All you need to do is type in your favorite order, delivery address and payment details when you first use the app. Next time you open the app, a timer counts down from ten seconds to zero.

If you do nothing during those ten seconds, your repeat order will be automatically placed.[31][32]

In addition to its commercial success, the app has had a neat side effect. Students in particular have turned it into a kind of 'Russian roulette' game to close the app at the last possible moment without making an order. This not only creates additional emotional attachment to the Domino's brand, but also generates additional turnover, because (surprise, surprise!) not everyone succeeds in turning the app off in time...

THE RAPID INCREASE IN AVAILABLE CHOICE: EVERYTHING UNDER ONE ROOF

The market leaders are also continuously and systematically increasing their range of products. This makes it super-easy for customers. What could be better than to know you can find almost anything you need at your favorite webshop! There are two aspects to this phenomenon. On the one hand, there is a broadening of the generalist's assortment: in addition to books and cds, Amazon now also sells diapers, toys and drills. But the specialists are also playing the same game: Zalando started with just shoes, but has since added clothing and accessories, followed since the start of 2018 by beauty products.

In addition to this broadening, the deepening of the product range is equally important: offering more choice within a single product category.

These evolutions in range composition seamlessly match the needs of homo economicus during the first wave of e-commerce. Once he has made a choice, homo economicus searches for a product on the basis of specifications. And if you don't have that specific article in your assortment, you don't make a sale!

The development of online marketplaces in recent years has boosted this growth in product choice into overdrive. Initially, the webshops behaved like traditional retailers: they purchased goods, stored them in a distribution centre, and, once sold, transported then from there to the consumer. The webshop compiled its own range, set the selling price for the customer, accepted the stock risk and bore the costs for shipment and eventual return.

But even if, as a webshop, you hold your stock at a central location instead of at shops spread over the entire country, there still inevitably comes a moment when you cannot keep on deepening your product range. This is simply unaffordable. However, the advent of new marketplaces has opened up alternative possibilities. Nowadays, the manufacturer/supplier – for example, Nike – no longer sells to the webshop – for example, Zalando – but directly to the customer, albeit through the Zalando marketplace, for which service Nike pays Zalando a commission on its turnover. Now it is Nike that compiles the range, sets the selling price for the customer and bears the shipment and eventual return costs. Zalando is simply the middle man.

In other words, its marketplace makes it possible for Zalando to continually expand its own overall range ad infinitum without the need to invest in stock. At the same time, Nike profits from the traffic generated in the Zalando webshop. In this way, the dominant position of the market leader is strengthened even further. The webshop with the most buyers becomes the most attractive partner for suppliers who want to sell via a marketplace. This means that the number of sellers in the marketplace grows, as does the range of customer choice. This in turn attracts even more new customers and more new sellers. And so the ball keeps on rolling.

THE DECLINING DIFFERENCE IN PRICE

Because it is so easy to compare prices online, price differences between comparable products have been significantly reduced. Webshops and retailers continually use software scans to monitor the prices of their competitors. If necessary, they then immediately adjust their own prices to remain as competitive as possible. Result: a narrowing of the price range. The knowledge of this fact means that the 'lazy' consumer becomes even less inclined to make the effort needed to actively compare prices before making a purchase. He just sticks with the company he knows. Webshops with a reputation for low prices like Amazon and Zalando benefit most from this phenomenon. In a variation on the same theme, the Dutch Coolblue promotes specific products as 'Coolblue's choice'. These products have a 'rock-bottom' price, which gives the consumer the feeling that it is not worth taking the trouble to compare prices elsewhere.

CUSTOMER LOYALTY PROGRAMS

Finally, the marketing campaigns launched by the webshops also help to generate additional customer loyalty. Once again, the champion is Amazon. Their pay-for-service Prime subscription is a mega-success. Prime customers can benefit first and foremost from fast and free delivery, irrespective of the order value. It also logically follows that the customers who 'invest' in Prime want maximum return for their investment – which means buying more and more products from Amazon!

Prime also offers a range of subsidiary benefits, such as a film and music-streaming service. These substitutes for Netflix and Spotify are automatically included free of change in the Prime subscription.

THE BALL KEEPS ROLLING…

The current e-commerce winners clearly profit from huge economies of scale, since they are not only the largest company within their product-market combination but also enjoy the clear preference of consumers. In this way, scale has a double effect: it creates a cost benefit, while simultaneously acting as an accelerator of growth.

Michel Schaeffer, the former marketing director at bol.com, puts it as follows: 'The good become big and the big become even better. This is a selective process that sees many companies fall by the wayside, so that at the end of the day it is only the very biggest who are sustainably successful in the long term.'[33]

The more transactions you conduct, the better you are able to optimize the operation of your webshop, the more effectively you can allocate your marketing resources, the more efficiently you can detect fraud, etc. This will ultimately increase your conversion and therefore your turnover on each euro you invest in advertising (ROAS or return on advertising spend).

A useful indicator in this respect is the source of the traffic coming into your webshop: if more and more customers consciously choose to shop in your online store, this free direct traffic makes you less and less dependent on paid searches. This leads to savings on marketing expenditure. Scale is again a key factor, with Amazon once more leading the way: Amazon derives less than a quarter of its visitors from search engines,[34] while the comparable figure for its rivals frequently exceeds 50%.[35]

Because of their sheer size, it is not only possible for companies like Amazon to spread their fixed costs over a higher turnover, but also to negotiate better terms with their suppliers. In general, market leaders pay less per package delivered than their smaller challengers. To get goods to the customers as quickly as possible, you need to keep your stock as close to those customers as possible. Within each single geographical market, it is only the largest players who can do this with maximum cost-efficiency. For example, Zalando has distribution centers in Germany, Sweden and France, while ASOS integrally services the European market from its stock base in the United Kingdom. In this way, market dominance provides Zalando both a cost benefit for the company and faster service for the consumer.

THE END OF THE WAVE OF CONSOLIDATION?

But are these current market positions stable? Is it possible, for example, for the specialists to keep the generalists at bay? In China, this battle has already been fought and won by the generalists. Market leader Alibaba (with a Tmall market share of 56%) and runner-up JD.com (25% market share) are head and shoulders above the rest, a dominance based almost exclusively on their activities as a marketplace for others.[36] Chinese consumers rarely buy directly from the webshops of existing retailers and brand manufacturers, so that this kind of sales only accounts for between 1 and 2% of online turnover. As a consequence, more and more of these retailers and brand manufacturers are now asking themselves whether or not it might be a smart idea to actually close down their own webshops, relying instead exclusively on the sales platforms of the giant online marketplaces.

In Europe, things have not yet progressed quite so far. As long as the specialists can continue to demonstrate that their expertise offers added value to consumers, they will be able to hold their own in the battle with the generalists. Zalando wishes to become 'Europe's leading fashion destination' and seeks to position itself as a 'love brand'. Their specialist knowledge currently makes it possible for them to provide a more emotional customer experience (see chapter 3: 'The second wave of e-commerce'), whilst at the same time making it easier to convince an increasing number of fashion brands to approach their customers through the Zalando webshop and marketplace. And as we have already seen: more sellers means more buyers, and more buyers means even more sellers...

Coolblue, the Benelux online specialist in consumer electronics, has chosen to place its focus on service and advice. Their high Net Promoter Score shows that their high levels of customer loyalty are not solely based on convenience, but also reflect a high degree of trust and a superior customer experience. A good example of this is the way in which Coolblue was the first pure player to set up its own logistics service for the delivery and installation of appliances that usually require two people to carry them (washing machines, large televisions, etc.). Of course, physical stores have been doing this for some time, but the Coolblue initiative clearly set them apart from Amazon, bol.com and the other generalists.

A second similar question is whether or not local and regional players will be able in future to fend off the threat posed by the international and worldwide giants. Once again, this is by no means an open-and-shut case. Alongside important economies of scale at the national level, there are also significant scale benefits at the international level. For example, Amazon and Alibaba can devote significantly more resources to investment in new technologies than their local competitors, like bol.com or Coolblue. What's more, they can also exercise far greater pressure on suppliers to negotiate more advantageous terms and conditions.

Can the local players continue to convince consumers of their added value? Only time will tell, but the initial signs suggest that the local 'minnows' are going to find it increasingly difficult to escape the sharp teeth of the international 'sharks'. To date, Amazon is mainly targeting larger countries. In Europe, it is no coincidence that they have created local webshops in the United Kingdom, Germany, France, Spain and Italy – the five largest economies within the European Union. Their approach to smaller countries is much more opportunistic. For example, Dutch-speaking consumers are obliged to use the German Amazon site, part of which has been translated into their native language (and often pretty poorly!). What's more, many of the products offered for sale on the site can only be delivered in Germany. Likewise, until as recently as November 2017, the site made no provision for the use of iDeal, the most popular system for making online payments in the Netherlands. To say that Amazon has so far only taken modest steps to adjust to the needs and norms of the Dutch market is an understatement! Even so – and this is the worrying thing for the local players – Dutch consumers have still found their way to Amazon in sufficiently large numbers to boost the company to fifth place in the Twinkle100 listing of the top e-commerce companies in the Netherlands. In Belgium and Switzerland, the situation is comparable. French-speaking consumers are required to make use of Amazon.fr., but this has not stopped Amazon from already shooting to top spot in the country rankings for major webshops.[37]

Click here today, wear tomorrow

Shop online here before
8pm and collect after
2pm tomorrow

➕ Or download our app
and scan any barcode

🎀 Free WiFi

in store | online | mobile

SAMSØE ♢ SAMSØE

CHAPTER 2

OMNICHANNEL: THE ANSWER TO E-COMMERCE

'E-commerce is the most stupid

business model in the world.'

Pieter Zwart (CEO and founder of the Coolblue webshop)

2013. The first wave of e-commerce is crashing like a tsunami over the retail sector, which has already been severely dislocated by the effects of the 2008 financial and economic crisis. Since then, the consumer has been keeping his hand in his pocket. The purchases he can delay are put off until 'later', although he is increasingly charmed by the tempting discounts offered by the webshops of the new online traders. And the traditional retailer? He licks his wounds and looks with trepidation towards the future.

It was during that same year that I wrote my book about omnichannel. It explained how traditional retailers could best deal with the exponential growth in online sales channels in general and with the competition posed by e-commerce pure players like Amazon, Alibaba and Zalando in particular.

THE BEST OF BOTH WORLDS

The basic idea is as simple as it is brilliant: combine online and offline and let the consumer decide which channel he wants to use, and when. But let me be clear on this point: I did not 'invent' omnichannel. The only credit I can take is that I developed the idea in a structured way in a book that even today is still regarded as a standard work on this subject.

In omnichannel we start by bringing the physical store into an online context. This involves much more than simply opening and operating a webshop. The surfing customer needs to be able to see which products can be tested in which stores and where those products are currently in stock. Perhaps he wishes to make an appointment with a salesperson or wants to check the hours of opening and locations of stores in his vicinity. Or maybe he wants to confirm online an offer that was made during his store visit, so that he can now finalize his order without any need to return to the store.

At the same time, omnichannel also means bringing the internet into the physical store. One customer might still be in the exploratory phase and wants to search for more general information online when he is in the store. Another might be further along in his customer journey and wishes to consult various online reviews while he has the actual product in his hands. A third customer, before making his purchase, might first want to check online to make sure he is not paying too much for the product of his choice. And a fourth might want to order a blue model, which is currently not in stock, and have it delivered to his home.

In other words, omnichannel is essentially a matter of seamlessly integrating all online and offline channels. In this way, communication channels like the website become sales channels (for example, as a webshop), while sales channels like the physical stores also become communication channels (for example, as a showroom where the customer can test and choose products, before ordering them online). The basic principle is that the customer is central at all times. He decides what he does, when he does it and via which channel.

Readers who are not yet familiar with the omnichannel concept can find a brief explanation in the following box. Better still, why not read my book *Omnichannel in retail...*

MONO, MULTI, CROSS AND OMNICHANNEL FOR DUMMIES

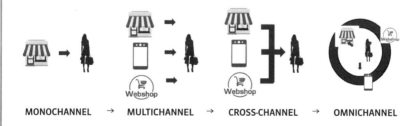

Before the advent of e-commerce, retailers made use of just a single sales channel: their network of shops and stores. All other touchpoints – the folder, the website, the customer contact center, etc. – were purely channels of communication. This was the era of monochannel.

In order to secure a slice of the cake created by the rapid growth of e-commerce, many retailers also decided to open their own webshop. This was later supplemented by a mobile shop and/or app. As long as the physical stores and the digital channels continue to operate independently of each other, we speak of a multichannel approach.

This could often be confusing for the consumer: he saw many different channels, but they were all the expression of the same single company and/or brand. So where should he actually go for what he wanted? This confusion led to a need for greater integration between the different channels. Comparable with the philosophy of 360° communication, retailers increasingly tried to ensure that both their physical stores and their webshop provided a consistent image to the consumer.

In the process, the distinction between communication channels and sales channels became increasingly blurred. The website and the mobile site evolved from communication channels into sales channels. At the same time, more and more customers began to use the physical store as a kind of showroom – a communication channel – before later making their purchase online. Likewise, it also became possible to collect or return products ordered online from and to the physical stores. This seamless integration of all sales and communication channels is known as cross-channel.

Eventually, people realized that cross-channel was still fundamentally based on the idea that the retailer controlled the process of interaction with the customers. All the channels might be carefully attuned to each other, but it was the retailer who still decided what customers were able to do and via which channels. For example, some promotions or even some products might only be available in stores, and not online.

This 'control' exercised by the retailer is no longer in keeping with the spirit of the times. In the digital era, power now rests with the consumer. He wants to decide for himself which channel to use and when and how to use it. This is omnichannel – a philosophy of extreme customer centricity.

TOWARDS A WIN-WIN RELATIONSHIP

The underlying idea is that while consumers like ordering things online and having them delivered to their house, this is not always the ideal solution for all people in all circumstances. Today, I might prefer the convenience of home delivery but tomorrow I may fancy a day out at the shops with the family. And the day after tomorrow the delivery man might find himself standing in front of a closed door, because I am away at work. Fortunately, I pass the store on my way home, so I can collect my package then. And maybe I will try on the new jacket while I am still there. It doesn't fit? No problem! I can return it on the spot and see if they have something in my size in their store display…

Research and practice have shown conclusively that consumers love combining the use of different channels. De Bijenkorf, a trendsetting department store chain in the Netherlands and part of the British Selfridges Group, has been omnichannel for years. Its customer loyalty card allows the company to see which customers are buying what, and with which channels.

And what does this information reveal? Omnichannel customers, who shop in both the webshop and the physical stores, make four times as many purchases as customers who only shop online and twice as many purchases as customers who only shop in the stores. In other words, omnichannel customers are the biggest spending and most loyal customers. But a second conclusion is even more striking: omnichannel customers also buy more frequently online than the customers who only buy online, just as they buy more in the stores than the customers who only shop in the stores![38]

The inference is clear: omnichannel customers love De Bijenkorf. They like going to the stores and they go there often. But if they don't have the time or they know exactly what they want, they will order online instead. By giving customers this freedom of choice, they end up buying more – much more – than would otherwise be the case. If De Bijenkorf did not have an excellent webshop, it would no doubt lose part of its online custom to the Zalandos and Amazons of the world. But the webshop is excellent, and so it becomes possible to create a true win-win relationship: customers happy and De Bijenkorf happy!

This insight offers omnichannel retailers the opportunity to develop a sustainable competitive advantage: retailers who already have a network of physical stores will find it easier to add on a webshop to those stores than the e-commerce pure players will find it to add on a network of physical stores to their webshop.

The billions invested by Amazon, Alibaba and JD.com in brick-and-mortar stores illustrate that they also believe in the power of the online-offline combination. Perhaps their seemingly inexhaustible financial resources will allow them to quickly develop a physical presence in our high streets – possibly by buying up existing retailers lock, stock and barrel. But even after its takeover of the 400 Whole Foods stores worldwide, Amazon still has fewer physical outlets than most supermarket chains in even a small country like Belgium. And the ambition of JD.com (which we mentioned in chapter 1) to open a million neighborhood supermarkets within the next five years shows that the development of a truly national coverage takes time – time which existing retailers can use to prepare their defenses.

During the past five years, I have travelled around Europe giving presentations and workshops about omnichannel. With great passion, I have tried to enthuse companies for a concept that could be the salvation of the traditional retail sector. Retailers and brand manufacturers, local and international players, huge organizations and relatively small ones: I have seen and talked to them all.

The good news is that the vast majority of retail professionals recognize that omnichannel is the strategic direction they need to follow. Eight out of every ten retailers now have an omnichannel strategy, which is twice as many as four years ago. Of the remaining two out of ten, half are currently in the process of elaborating such a strategy, so that only one in ten believes that omnichannel has nothing to offer them.[39]

So far, so good. But the real challenge is in the implementation of the strategy. More than half describe omnichannel as 'a work in progress'. This means that in theory we should gradually see more and more retailers making the step from cross-channel to omnichannel. But the current reality is more worrying. Only 8% claim to have made this transition successfully. A quarter describe omnichannel as a 'battle' or even 'a castle in the air'. CEOs say that budgetary limitations are the biggest stumbling block for the successful implementation of an omnichannel strategy.

In other words, the retail sector is full of good intentions. But will it ever be able to put those good intentions into practice? The available information suggests that currently far too many attempts to carry through ambitious projects for digital transformation end in disappointment. There are numerous studies to show that on average only 10% of retailers are able to bring the implementation of their omnichannel strategy to a successful conclusion.[40] My own survey yielded similar results.[41]

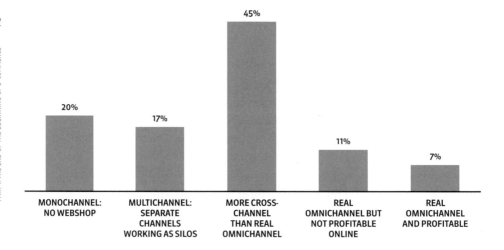

1. **Monochannel:** a fifth of all retailers do not yet have a webshop. Some have acceptable and rational reasons for this omission. For example, discounters wonder whether they can cover the costs of delivery with their ultra-low margins. After all, it costs as much to ship a five-euro t-shirt as a fifty-euro t-shirt. Because the discounters currently continue to grow without e-commerce, they are inclined to turn their backs on omnichannel – for now. This explains why fast-growers like Primark and Action have not yet launched a webshop. But many others have simply got cold feet. They give a new meaning to the term 'a head-in-the-sand' policy! They start off by saying 'My products are not really suitable for online sale', but this later develops into 'Perhaps my products are suitable for online sale abroad, but not at home', before ending the denial phase with something like 'Our customers don't want to buy our products online'. In other words, we go all around the houses but end up back at square one. Lots of blah, blah, blah, but in essence nothing changes. When these companies do finally decide to launch a webshop, the project typically suffers from delay after delay. And it is worth noting that it is not only small companies that behave in this manner; some big names have been equally culpable: Inditex/Zara, MediaMarkt and Ikea have all only recently launched their own webshops. True, MediaMarkt opened a webshop as long ago as 2004 in its domestic market in Germany, but then closed it down again in 2008 because it was not profitable...

2. **Multichannel:** you might expect that most retailers should be able to integrate their various channels more or less seamlessly. However, my research demonstrates that for 17% of retailers this is a bridge too far. They have a webshop, but it operates as a separate silo alongside their stores. One of the most frequently offered explanations for this is that the company's shops – either in part or in whole – are run by self-employed owners, often on a franchising basis. Finding a way to involve these owners in an online context is far from simple. Do you pay them part of your margin to reflect the fact that people have ordered via the website instead of in their store, even though they have had no direct role in the online sale? Or do you offer them a small commission in a 'click-and-collect' role? Whichever option is chosen and for whatever reason, these are matters that understandably concern the company and its management, but are of no interest whatsoever to the consumer.

3. **Cross-channel:** fortunately, many retailers are able to successfully integrate their different channels. At 45%, they represent the largest group. So what is stopping them from going the extra mile? What prevents them from becoming fully omnichannel? First and foremost, they prefer to remain cross-channel and make a profit, rather than becoming omnichannel and risk making a loss (see the next group). Going omnichannel requires a significant investment, because the company's existing systems are seldom suitable for an omnichannel approach. For example, a consumer might like to check if a particular product is in stock in his local store, but is unable to do so because the existing systems do not allow the real-time updating of stock totals. Or a retailer might like to develop an app that can also serve as a customer loyalty card, but his cash register system is unable to make the necessary connection with the consumer's smartphone.

4. **Omnichannel but unprofitable:** fewer than one in five of all retailers regard themselves as being 'truly' omnichannel. What's more, the majority of them have an online channel that is making a loss. One of the explanations for this is that you first have to incur costs before you start to reap the rewards. Speculate to accumulate, if you like. The initial online turnover is often so limited, that the scale of the investment in e-commerce can only be written off against relatively low sales. Moreo-

ver, e-commerce in general is structurally less profitable than store sales. As in so many other ways, Amazon is a classic example. Amazon Web Services (AWS) is a business-to-business cloud service that in 2017 represented just 10% of the company's turnover but was equivalent to more than 100% of the company's profit.[42] In other words, the money that the company earns with AWS needs to be used – partially or completely – to make good the losses the company incurs in its online retail operations. In this respect, Zalando is perhaps an even better example. Since 2014, the Berlin-based fashion giant has been in the black for several years in a row. Even so, the company's profit expressed as a percentage of turnover remains extremely modest. In comparison, the figures for Inditex – the mother company of Zara, a largely physical retailer – are three times higher. Even the battered and bruised H&M chain, which saw its profits plummet in 2017, is still 50% more profitable than Zalando. More about this in chapter 10: 'The new reality'.

5. **Omnichannel and profitable:** at last! But at just 7%, this is by far the smallest group of retailers. Nevertheless, it is comforting to know that some at least have managed to crack the code that allows them to be both omnichannel and make money.

What are we to make of all this? It leaves us with a kind of double feeling. Yes, it is positive that the majority of retailers wish to become successful omnichannel players. But it is disappointing that so far less than 10% of them have been able to do it.

So what are this 10% doing that the others aren't? And how can we improve their approach still further? That will be the subject of the rest of this book. For now, suffice it to say that omnichannel really does work. And not just in Powerpoint.

OMNICHANNEL AND THE BRAND MANUFACTURER?

Omnichannel has its origins as a strategy for retailers. The 100% seamless integration of all channels implies that you need to have control over all these channels. Retailers do. Brand manufacturers don't.

Even so, Bosch, Puma or Panasonic still want to see as much of their range as possible for sale in the local stores of Hornbach, Footlocker or MediaMarkt. What's more, they hope that POS communication will help to create an experience around their brand, in the further hope that this will convince the retailer to respect the recommended selling price.

In practice, of course, these are all matters that the retailer decides for himself. Limited floor and shelf space means that it is impossible for a retailer to include every brand of a product in his assortment, never mind display the entirety of each brand's range. In general, the retailer understandably gives priority to his own store brand, so that the Panasonic headphones end up anonymously among a hundred and one other brands on MediaMarkt's discounted red shelf. If a manufacturer wants to have his brand more specifically highlighted, he needs to pay for the privilege. Last but not least, it needs to be remembered that price is one of the easiest weapons for retailers to use in their battle for consumer hearts and minds. As a result, you will seldom find Puma sneakers or Bosch drills sold in different stores at the same price.

OMNICHANNEL COMMUNICATION

Notwithstanding all these caveats, brand manufacturers have increasingly embraced the term 'omnichannel' in recent years, also for their indirect sales. This has led to the necessary degree of confusion and misunderstanding, since the concept as interpreted by brands is less completely applied than by retailers. In the retail sector omnichannel relates to both sales and communication channels. Brand manufacturers are only concerned with the latter, and not with the former.

The underlying idea behind omnichannel communication is the same in both instances. To begin with, all communication needs to be seamlessly integrated – what used to be called 360° communication. If, during his customer journey, the consumer looks up information online to find out which Kärcher high pressure washer best suits his needs, 360° communication must ensure that he gets the same information on the websites of Kärcher, Amazon and Hornbach, but also on the shop floor and on the product packaging. The decision about which channel he uses to find this information is then left to the customer.

If he contacts Kärcher by e-mail for a repair and later telephones with some additional questions, he does not want to repeat his story all over again. The operator on the phone must be able to see immediately what information has already been exchanged in the mails. In this way, the customer is given a more efficient experience. In a world where convenience has become the new customer loyalty, companies use omnichannel communication to achieve higher levels of customer satisfaction and customer retention, and, consequently, higher turnover.

The new element in all this is that the brands now surrender to the customer the choice about the best way for him to communicate with the company. In this respect, it is possible to cite dozens of examples. Whoever subscribes to a newsletter is immediately asked how often and about which subjects he wishes to be informed. Today, you cannot only phone companies, but also mail them or chat with them, if you prefer. And every new app comes complete with a palette of different settings that allow you to interact with the company in the way most appropriate to your needs.

The customer journey remains central at all times: throughout the different steps of this journey, it is you, the consumer, who decides which channels of communication and which touchpoints you want to use. How do you want to receive your boarding pass for your next flight: as a pdf or via a text message? Or would you prefer to install our app? If the departure gate for your plane changes, should we phone you, mail you, text you or contact you via WhatsApp?

CHAPTER 3

THE SECOND WAVE OF E-COMMERCE

'I can resist everything except temptation.'

Oscar Wilde (Irish writer)

If it rains for a day during the summer holidays, the lines of waiting customers at the Ikea check-out get longer and longer. The rain forces the kids to stay inside. No problem as long as they are allowed to amuse themselves with their PlayStation, tablet or smartphone, but if mum and dad decide that their offspring could do with a little digital detox, boredom soon sets in. So what to do? 'What about a day out?' suggests someone. 'A day in you mean – look at that weather?' 'Okay, so what about Ikea – at least it's dry there!'

The funny thing is that we seldom do this online. Would you surf to the Ikea website just for fun? Watching films on YouTube, contacting your friends via Facebook and Instagram, or keeping up-to-date via news sites: sure! But funshopping online? Most people would still shake their heads in disbelief – but a growing number are starting to think 'why not?'

THE HEART AND THE BRAIN

What is going on? In chapter 1 we saw that during the first wave of e-commerce we search for and buy the things that we need. We make purchases rationally and functionally, and are difficult to tempt when it comes to impulse buying. E-commerce appeals primarily to our brain.

But what if e-commerce was also able to touch our hearts? What if we started to visit online webshops not because we need something, but simply to have a look around, to see what's new? That would create amazing opportunities for growth, especially in product categories where fun shopping is important. This explains why webshops in the fashion sector have already been exploring for some time the best ways to allow their customers to 'nose around' online.

For example, Zalando has known for years that the number of visitors to its website always increases if there is football on the television. As a result, on evenings when matches in the Champions League are scheduled the company makes use of traffic-generating marketing to attract even more customers. While the men are watching the game on the sofa, the women are behind the family computer doing a little extra shopping. But there is a difference with the Ikea example. We are happy to spend half a day in Ikea, simply to pass the time and have a look around. But webshops are unable to hold our attention for that long. We very quickly succumb to the alternative attractions of Facebook and Instagram!

In other words, it is clear that the second wave of e-commerce has begun, but it is still very much in the embryonic phase. So far, only a few webshops are trying to exploit these new opportunities and the resulting turnover is limited. Even so, this growth is exponential. What's more, the second wave will be 'in addition to' and not 'instead of' the first wave.

1st wave		2nd wave
reason/brain	→	emotion/heart

FROM SEARCH...

In a world in which convenience is the new customer loyalty, webshops have been developed in ways that allow the customer to find what he wants with a minimum of fuss and bother. This is why every webshop has a search function and a menu bar. On the Zalando site, for example, you must first choose between the obligatory 'men', 'women' and 'children' categories. You can also flag particular brands, which you can find alphabetically. But it all still has a very rational look-and-feel. It appeals primarily to the brain.

The product assortment is then shown in a continual stream of individual images. If you are looking for a dress, you will be offered about 15,000 of these images. Once again, it is the rational brain that is activated, because each image is exactly the same size and shows just a single product. It's a bit like the advertising folder you get each week from your local supermarket – only bigger. What's more, there is still a lot of text on the screen: on the left, the menu with the different types of dresses (summer dresses, business dresses, jeans dresses, etc.); at the top, the standard filters (brand, color, price, size, etc.).

A LITTLE BIT OF HISTORY: HOW FASHION HAS BEEN PRESENTED VISUALLY ONLINE

In the early days of e-commerce, the visitors to fashion websites were offered 'flat' product photos. A dress would be arranged on a special shooting table and then photographed from above. The power of these photos to 'tempt' customers into making a purchase was limited.

This explains the subsequent rapid success of the so-called 'invisible man' photos. The dress was now draped over the torso of a kind of tailor's dummy, in a way that also made it possible to see the inside of the neck. It looked as though the dress was being worn by an invisible person, creating an effect that was much closer to what you can see in a physical store. This significantly increased the 'temptation' factor.

This factor was increased even more when the switch was made to model photography. It was now a live person wearing the dress. On the upside, there was more emotion. On the downside, there were higher costs. The model needed to be paid and it took a lot of time to get all those dresses on and off, and then find the right pose. For this reason, Zalando, for example, uses a live model for just one color of each dress, using 'invisible man' photos to shoot the remaining colors. Other companies prefer to use both types of photo, so that customers can get a better impression of the neck.

The 'body model' photo is also quite popular, primarily because it is cheaper. This makes use of live models, but with their heads removed in the finished images. Costs are considerably lower: quicker poses (because facial expression is no longer relevant), no make-up, no portrait rights, etc. But the end result is less visually appealing: the photos nearly all look the same, since there are only a limited number of ways you can frame a 'headless' model.

For years, the British ASOS company has been taking things a stage further. They make use of videos on their product pages. In short clips lasting no longer than 10 seconds, you can watch a model 'parade' the dress, almost as if she were on a catwalk, allowing potential customers to see in detail how the dress falls in movement.

...TO DISCOVER

More and more webshops are trying to respond to the needs of 'fun shoppers'. One simple way to do this is to add a 'new collection' option to your menu bar. This makes things as easy as possible for your loyal customers and frequent visitors: on their landing page they are automatically shown the very latest things you have to offer. People visiting the website for the first time can be shown a different selection of products, usually your best-selling lines.

If you click from the landing page overview to the relevant product page, you will generally now find a 'shop the look' button. This allows you to see all the products worn by a model, but in combination with a range of other products, such as shoes, a scarf, a handbag, jewelry and other accessories, cosmetics, etc. These secondary products are not always visible in the original product photo, but they complement the dress perfectly. This allows the customer to 'discover' the potential offered by the new dress, while the shop can promote cross-selling in a new and attractive manner.

The Dutch Miss Etam primarily uses 'invisible man' photos on its product pages. This means that they cannot use the 'shop the look' method, because customers only see a single product at a time. To get around this, the company has added an 'Outfits' button to its basic menu. In contrast to the product pages, this option does make use of model photography. The surfing customer is presented with a series of full silhouettes and with a simple click is immediately shown the product photos of the various items on display.

1st wave		2nd wave
reason/brain	→	emotion/heart
search	→	discover

FROM A PRODUCT...

Choosing and buying a drill online is child's play. There are numerous buying guides that will navigate you through the fascinating world of drilling technology. These guides will tell you what you should look for and what you need to be aware of. Once you have made your choice on this basis, you go in search of the cheapest webshop that you feel you can trust and currently has your product in stock. You then drop the said product into your shopping basket, click on the pay button, and Bob's your uncle!

For this reason, the buying guide of smart webshops seeks to lead customers to a machine that can only be found in their shop or that no-one else is offering at a lower price. This reduces the chance that a customer will come to your site to make his choice, but will then end up buying somewhere else. Ideally, the margin should also be sufficient, so that you actually make money on the transaction. This should usually be the case: because you will sell a high volume of the recommended products, you will be able to negotiate favorable purchasing terms with your suppliers. Having said that, this tactic is not without risk: the customer's confidence in your webshop will be eroded if he gets the feeling that he is being led to the product that gives you the most profit and not the product that is best suited to his needs.

...TO A SOLUTION

Now imagine that you don't want to buy a drill, but want to insulate your attic instead. I expect that many do-it-yourselfers would find it useful if they could order everything they need online and arrange for it to be delivered to their home early on Saturday morning, just before they are ready to start.

Unfortunately, that is not possible. Or should we say: not yet? In addition to the fact that you can probably find all the products you need more quickly with a visit to your local builders' merchant than with a visit to a webshop, there is also a second problem: you seldom know in advance exactly how much of each product you need.

What is the current position with the customer journey in this scenario? In the best case, the do-it-yourselfer may be able to find sufficient information online about how to insulate an attic and what products are needed. After that, he drives to the local building materials store, asks for a bit of advice from the sales staff, searches for the things he wants, loads them into his car, and drives home. A few hours up in the attic and it's mission accomplished!

Sadly, it's not quite as easy as that. The first problem is that the information you find online seldom closely matches what you really want to know. It is either too brief and too superficial, or else too long and too technical, so that you can't understand it. For example, the current state of your attic can make a big difference to your task. Does existing material first need to be removed or not? Does the roof lining need to be replaced? There is no standard solution that covers every situation.

Even when you finally get to the shop, the problems can continue. The insulating material they sell has a different method of fixation from what you saw online. And when you ask the seller for advice, you discover that you haven't taken all the necessary measurements. Not that it matters, because you are going to have to come back next week anyway: the profile you need is currently out of stock. When, after your second visit to the suppliers, you finally start to work in your attic the following weekend, you realize you have forgotten to buy enough screws. So back to the shop you go!

This kind of scenario offers lots of potential opportunities for smart builders' merchants. If they can offer the right kind of DIY advice online, this can be geared to the recommended products available in their store's product range, adjusted where necessary to take account of products temporarily out of stock. What's more, by making the products referred to in the advice clickable, the customer can immediately add them to his shopping list. This is known as the blending of content and commerce, and saves the customer a lot of searching. You can even suggest a complete list to the customer that he can accept integrally with a single click.

Of course, your DIY-er still needs to know how much of each product he requires. A smart website will help customers to make the correct measurements. For example, it may be possible to develop a useful online calculator that converts measurements into amounts of specific products. This type of calculation could then be linked back to your product list. And if the customer still needs additional advice, via a 'click to call' button he can be put in instant telephone contact with a member of your sales team. If need be, this salesperson can invite the customer to the store, especially if you have a demo-area where the different layers of an insulated roof can be viewed. This will allow the salesperson to demonstrate in a very hands-on way exactly how the work should be carried out and what alternatives are available.

The customer now has a provisional list of products and measurements, which he can save on the store's website. If he wants, he can also install an app on his smartphone that synchronizes everything with the site. In the shop, he runs through all the details with the salesperson, to make sure he hasn't forgotten anything. He can also be given answers to any last questions he might have.

Now he is in a position to finalize his list and start searching for everything he needs in the store. The app can help him, by showing him where the various products are located amongst the shelves. Alternatively, he can add his list to an online shopping basket and have everything delivered direct to his home. But it doesn't stop there. While he is carrying out the work in his attic, the DIY-er can still phone the store's help line for any last minute advice he might still need.

Sounds too good to be true? It is – at least for the moment. But builders' merchants are already working to turn this kind of dream scenario into a reality in the not too distant future. And this future looks bright. Whereas in the first wave of e-commerce the traditional retailers of drills, tools and building supplies lost market share to Amazon or Alibaba, they are now much better placed than the online giants to provide customers with the ideal customer journey. They have the know-how to give the right advice and possess the necessary infrastructure to optimally combine the online and offline channels in an omnichannel environment.

1st wave		2nd wave
reason/brain	→	emotion/heart
search	→	discover
product	→	solution

FROM SPECIFICATION TO INSPIRATION

During the first wave of e-commerce, at the moment of truth the consumer goes in search of the product he has chosen on the basis of concrete specifications at the cheapest price from a reliable supplier.

But during the second wave, discovery and inspiration go hand in hand. Let's return briefly to the world of fashion. On each product page you can find 'comparable products'. A company like Zalando explicitly invites you to browse with its 'Discover more' button.

All that is lacking is the creation of the right atmosphere: the seductive power of the shop floor. Modern consumers expect the webshops of the future to provide this same kind of mood enhancement. At the moment, all they see is product photos, which come across as a series of isolated and sterile images that do very little to inspire.

So how to improve things? Dimmed lighting, atmospheric music and perhaps even a glass (or two) of alcohol help to set the scene for seduction during the mating game. The same seducing effect can be achieved in a webshop by adding content that is relevant to your visitors. At Zalando, for example, there is an 'Editorial' option in the main menu. The equivalent ASOS button is called 'Inspiration'. These buttons transport you to a different world. You can read articles and blogs, watch videos, pick up style tips... In this way, the website becomes an alternative to a fashion magazine – but with one important difference. If you see a photo-shoot of a dress you like in a fashion magazine, you can't view it in detail with just the single click of a mouse, nor immediately buy it if your favorable first impressions are confirmed. This is where the webshop has the advantage: it blends content and commerce.

Or to put it in ASOS's own words: 'Content is an important part of the experience and a key part of what makes us stand out from the crowd. We really believe ASOS is more than a shop – it's not just about pushing products, it's also about being the fashion-forward friend who you trust to say: "try this".'[43]

NET-A-PORTER.com takes this idea so far that no less than 50% of their webshop consists of content. It is a veritable Valhalla for fashionistas who want to do a little fun shopping. On their home page you will not find just any old ordinary product photos. Instead, each month you will see a prominent image of the newest edition of *The Edit* – an online mag devoted to the very latest and best in fashion and lifestyle. And every product is just a click away...

1st wave		2nd wave
reason/brain	→	emotion/heart
search	→	discover
product	→	solution
specifications	→	inspiration

CURATED COMMERCE

The winners in the first wave of e-commerce use their assortment to make the difference. Certainly in terms of the marketplaces, it is even possible to speak of a self-perpetuating phenomenon: whoever has the most buyers attracts the most new sellers, which in turn attracts even more new customers, which attracts more new sellers...

However, when I am not searching for a product on the basis of specifications, but prefer instead to discover a solution and be inspired, having the largest choice is no longer relevant. What I want is the right choice – for me. In other words, the offer needs to be tailor-made to the needs of the customer.

Once again, it is possible to see interesting moves in this direction in the world of fashion. The Cloakroom, Outfittery and Suitcase all profile themselves as online personal shoppers for men. They offer personalized style advice to men who want to look good, but don't have the time or interest to go shopping for themselves. As a customer, you first need to answer a few questions online. Next, you speak to the stylist of your choice on the phone to finalize your preferences. Within a matter of days, you then receive a delivery with a number of complete outfits: jackets, trousers, shirts, pullovers, shoes, accessories, etc. You keep what you like (at the recommended shop price) and send back the rest. The advice, delivery and return are free.

In all these cases, customers are buying a solution. This is also known as 'curated commerce', because the products are chosen to match the customer's specific requirements. In addition to the convenience of the service, the men also enjoy being pleasantly surprised by the contents of the deliveries, and often end up buying articles they would never have chosen for themselves: this is the power of discovery and inspiration. Success is dependent on the quality of the styling advice: the better the selection and the closer it matches the customer's taste, the greater the level of retention and the lower the level of returns. Even more important: satisfied customers are likely to request further deliveries. Our rolling ball from the first wave is no longer being kept in self-perpetuating motion by scale, but by personal service: the more often a customer makes an order, the better you learn to understand his preferences.

The strength of the above models – but at the same time also their limitation – is that the selections are made by people. This means that scalability is a problem: to grow, you need more style advisers.

Several of the established webshops are now also trying to provide this kind of service. For example, Zalando offers personalized style advice under the name of 'Zalon by Zalando'. However, their version of the concept is weaker: you can speak to a stylist on the phone if you want to, but it is not an integral part of their procedures. The choice of the clothes they send you is based on the online information you provide, including any photographs of your favorite clothes you choose to submit. This information is then processed not by humans, but by algorithms and artificial intelligence. The end result is an e-mail sent to you with a preview of the selected items, which you can either reject or ask to be delivered to your home. This reduces the surprise effect for the customer but saves a lot of money for Zalando, as well as providing useful additional data that helps to make their algorithms even smarter.

I am convinced that even today, in our high-tech age, the human, personal approach – including the warmth of telephonic contact – leads to a better selection and a higher degree of customer satisfaction. But be that as it may, the future still looks set to be taken over by an algorithmic form of curated commerce.

THE AMAZON VOICE

In its earliest days, Amazon employed a team of book critics, who decided which books should be given extra attention in the company's webshop. They were known collectively as the Amazon Voice. An article in the *The Wall Street Journal* described them as the most powerful critics in the world, because they had such a strong influence on the purchase of books. At the same time, the company went in search of possibilities to make personal recommendations to customers. The first attempt was a failure. It was based on the idea of looking at the books customers had previously purchased, but this resulted in recommendations that were too similar to what people had already read. For example, if someone had bought a travel guide for Poland, they received recommendations for lots of other travel books about Eastern Europe. The second attempt was more successful. The analysis no longer examined what just a single customer had purchased, but looked at the other books that all the purchasers of one specific book had bought. A real market test was conducted to measure what effect the recommendations made by the critics and the algorithms had on turnover. The difference in results was so glaring that the critics were very quickly pensioned off.[44]

In order to gather more data about the preferences of customers, webshops not only analyze what you buy and send back, but also your general surfing behavior in their online store. Which product pages do you look at? How much time do you spend on each page? On which specific items do you zoom in? Nowadays, you are increasingly given the opportunity to 'like' particular products via social media, which is again designed to help better map out your preferences.

The ultimate goal of all this analysis is to create the made-to-measure webshop. For functional purchases, this means drawing up a made-to-measure shopping list, with convenience as the new customer loyalty. But for recreational purchases, people now want to be surprised with products that they don't yet know but like once they have discovered them. In both cases, the future rests with curated commerce: choice tailor-made to the needs and desires of the customer.

1st wave		2nd wave
reason/brain	→	emotion/heart
search	→	discover
product	→	solution
specifications	→	inspiration
largest choice	→	personalized choice

FROM LOWEST PRICE TO SHOP LOYALTY

The first wave of e-commerce encouraged a 'race to the bottom': because the internet created almost complete price transparency, making consumer price comparison far easier than ever before, rival companies soon found themselves involved in a non-stop price war. This put margins under greater pressure, so that having sufficient scale became a prerequisite for survival. This urgent need for scale went hand in hand with ambitious targets for growth, which were necessary to keep investors and shareholders satisfied.

The second wave of e-commerce breaks through this downwards spiral. In this second phase, love is the language of the heart. By creating an emotional bond, customer loyalty transcends the dimensions of convenience and low price. Online stores now seek to inspire the consumer, allow him to discover new things and put him in the right mood. This is effectively declaring war on the rational brain. If you receive a surprise box with a new outfit that you love as soon as you see it, you are not going to spend the next half hour hunting around the internet to see if you can find the same outfit at a cheaper price elsewhere. On the contrary, you are delighted with what you have received and want to wear it as soon as possible! What's more, this kind of curated commerce or personalized shopping gives the customer the feeling that this webshop is different and better than all the rest: they are always sending you such wonderful things…

In other words, these sellers of solutions generally avoid price comparison by the customer. If you have gone to the trouble, with the help of your builders' merchant, of drawing up an exact list of everything you need to insulate your attic, there doesn't really seem a lot of point to then start comparing prices for each individual item. Even if you make the effort, you will soon discover that no two shops sell precisely the same products. Sometimes the brand will be different, sometimes the package size, etc. This makes accurate comparison very difficult. What's more, the 'gratitude factor' also often plays a role: even if the prices at your supplier are a little higher, you are prepared to pay them because you are satisfied with the smoothness of your customer journey and the quality of the advice you have received. In this way, the shop becomes a brand, creating a higher form of customer loyalty.

1st wave		2nd wave
reason/brain	→	emotion/heart
search	→	discover
product	→	solution
specifications	→	inspiration
largest choice	→	personalized choice
lowest price	→	shop as brand

CHAPTER 4
OPTICHANNEL RETAIL

'Arrive too early at the party and there are no guests,

arrive too late and you are cleaning the trash.'

George S. Day (professor at the Wharton Business School)

Even when you are writing a book, you are subject to the Messi syndrome. You want to go for gold. You hope that you are unleashing a classic on the world. At the same time, you realize that the sell-by date for most management books is just a few years. And if you are writing about the impact of new technology, this few years can even be reduced to a few months.

For this reason, I am proud that my book *Omnichannel in retail* has lost surprisingly little of its relevance and can still be found in most good bookstores. So if you think, when reading the title of this chapter, that it perhaps sounds a little dated, you are wrong. I am not trying to put new wine in old barrels; the old wine is still good.

EVERYONE A RETAILER, EVERYONE A (BRAND) MANUFACTURER!

In other words, omnichannel is still of considerable importance in the field of direct sales. This is the only way a retailer can control all his different sales channels and provide an integral customer experience to the consumer.

As we saw in chapter 2, this is most difficult for brand manufacturers like Bosch, Puma and Panasonic, because their products and services are largely sold by third parties and therefore through indirect sales channels. Until recently, this was in physical stores; today and in the future, it will be increasingly via webshops. If the brand manufacturers open their own stores and webshop, the resulting turnover as a proportion of total sales is usually not much to write home about. This means that in the narrow sense of the term they cannot create a true omnichannel environment: they remain too dependent on their third-party sellers for the final customer experience. This is particularly the case in terms of the price paid by the customer: this is fixed not by the brand, but by the selling store or webshop. Otherwise, the brand would be sold at the same price everywhere.

In recent years, we have seen that the boundary between retailers and brand manufacturers has become increasingly blurred. This is an evolution that started some time ago in the fashion sector. In addition to their traditional sales channels in multi-brand stores, brands like Esprit and Nike began to develop their own retail networks.

In the professional jargon, we refer to 'wholesale' (indirect sales) and 'retail' (direct sales). The balance between wholesale and retail differs significantly from company to company and from brand to brand. In 2017, 28% of Nike's turnover was derived from direct sales to consumers, compared with just 4% five years previously.[45] This means that their direct sales have been growing two and a half times faster than their indirect sales.[46] For the Belgian fashion house FNG, mother company of Claudia Sträter, Miss Etam, CKS and Fred & Ginger, the direct-indirect split is roughly fifty-fifty. For Esprit, direct sales now account for 70% of turnover.[47]

In the meantime, brand manufacturers have opened direct sales channels in many other sectors. The Apple Stores are perhaps the best-known and appeal most strongly to our imagination, but companies like Dyson, Sonos and Samsung also now have their own high street outlets.

The rise of e-commerce has further accelerated the pace of this 'direct sales' development. Nowadays, brands without their own webshop are the exception rather than the rule. The Esprit e-shop now represents a quarter of the company's turnover and a third of all direct sales. In short, brand manufacturers are increasingly becoming retailers.

Among retailers we can see a move in the opposite direction. Today, it is possible for fans of Mango, OYSHO (Inditex) or Weekday (H&M) to buy their products from ASOS, Zalando or About You. More and more retailers are finding their way to the dominant e-commerce pure players and their marketplaces. Even the multi-brand retailers are starting to become active on these platforms. The collaboration between BCC, part of the Fnac Darty Group, and bol.com is a notable example. As a result, retailers are becoming increasingly engaged in indirect sales and are therefore losing control over a growing part of their turnover. In fact, they are behaving like suppliers, comparable with (brand) manufacturers. The blurring of the boundaries between the different protagonists is complete! Nowadays, everyone is a retailer and everyone is a brand manufacturer/supplier!

Precisely because today's companies now operate with a mixed model incorporating both direct and indirect sales, we need a new and broader approach than the original omnichannel concept, an approach that is immediately relevant for both retailers and brand manufacturers.

THE CHALLENGE OF OMNICHANNEL

But even within the direct sales segment many retailers are also struggling to develop an effective omnichannel strategy. We have already seen in chapter 2 that this is more a question of 'not being able to', than of 'not wanting to'. Fewer than 10% describe themselves as successful in terms of actually earning money from omnichannel. A lack of budget is the reason most frequently quoted by CEOs for this failure.

This is the logical consequence of wanting to offer the best of both worlds: a physical store and a webshop. This means, of course, that you need to bear the cost of both worlds. Retailers are obliged, as it were, to build up an e-commerce value chain on top of their existing high street shop network.

In addition to the necessary investments in a webshop and e-logistics, there are also variable costs for digital marketing, home delivery and the recruitment of a digital team. Costs also increase in the shop network; for example, for the training of staff, the introduction of digital shelf labels, interactive screens and an amended cash register system. Unfortunately, in this respect omnichannel is an 'and-and' story.

For brand manufactures who want to try their hand at omnichannel, the main cost relates to the development of the direct sales channel; in other words, their own webshop and physical stores. What's more, the brand manufacturers also now need to carry the stock risk and the financial burden inherent in direct sales – matters that in traditional indirect sales can be passed on to the retailers.

On the other side of the coin, the benefits of omnichannel often remain below expectations. The race to the bottom, which makes it easy for price-sensitive customers to compare prices in the transparent online world, has put margins under pressure: the retailer is now earning less and less per product sold than he used to, not just online but also in his shops. To make matters worse, a small number of large pure players are dominating the fast-growing e-commerce market, so that it is difficult to compensate for the falling unit margin through a growth in volume. In reality, for many retailers omnichannel turns out to be little more than a question of making good falling shop turnover by creating new online turnover. The growth they are able to achieve is too low in relation to the costs incurred. This also has negative implications for the brand manufacturers: the retailers try to compensate for margin pressure by insisting on bigger purchase discounts from their suppliers.

If only 10% of retailers succeed in making money from omnichannel, this means that it is no longer good enough to belong to the top 20% of performers – our criterion for success. This means that we need to search for a different approach to omnichannel that will make it more accessible and more efficient.

OPTICHANNEL COMMUNICATION

It is not just omnichannel retail that is fraught with difficulties and challenges. Omnichannel communication is also under fire.

To begin with, all companies face exactly the same problem: the need to seamlessly integrate all their interactions with the customer throughout the entire customer journey. This is no easy task. It is technically possible, but demands heavy investment in ICT solutions.

Secondly, the expected positive effect on customer satisfaction is often well below par. It seems that the customer is not as excited as many companies had hoped about the possibility of choosing his own preferred channel of communication at the different moments in his journey towards a purchase.

This certainly gives the customer a high degree of control, but the explosion of online forms he receives to discover his preferences often work as an irritant that creates a mild form of choice stress. This can actually make the customer journey more difficult, instead of easier. As a result, the customer often makes choices in a kind of 'automatic pilot' mode; choices that are often sub-optimal.

In other words, the effect of omnichannel communication on customer loyalty is, on balance, disappointing: the costs tend to outweigh the benefits. Consequently, companies complain that the return on their investment is too low to be sustainable.[48]

In view of this negative situation, the alternative concept of optichannel is increasingly gaining ground. Optichannel proposes that while the customer should always remain in the central position, he should no longer be encouraged to choose his own preferred channel of communication at the different points in the customer journey. Instead, the company will encourage him to choose a specific channel in specific contexts and for specific purposes. This is the optimum channel. The starting point for this concept is the idea that not every channel of communication is suitable for every purpose. Text messages, for example, are ideal for sending short and urgent messages: 98% of all text messages are opened, 95% of them within three minutes. Compare this with e-mail: 78% of all commercial e-mails are never opened. But e-mails are much better at fulfilling an archive function than text messages. For this reason, sending a flight confirmation by e-mail is a much better idea than doing it by texting.[49]

OPTICHANNEL COMMUNICATION AT THE DSB BANK

A good example of optichannel is the way in which the Singa-pore-based bank DSB deals with the reporting of lost or stolen credit cards. The bank has learnt that customers often lose their wallet/purse and everything in it. As a result, they are generally upset when they contact the bank to report the loss of their card. Typically, they ask themselves three questions:

1 How am I going to get the money I need to get home?
2 Can someone use my credit card to illegally make payments or withdraw money from my bank account?
3 How can I get my life back in order?

Given the nature of these questions, the bank has decided that the reporting of credit card loss can only be made by telephone. In this way, the bank's staff can first reassure the customers and put them at their ease, before establishing precisely what has been lost and giving practical advice about what best to do.[50]

In the following step, the bank sends the customer a text mes-sage with relevant telephone numbers. They prefer not to dic-tate these numbers during the telephone conversation, in case the upset customer hasn't got a pen and paper handy or makes a mistake when jotting down the numbers. This also allows the customer to directly call one of the numbers without the need to dial.[51]

By guiding customers in this specific way, a standard customer journey can be developed for a particular type of customer in a particular context, instead of having an endless number of vari-ants generated by the customer himself.

The benefits for the bank are obvious: by focusing on a limited number of standard customer journeys making use of standard channels and touchpoints, it is possible to optimize the customer experience in a more targeted manner. Moreover, this often leads to cost savings, because in this context the company only needs to seamlessly integrate a limited number of communication channels, not all of them.

Last but not least, there are also benefits for the customer: he avoids choice stress and enjoys a better customer experience if he follows the customer journey chosen for him by the bank. Of course, the essential precondition is that this journey must fully meet his needs and is not simply a quick way for the bank to save money. This explains why DSB has chosen for the more expensive option of telephone support via a contact center, since this channel better meets its objective: reassuring and helping the customer.

OPTICHANNEL RETAIL?

The similarity between omnichannel communication and omnichannel retail is a close one: in both cases companies are wrestling with the implementation of a well-intentioned strategy for which the costs often exceed the benefits.

One possible reason for this is that companies have taken things too far in a dogmatic approach to the concept of customer satisfaction. The idea that the customer must be able to choose at all times from all available channels may sound good, but it is a two-edged sword. It leads to a countless number of different customer journeys, resulting in a complexity that is difficult to manage. Costs shoot through the roof, the customer journey continues to be sub-optimal and money is lost below the line.

Hence the appeal of optichannel retail, where smart companies seek to establish a healthy balance between customer focus, competitive strength and sound financial management.

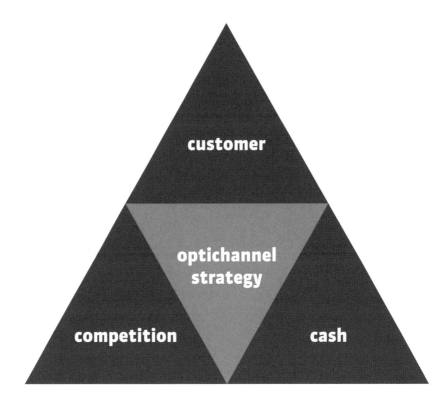

OPTICHANNEL IN PRACTICE

In a similar way to optichannel communication, optichannel retail steps away from the idea that the customer must have full control over all stages of the customer journey. Instead, the customer is guided towards the retailer's own view of the best possible journey, based on the customer's profile, the product category in which he wishes to buy, and the context in which he is situated (see chapter 5: 'Choose a target market').

In the most extreme cases of optichannel, the customer is no longer left any freedom of choice at all. In more moderate versions, the customer is merely 'nudged' in the direction of the ideal journey, but can still deviate from the company's chosen route, if he so prefers.

In this respect, the Belgian telecom operator Proximus offers a good example. When a decoder malfunctions, the customer has a choice between having a new decoder delivered to his home or collecting it himself. In the past, this self-collection was possible from any Proximus store. This seemed to be the ideal scenario: the logistical costs are lower and you have the chance to tempt the customer to make additional purchases when he visits your premises.

The reality, however, is different. The rent of shops in city centers is high and the time of your highly trained sales staff is valuable. As a result, self-collection is actually a more expensive option than home delivery. Moreover, the customer who collects the decoder himself is primarily concerned with efficiency, so that he is unlikely to fall for your cross-selling gambit.

Given these factors, Proximus made the sensible choice of trying to dissuade people from self-collecting. Self-collecting is still possible but only from one of the 1,250 post offices operated by bpost, the Belgian postal company.[52] It is no longer possible from Proximus stores. This has narrowed the customer's freedom of choice, but without eliminating it altogether. What's more, it has also reduced waiting times in the Proximus stores, not only for people who want to collect a decoder, but for all other Proximus customers as well.

It may seem that the idea of scrapping channels and limiting choice is alien to our modern digital age, where the customer is king and his every whim must be catered for.

Even so...

It is clear that some of the leading e-commerce pure players are also increasingly adopting an optichannel approach. For example, some people may prefer to buy things from Alibaba, Amazon or Zalando in physical stores – but they can't. These online pure players have decided that online is the only ordering option.

Hello Fresh has taken things even further. The meal delivery service works exclusively with a subscription formula. Simply ordering a single meal is not possible. The delivery process is equally inflexible: in Brussels, they only deliver on Saturday, Sunday, Tuesday evening (16.30 to 21.00) and Wednesday (14.30 to 21.00). These timings aren't convenient for you? Tough luck!

The explanation for this strategy is very simple:

» Every company chooses a target group and attempts to service it in the best possible manner. This involves an interaction between the defined target group and the company's chosen value proposition. As long as sufficient customers are interested in the Hello Fresh offer, the company will still be able to prosper, even with its 'imperfect' proposition.

» Competitive strength also plays a role: as long as no other company is able to come up with a more perfect proposition – for example, more flexible hours of delivery – customers have no real alternative. If Hello Fresh continues to satisfy the Olympic minimum, customers will continue to order.

» Every company develops a value chain that offers the prospect of profitability in due course. Hello Fresh has opted for a subscription formula, because it significantly reduces marketing costs. Moreover, the lifetime value of a new customer is high, because the subscription immediately results in repeat sales. At the same time, the formula makes it possible to more accurately predict sales volumes, thereby eliminating product loss (Hello Fresh, as the name implies, works with fresh products). Finally, the delivery model also contributes to lower costs, thanks to the optimization of route planning, with a higher number of drops per driven kilometer.

If even the e-commerce pure players are no longer offering unrestricted freedom of choice to their customers, why should traditional retailers and brand manufacturers feel obliged to do it?

'OBSESS OVER CUSTOMERS'

In the eyes of the digital gurus, it is not a good idea to make customer focus less of a priority than competitive strength and sound financial management. 'Customer centricity' is undoubtedly the most hyped term in this age of digital hysteria. The evangelists of this dogma insist that customer focus must always come first and that no compromise is possible. This has created the perception that companies in the past were not customer-oriented.

In this context, the first letter that CEO Jeff Bezos wrote to the shareholders of Amazon is repeatedly quoted with the same reverence as holy scripture. This 1997 letter set out the Bezos vision for the future of the company. Since then, it has been included each year in the Amazon annual report:

'Because of our emphasis on the long term, we may make decisions and weigh trade-offs differently than some companies. (...) We will continue to focus relentlessly on our customers. (...) Obsess Over Customers. From the beginning, our focus has been on offering our customers compelling value. (...) We maintained a dogged focus on improving the shopping experience and in 1997 substantially enhanced our store. (...) Word of mouth remains the most powerful customer acquisition tool we have, and we are grateful for the trust our customers have placed in us.'[53]

As is so often the case, the digital evangelists are very selective when it comes to interpreting the words of the Amazon pioneer. But more of this later.

It is certainly true that Amazon places the customer centrally in its long-term vision for the future. And this is something that I agree with completely. In the long term, customer centricity in an absolute sense must also be the concern of an optichannel strategy. The highest priority is to develop a vision of the ideal customer journey, without taking too much account of today's practical objections. Because the future competitive landscape is highly uncertain, competitive strength also offers no real long-term security. We do not know who our competitors of tomorrow will be, just as we do not know what technological developments will take place in the years ahead. In other words, competition is not a benchmark for helping to determine your ideal customer journey. Likewise, long-term financial performance need not be a subject of concern. Whoever has the courage to dream, need not worry unduly about the financing of the distant future. Such dreamers take as their starting point the conviction that a winning vision of the customer will automatically lead to success in the market – and therefore also attract the necessary investors.

OPTICHANNEL: A DYNAMIC MODEL

In an optichannel strategy, the desired balance between the different key elements evolves over time. It is a dynamic model.

In the short term, all three objectives must enjoy an equal priority. The first reason for this is that customer satisfaction and competitive strength are closely interwoven: competition determines the expectations of the customer. Even indirect competitors help to shape these expectations: customers who never need to pay for a delivery from Zalando soon come to expect the same thing from their supermarket or garden center, even though these enterprises sell totally different products. This is equally true for speed of delivery.

In this respect, we need to make a distinction between competitive conditions and competitive advantages. Competitive conditions are a kind of 'Olympic minimum' that you need to satisfy as a company. This doesn't win you any medals, but it is a prerequisite for competing at all. If you fail to meet this minimum, customer satisfaction will decline and you will lose turnover. In the terminology of the Net Promoter Score, you will create 'detractors'.

Competitive advantage is achieved when you do things better than your rivals: by making a difference, you can go for gold! Customer satisfaction increases and you create 'promoters'.

But cash is also important: it is only the financially healthy companies that have the resources to invest in their long-term vision, which, sadly, will yield little return in the short term. It is precisely for this reason that you must invest in your transformation while things are going well, and not wait until the water has almost reached your lips.

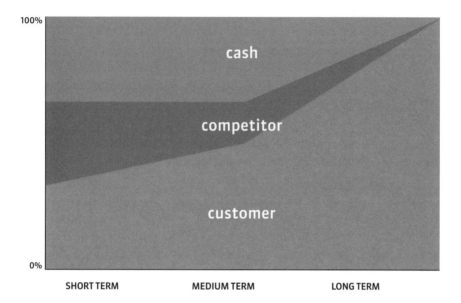

During the transition from the short term to the long term, it is the relative weight of the competitive strength factor that first decreases. Because successful companies on their way towards their ideal customer journey innovate more quickly than others, they enhance their lead over the competition. As a result, they focus less on the Olympic minimum (which is determined by their rivals) and more on the winning of medals, preferably gold (how can we serve the customer even better?).

Financial health continues to be an important factor in this middle phase: successful companies keep the ball rolling, so that sufficient cash is generated to keep investing in the future. This implies a more frequent choice for investments with a short payback period.

As we get further and further into the future, so the focus shifts increasingly to the customer. We have no idea who our competitors will be in the long term, nor can we know how well they will perform. Financially, we assume that by then we will have been able to yield the benefits of our ideal customer journey, so that financing will no longer be a problem.

In short, the dynamic of the optichannel model emphasizes the importance of concentrating on the right priorities at the right moment.

One of the remarkable things about the famous Jeff Bezos letter is that it describes precisely these same priorities. He attributes his initial success in online book sales to an ability to differentiate from the leading American bookstore of the day, Barnes & Noble:

'Therefore, we set out to offer customers something they simply could not get any other way, and began serving them with books. We brought them much more selection than was possible in a physical store (our store would now occupy six football fields).'[54]

At the same time, Jeff Bezos implicitly underwrites the basic premise of an optichannel strategy: because you cannot possibly do everything, you need to make choices about what to do and what not. This has crucial consequences for your investments:

'To be certain, a big part of the challenge for us will lie not in finding new ways to expand our business, but in prioritizing our investments.'[55]

The only difference is that digital companies are judged by investors on the basis of their growth objectives. They assume what is known as the 'hockey stick' effect, which at some point foresees an exponential increase in turnover and profitability.[56] This means that such companies have almost continual access to extra resources, if they need them. In contrast, existing companies are judged much more critically by the financial analysts. Their growth potential is estimated to be more modest, because they are more heavily assessed on the basis of traditional indicators relating to financial performance. Consequently, a healthy financial basis, with an emphasis on a strong operating cash flow, is vitally important for the successful implementation of an optichannel strategy.

THE FUTURE OF OMNICHANNEL?

Does optichannel mean the end of omnichannel? Not at all! The following table shows the various differences and agreements:

	OMNICHANNEL	OPTICHANNEL
TYPE OF SALE?	direct	direct and indirect
FOR WHO?	retailer	retailer and supplier
FOCUS?	customer	ST/MT: customer, competitor, cash LT: customer

In the long term, omnichannel and optichannel both place the customer centrally. Omnichannel has a narrower scope, being confined to direct sales by retailers.

In optichannel, it is necessary to make compromise in the short and medium term between customer focus, competitive strength and the need for financing. For direct sales, this approach will ultimately coincide in the long term with an omnichannel approach.

For indirect sales, optichannel is complementary to omnichannel, which can only be used in direct sales.

In the next two parts of the book we will discuss the building blocks of an optichannel strategy in more detail.

PART 2

OPTICHANNEL CUSTOMER FOCUS

INATION

E Y BREW
CUP   3.00
BREW   4.50
SSO   4.00
ER   3.00
K   MINI   3.00
K   SML   3.50
K   MED   3.50
K   LRG   4.00
COLATE   +1.00
MOND   +1.00
                                 5.00
                                 4.00

DEPARTURE

SEE SIGNATURE MENU

The WHEELHOUSE

CHAPTER 5

CHOOSE YOUR TARGET MARKET

'Most people don't choose what they want,

they choose what they think is safe.'

Phillip McGraw aka Dr. Phil (American television psychologist)

What do you sell? And to whom? And in which context? The answers to these three questions define your target market. Since it is impossible for you to be all things to all men, a successful optichannel strategy always begins with the careful consideration and choice of a target market. Even in this digital era of ours, the principle put forward decades ago by the American economist Michael Porter remains valid: the essence of strategy is choosing what you don't want to do. In other words, you need to choose what you will not sell, which target groups you will not approach, and in which contexts you will not attempt to serve the customer.

Mrs Smith needs a new vacuum cleaner. A second one. She lives in a nice house, but it has two floors and she is tired of carrying the vacuum cleaner from one floor to the other. Even though she is now 63 years old, she still likes to keep up with the times. She has a smartphone, a tablet and often Skypes with her grandchildren, not to mention regularly buying things online from Amazon. But for an important purchase of this kind, she prefers to go to the shops. That's the only way to really see a product before you buy it. It also gives you the opportunity to ask face-to-face advice from the sales team.

Mrs Jones also lives in a nice house with two floors and likewise wants a second vacuum cleaner, for precisely the same reason as Mrs Smith. She is a 43-year-old single mother of the twins Lucas and Milan. Ever since the birth of the boys, she has been constantly rushed off her feet. It's always 'go-go-go'! In recent years, she has discovered the time-saving ease offered through buying things online. Amazon is her favorite webshop and after using the relevant filters to search through the store's extensive range of a thousand or more vacuum cleaners she eventually makes her choice, which is largely dictated by the high ratings and clear reviews she finds on the site. So easy!

Mrs Smith and Mrs Jones are two consumers who want to purchase the same product, but have different needs. As a result, their ideal customer journey is not the same. Consequently, they end up buying the same vacuum cleaner, but from different vendors.

IN WHAT CONTEXT DOES YOUR CUSTOMER PURCHASE?

But let's now change the context slightly. Mrs Jones still needs a new vacuum cleaner, but this time because the old one is broken. What a nuisance! And just on the day before she is expecting guests for dinner! Obviously, she needs a replacement as soon as possible, so that she can clean her home before her guests arrive. She surfs to Amazon, but now she has no time to read through all the reviews and ratings, even after the filters have narrowed down the huge range of available vacuums. Consequently, she switches to the Currys website, but even here she is faced with making a choice between more than 150 different products. Fortunately, she notices the first vacuum cleaner in the list: a Miele with high ratings and a single clear review, which is also being offered at a 60% reduced price. That will do nicely! She orders instantly, with a guarantee of delivery the next day. Now she can get on with the preparations for her dinner party!

The situations in which we wish to buy the same product can vary significantly. This has a strong influence on our specific needs. People who want to shop for groceries at the weekend to buy everything they need for the coming week will take the car and drive to the hypermarket on the edge of town, where the range is bigger, the prices are cheaper and there are always lots of interesting special offers to be had. But if all you need is a loaf of bread and a tube of toothpaste, you will probably nip around the corner to the neighborhood supermarket in the next street, even though it's a bit more expensive and has a smaller assortment of brands and products.

In short, we are 'chameleon consumers'. We shop from moment to moment. And how and where we buy are strongly influenced by the nature of those different buying occasions.

The same principle applies for the use and consumption of the product. Do we offer people bottled water when they come to visit? Or do we give them the same tap water that we drink all the time at home? And if we go for the bottled water option, do we buy an ordinary brand if our boss is amongst the guests, or do we feel a need to splash out on a more exclusive brand like Perrier?

WHAT DO WE SELL?

Let's change products. Mrs Jones now needs a new television. The old one is being taken upstairs to the kids' room, so that they can occupy themselves with PlayStation while their mum enjoys her favorite soaps. In keeping with her habits, Mrs Jones chooses a new set online. Thanks to the ratings and reviews, she is convinced of the wisdom of her choice. But because the TV occupies a central position in her living room, this time she actually wants to see it 'for real' before she confirms her decision to buy. Is the design attractive? Will it match her other furniture? Via Google Shopping she notices that Currys currently have the model of her choice at a reduced price. Consequently, she decides to pop into town on Saturday afternoon to have a look for herself. When she arrives in the store, she likes what she sees and so she makes up her mind on the spot to buy it, at the same time arranging delivery to her home on the following Monday.

The same customer, Mrs Jones, has a higher level of engagement for a television than for a vacuum cleaner. As a result, her customer journey for the respective products looks very different.

THE SHOP FOR EVERYONE?

You can define your target group very broadly. Amazon, for example, wants to be the shop for everyone and with Amazon Prime has already managed to reach over 50% of the American population. However, its value proposition is based on wide choice and limited advice – a model that is not suited to every product and every buying occasion.

In terms of penetration, supermarkets often do even better than Amazon. In the Netherlands, two thirds of all Dutch families buy their groceries from market leader Albert Heijn. In part, this is due to their huge number of stores. Even so, there are some interesting variations within the customer base: the company attracts more than 70% of singles, but 'only' 56% of families of four or more people.[57] In addition, Albert Heijn also tries to cater for different types of buying occasions by using different shop formulas: the AH to go stores primarily sell food products for immediate consumption, while its ordinary supermarkets focus on food for consumption at home and all other non-edible groceries.

Sometimes, your target market develops organically. Sometimes, it is the result of a conscious strategic choice. Sometimes, it is a combination of both. Right from the very start, Jeff Bezos intended to grow Amazon from an online bookshop to a general store selling just about everything. In contrast, the Dutch bol.com began life as part of the Bertelsmann media group and had no ambition to sell anything other than books. But today bol.com has become the Amazon of the Netherlands and Flanders.

Irrespective of how your target market came into being and has changed over the years, when you want to develop or update an optichannel strategy you really need to carefully re-examine that market and what you expect from it in the future. It is only once you have confirmed or amended your ideas about the market that you should move on to trying to define your ideal customer journey for the years ahead (see the following chapter).

This is not a linear process: thinking about the customer journey of tomorrow will often lead you to new insights that make necessary the further re-defining or fine-tuning of your target market.

When choosing your new target market, the following four factors need to be taken into consideration:

1. The DNA of the company: are we making use of synergies with the existing target market?
2. The ability to differentiate: do we have sufficient competitive power?
3. The size of the target market: is our choice financially viable?
4. The expected evolutions in the medium and long term: is our choice sustainable?

THE DNA OF THE COMPANY

It is in the best interests of existing players to try and match their new choice of target market to their past history, so that the effect of possible synergies can be exploited. This will give them a lead over start-up rivals.

The most obvious choice in this respect is to develop an optichannel strategy for the existing target market. In the market of tomorrow Carrefour, Tesco, MediaMarkt, H&M, Lush and Esprit will continue to sell the same products during the same buying occasions to customers belonging to the current target segment. The customers who visit their physical stores will also be the first target group for their webshop. In fact, they can use the stores to activate these customers online. What's more, thanks to the loyalty cards of existing customers they already possess lots of valuable customer data. This helps to explain why companies such as H&M and Hema have recently launched loyalty programs: they not only want to know about the online shopping behavior of their customers, but about their offline behavior as well.

It is for precisely this same reason that the Dutch webshop wehkamp has chosen the family as its target group, with a special focus on purchases for which women make the final decisions. This is fully in line with the company's past as a mail-order specialist.

The same synergy benefits also apply to your range: whoever offers the same products online and offline can make best use of existing supplier relationships.

Synergy does not need to be sought in all three dimensions of the target market. Eriks, an international player specialized in the business to business sale of maintenance, repair and overhaul supplies – also known as MRO material[58] – has developed an optichannel strategy based on its existing assortment, but marketed via a new start-up to a new target group. Traditionally, Eriks has always been strong in sales to large industrial companies, but with its Zamro start-up Eriks is now aiming to reach smaller entrepreneurs and even consumers. The synergy between the mother and daughter companies in terms of sourcing and logistics is as good as it gets, yet even so Zamro still markets the Eriks range as an independent digital entity.

Of course, new entrants into the market have no past history to rely on. This means that they are unable to enjoy the benefit of synergies derived from an existing activity. On the other side of the coin, they have the advantage of being able to start with a blank sheet of paper, so that they can choose a target market in full freedom – as we shall shortly see with ASOS.

Manufacturers are confronted with the same question: should I make a vacuum cleaner for Mrs Smith, Mrs Jones or for both of them?

THE TARGET MARKET FOR ASOS

In contrast to what some digital gurus would like you to believe, segmentation and targeting continue to be highly relevant, even in our new digital era.

This is clear, for example, from the case of the British online fashion giant, ASOS. In its communication with investors, the company describes its target market in unambiguous terms.[59]

Its core customers are young people in their twenties who love fashion and live in Great Britain, continental Europe and the United States:

'Our mission remains: to be the world's no.1 fashion destination for 20-somethings.'

- 'ASOS is a true home for young fashion lovers.'
- 'It's for all fashion-loving people, whatever their shape and size, whatever the occasion.'
- 'We have a real understanding of our customers because 2,000+ of them are ASOS employees!'
- 'Geographically, we're currently focusing pricing and capital investment in three target markets: the UK, continental Europe and the US.'

In contextual terms, they focus on 'fashion as a hobby online':

- 'Content is an important part of the experience and a key part of what makes us stand out from the crowd.'
- 'We really believe ASOS is more than a shop – it's not just about pushing products; it's also about being the fashion-forward friend who you trust to say: "try this".'

This translates into a clear product offer:

- 'We champion inclusivity with our product offering.'
- 'Our Petite, Tall, Curve, Maternity and Bridal ranges – to name just a few – are growing fast.'
- 'Our future expansion plans include specialist sizes for menswear, plus beauty and grooming additions for both men and women.'

The biggest challenges of all occur if a company's existing product can be digitalized. When this happens, the physical store loses the reason for its existence.

This explains why retailers such as Virgin, Tower Records and Free Record Shop have all gone under in recent years. In a first stage, illegal downloads helped to weaken the market. This process was intensified when Apple created a new business model with the introduction of iTunes, which allowed music to be downloaded legally. The final blow came when Spotify launched its streaming service, which gave the new music market its definitive shape – at least for the time being.

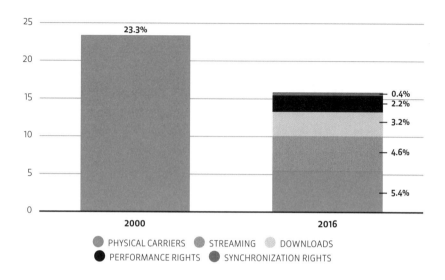

Worldwide turnover in the music industry (in billions of dollars). Source: IFPI

The record companies – effectively the 'manufacturers' of the music industry – have also been affected by this dislocation of their market. During the past fifteen years their turnover has dropped by 40%, although it is now slowly starting to rise again. Turnover relating to physical carriers (CDs and vinyl) has fallen by as much as 75%. In 2016, digital music for the very first time represented more than half of total turnover (59% from streaming and 41% from downloads). One of the most remarkable things about this situation is the way in which the record companies responded almost passively. Instead of trying to develop the digital market themselves, they devoted most of their energy to pursuing and prosecuting the illegal downloading services, like Napster.

That being said, the Dutch-based Free Record Shop was quick to recognize the potential of e-commerce and launched its own webshop in the late 1990s. Even so, this was simply postponing the inevitable. The only way to survive the disruption of the market was for 'traditional' music companies to start up their own legal download or streaming service, or to change their target market by switching to a different product category.

The first of these options was difficult, but not impossible. Netflix began in 1997 with the distance sale and hire of DVDs and only switched to streaming activities in 2007. In comparison with Free Record Shop, Netflix had the double advantage that it was not weighed down by having an existing shop network, whilst at the same time also being able to develop its services in the much larger American domestic market.

Bol.com was another Low Countries victim of the dislocation of the multimedia sector. Just as the company was set to become the largest seller of music in the Netherlands, downloads threatened to decimate the CD market. As a result, in 2003 bol.com attempted to launch its own download service. However, because the company's negotiation with the record companies failed to deliver a financially viable model, these plans soon had to be shelved.

However, in contrast to Free Record Shop, bol.com was eventually able to secure its future by selling a new range of product groups to its existing customers within the same commercial context. In essence, the company switched its focus in 2004 to small consumer electronics.[60] In a later phase, toys were added to the assortment – and the rest, as they say, is history: bol.com is now the largest seller of toys in the Netherlands.

It is also possible to find good examples of successful transformations among the classic retailers. Before the digital era, the French-based Fnac chain of stores generated its turnover from the sale of books, multimedia (music, films and later also videogames), photography, brown goods (TVs, hi-fi, etc.) and informatics. It was like combining a bookstore, a multimedia store and a consumer electronics store under a single roof: three types of store that have largely disappeared out of many European high streets in recent years.

In the past, Fnac's customers – an urban public, more male than female and with an above average income – visited the company's stores to discover products (rummage through the books and CDs) and buy presents. In line with this existing target group and their buying occasions, Fnac now also sells an exclusive range of small household products, running from high-end coffee machines to the latest Dyson hairdryers (you won't find an ordinary Senseo or BaByliss!). In addition – and not dissimilar to bol.com in a different context – a carefully chosen selection of toys is also now offered. In this way, Fnac has been able to successfully add two new categories to its assortment to replace the turnover it has lost from photography and multimedia as a consequence of the digital revolution. It almost goes without saying, of course, that the company has also developed an online sales channel!

THE ABILITY TO DIFFERENTIATE

As a company, you always need to find a way to be different – and this applies equally to an optichannel strategy.

Even the so-called 'big box' retailers are faced with this challenge. In the introduction, we saw how the 'category killers' like MediaMarkt, Ikea, Best Buy, Toys"R"Us and Decathlon ('real' specialists) succeeded in hollowing out the competitive advantage of the hypermarkets, by forcing a change in customer perception away from the positive 'everything under one roof' towards the more negative 'a little bit of everything but nothing in depth'.

Nowadays, thanks to the growing pressure of e-commerce, it is the category killers who need to reinvent themselves. For example, in consumer electronics MediaMarkt conquered Europe by building bigger stores, which allowed it to offer a much wider range than its competitors. But in the digital era customers can find an even bigger range online, so that MediaMarkt now needs to go in search of a new form of competitive advantage.

In the toy sector it is not just the big box retailers like Toys"R"Us who are starting to struggle. Nearly all the classic toy stores are fighting for survival – think of the 'reorganizations' that have already taken place at Toytown and Maxi Toys. The problem is, of course, that toys are very suitable for online sales. Children are strongly influenced by advertising ('I want the Lego Duplo toy train!'), so that parents – in the spirit of the first wave of e-commerce – go online to see where they can find the cheapest offer.

Attempting to differentiate by creating a superior store experience seldom offers a way out. Because a large part of toys turnover is generated from gifts that are not purchased when the children are present, there is a risk that toy stores will soon be nothing more than a showroom for Santa Claus and Father Christmas!

What's more, the toy market in general continues to shrink, as 21st century children reach maturity at an increasingly early age. They are much quicker than they used to be to say farewell to Barbie dolls and model train sets: nowadays, they prefer to 'play' with smartphones, tablets and videogames – products that are also on sale at other specialist outlets like Currys, Fnac and Game Mania. To make matters even worse, gaming – like music – is ideal for digitalization.

Toy stores that are able to differentiate on the basis of a specialist offer – for example, those who focus on wooden or educational toys – will probably find it easier to weather the digital storm.

We will look at this in more detail in chapter 11, when we discuss competitive power.

THE SIZE OF THE TARGET MARKET

The more narrowly you define your target market, the more specifically you can satisfy that market's needs. But as you can read in any standard book on marketing, the golden rule is to choose a target market that is sufficiently large to be financially viable.

In chapter 1, where we looked at the first wave of e-commerce, we already highlighted the difference in scale between local players like bol.com and Coolblue, and the international players like Amazon, ASOS and Zalando. Scale can be created in different ways. By focusing on 'twenty-somethings' ASOS has consciously opted for a smaller target market than Zalando. But in contrast to Zalando, ASOS does not restrict its operations to Europe, but also seeks to penetrate the huge American market.

Whichever options you choose, it is becoming increasingly clear that digital excellence requires the availability of significant resources and, consequently, a minimum level of scale. In his 1997 letter to his shareholders, Jeff Bezos was already arguing that: *'We have a window of opportunity as larger players marshal the resources to pursue the online opportunity. (...) The stronger our market leadership, the more powerful our economic model.'*[61]

Companies that are unable to achieve this minimum scale will need to find some other way to differentiate themselves. In the toy sector, the British Hamleys is an outstanding example. The 5,000 m² of their flagship store in London's Regent Street makes it the largest toy shop in the world. Everything is focused on maximizing customer experience – a factor in which their friendly and enthusiastic sales staff and product demonstrators have a crucial role. Children can play to their heart's content, while adults become kids again and enjoy sharing the pleasure of their young sons and daughters. At the same time, it is worth noting that while you will certainly find the obligatory sets of Lego and Playmobil in Hamleys, the biggest part of their turnover comes from relatively 'unknown' and more specialized brands and products, presented in a highly creative context. The temptation on the shop floor is so huge that it is almost impossible to avoid buying something!

The store's exploitation costs are high: a large number of very expensive square meters combined with a labor-intensive sales model making use of well-trained and well-motivated personnel. The customer experience is very personal, authentic and definitely non-digital. You can only make this kind of store viable if you can attract sufficient paying customers seven days a week and 365 days a year, and not just during the weekends and at peak periods like Christmas and New Year. This is what Hamleys does so well. Its perfect location means that it is mentioned in every travel guide, allowing the store to profit to a maximum extent from the 20 million tourists who visit London each year. [62] And as tourists, they often have no option but to make their purchases in the presence of their travelling children.

This makes it possible for Hamleys to survive and even thrive, but only on a limited scale.[63] The kind of experience they offer is only feasible at a select number of unique locations, as the Hamleys stores in Moscow and Dubai clearly demonstrate. This means that the overall scale of operations inevitably remains 'small', so that the Hamleys model cannot serve as an example for more 'ordinary' toy sellers like Toys"R"Us.

EXPECTED EVOLUTIONS IN THE MEDIUM AND LONG TERM

You develop an optichannel strategy to give your company a future. There is not much point in focusing on your ability to differentiate and upscale in the short term only. For all you know, the Mrs Smiths of the world, who want to see and handle their vacuum cleaner before they buy it, may represent a rapidly shrinking customer segment. How many Mrs Smiths will there still be in five years' time? Or in ten years? And what proportion of vacuum cleaner sales will they represent? After all, older people generally buy fewer vacuums than younger people. And what if Mrs Smith's children decide to order a new model for her online? Viewed in these terms, the future for stores that focus on the physical display of vacuum cleaners strikes me as being very limited indeed...

One of the biggest challenges in this context is correctly assessing the likely impact of new technologies on consumer buying and consumption behavior.

How will artificial intelligence influence the way in which we orient our search for a new vacuum cleaner? Will we ask for advice from a virtual salesperson? Or will we conduct a Skype conversation with a real 'flesh and blood' assistant? How will self-driving cars influence our purchasing behavior? Will these cars be a blessing in disguise for high street shopping, because we will be able to reach city centers without traffic jams and parking problems? Or will they stimulate even more e-commerce, because they will make deliveries cheaper and more convenient? In a similar vein, car manufacturers are asking themselves whether or not personal car ownership will soon be a thing of the past. Will we all be happy to use shared transport or will the desire for privacy and convenience still dominate? What's more, these are only some of the dilemmas we are already able to predict. Who knows what other surprises new technological developments may hold in store for us further down the line?

In view of all this uncertainty, it is unwise to make firm predictions about the future. Instead, it is wiser to develop a number of possible scenarios whose relative probabilities you can assess. These can then form the basis for a vision of the future that you can adjust as time goes by. To make this possible, retailers and manufacturers must ensure that their organizations are sufficiently flexible to respond quickly to changing circumstances, just in case the future does not turn out exactly as they had planned. We will be looking more closely at the importance of an adaptive strategy in chapter 13.

That being said, even in these fast-changing times it is still possible to develop a vision for your company that can last for two decades or more. To prove my point, I will refer for a final time to Jeff Bezos's remarkable 1997 letter to his shareholders, which set out a future course for Amazon that is still as relevant today as it was then:

'Today, online commerce saves customers money and precious time. Tomorrow, through personalization, online commerce will accelerate the very process of discovery'.[64]

CHOOSE YOUR TARGET MARKET

1. Which target market do you want to serve?
    a. Who do you want to sell to (customer profile)?
        Which segments are you going to target?
    b. In which context do you wish to serve your customers?
        For which buying occasions? For which consumption
        moments?
    c. In which product category/categories do you want to
        compete?

2. The DNA of the company: does your choice of target market
    allow you to make beneficial use of synergies with your
    existing target market?

3. The ability to differentiate: do you have sufficient
    competitive power?

4. The size of the target market: is your choice financially
    viable?

5. The expected evolutions in the medium and long term: how
    sustainable is your choice?

CHAPTER 6

THE IDEAL CUSTOMER JOURNEY

'It's really hard to design products by focus groups.

A lot of times, people don't know what they want

until you show it to them.'

Steve Jobs (co-founder and former CEO of Apple)

'*Imagine...*' sang John Lennon, and in three telling verses set out his vision for an ideal world: a world without religion, war and personal possessions. A naive and utopian vision? History would suggest that it is. Perhaps even a hypocritical and scarcely believable message? It was bizarre to say the least that a pop star with millions in the bank should unleash on the world his own communist manifesto in the form of a song that was destined to earn him millions more...

Even so, *Imagine* is an excellent source of inspiration for what we want to do in this chapter. In the following pages we will need to use our imagination to devise our ideal customer journey. And to do this, we must ignore possible practical objections and take no account of our current business model, with one important exception: our target market.

But there is a crucial difference between this exercise and John Lennon's worldwide hit. Our ideal customer journey is more than just a 'no-obligation' intellectual mind game. It is not a dream; it is an ambition. What's more, it is an ambition that we intend to make good in the foreseeable (albeit long-term) future, by systematically removing all the practical objections that stand in the way of its realization.

THE CUSTOMER JOURNEY

The concept of the customer journey is central to the current desire of the business world to achieve maximum customer focus. The aim is to obtain a holistic view of what the customer experiences at each point of contact with your company, your products and your services. This will allow you to gain insights into what your customer does, why he does it and how it makes him feel. In other words, you look at the customer experience through the eyes of the customer, with the ultimate objective of improving that experience and, as a result, customer satisfaction.

The customer journey typically consists of two parts. The path to purchase sketches the route the customer follows to arrive at his purchase. Every step he makes is carefully mapped out, from the origins of his initial need for a product, right through to the actual buying, delivery and, where appropriate, installation of that product.

The second part of the customer journey is the consumption phase, in which the customer uses his purchased product, whatever it might be: a can of cola, a bottle of washing-up liquid, a vacuum cleaner, a car (toy or otherwise), etc. In some cases, an after-sales service may be necessary, to keep your car in good working order or repair your vacuum cleaner if it breaks down. Finally, there is the question of how you dispose of your product once it comes to the end of its useful working life.

In contrast to optichannel, omnichannel retail focuses exclusively on the path to purchase. Omnichannel takes as its starting point the perspective of the retailer, who first and foremost wishes to sell a product or service, as a result of which he is less concerned about the consumption phase.

	OMNICHANNEL	OPTICHANNEL
TYPE OF SALE?	direct	direct and indirect
FOR WHOM?	retailer	retailer and manufacturer
FOCUS?	customer	ST/MT:customer/ competitor/cash LT: customer
REACH?	path to purchase	the entire customer journey

Optichannel embraces the entire customer journey. This not only blurs the boundaries between retailers and manufacturers, but also encourages greater out-of-the-box thinking, which in turn requires consideration to be given not just to the path to purchase, but to the use phase as well. The above table summarizes the main differences between omnichannel and optichannel.

THE DIFFERENT PHASES IN THE CUSTOMER JOURNEY

We usually draw the customer journey as a matrix, in which the different phases are positioned in separate columns. Regrettably, there is no generally agreed list of phases. For one thing, each consultant has developed his own model. In addition, the number and type of phases can vary, dependent on the nature of the product or service.

A good way to start is to divide up your matrix into sections for the path to purchase and the consumption phase:

» Path to purchase:
origin of the need ➡ investigation ➡ choice ➡ purchase ➡ delivery or transport

» Consumption phase:
initial use ➡ routine use ➡ after-sales service ➡ disposal

The origin of the need

This phase marks the start of the purchasing process. We try to understand how and why the customer wants something. Is this the result of a physiological need (for example, hunger), a latent need ('This laptop works too slow'), a stimulated need ('Research shows we should eat less red meat'), an imposed need ('My doctor says I must go on a diet immediately' or 'this vacuum cleaner is beyond repair, so I need to replace it'), a derivative need ('If you are flying to Rome, why don't you hire a car as well?') or a created need ('Can you really live without a smartwatch?')?

Investigation

The customer actively goes in search of something that can satisfy his need. The importance of this phase is dependent on the level of commitment he has towards his purchase. This varies from customer to customer. John likes having nice clothes and enjoys shopping for them. Peter sees clothes as a necessity and has a more functional approach to their purchase. The product itself also plays a role. For example, we attach greater importance to buying a coffee machine than we do to buying a pack of coffee. Finally, the context can sometimes be important as well: standard repeat purchases require little or no investigation, whereas non-standard repeat purchases require a little bit more and first-time purchases a whole lot more.

Choice

After the consumer has explored the market, he chooses what he wants to buy and where he wants to buy it. He compares the different vendors and opts for the one that best meets his needs.

Purchase

This phase relates to the actual physical process of purchasing. In a shop, this means how the customer gains access to the product and pays for it. Is the product in a self-service area? Is it easy to find? Or do you need to talk to a member of staff and get it from a collection point? Can you make the necessary payment to that same member of staff or do you need to go and stand in a queue at a separate cash desk?

In webshops this is a critical phase. More than 75% of potential customers never cash in their shopping basket but instead break off the purchase at the last minute. Typical reasons for this are the addition of unexpected transport and/or other costs or a too long and/or complex purchasing process (for example, the need to set up an account). Another classic is the instance where the customer sees a box marked 'promotion codes' and so delays completing the transaction while he goes in search of that code – which he never finds…

Delivery and transport

In the past, it was the custom in classic retail only to make home delivery for large and heavy products, such as furniture or washing machines. With the advent and explosive growth of e-commerce, more attention, time and money is now being devoted to the delivery of a much wider range of goods. Even for 'ordinary' shopping in supermarkets, greater concern is being shown for how consumers actually get their purchases back to their homes. Crates of beer now have a handle for ease of carrying and the societal discussion about environmental sustainability has had a huge impact on the use of plastic (and other) shopping bags.

Initial use

Whether in traditional retail or e-commerce, at some point the customer takes his purchase out of its packaging. Perhaps the product needs to be installed or connected, as is the case with a TV set or dishwasher. Even a simple coffee machine must first be rinsed through before it can be taken into use. Similarly, Ikea furniture needs to be put together, while new smartphones need to be properly configured, so that we can transfer all our favorite apps and contact details. And how exactly does that new navigation system in your car work?

Routine use

We make a cup of coffee each morning. We watch the television each evening. We do the washing each week. But what if we only want to make a screenshot of our smartphone once every four months and no longer know how to do it? Fortunately, you have a neighbor who can show you and he also points out that you can use the phone as a torch. That's great – but what a pity you didn't know that when you first bought the thing a year ago. Frustrating? Maybe – but not as frustrating as trying to work out how you change that damned filter in your vacuum cleaner!

After-sales service

Help: my washing machine is flashing me a malfunction message! Where on earth did I put that instruction manual? Perhaps I can find a copy online? Ah, there it is! Hmm. Not as simple as I thought. The instruction for malfunction message E7 is: 'Contact a service professional'. That's the third time this week. First, the brakes and gears on my bike needed adjusting and then I had to take the car in for its six-monthly service...

Disposal

What do we do with empty packaging or with our washing machine, vacuum cleaner, coffee machine, smartphone, television, shoes, clothes, etc. when they reach the end of their useful life, so that we no longer need them?

THE CUSTOMER JOURNEY VS. THE SALES OR MARKETING FUNNEL

It is important not to confuse the customer journey with the sales or marketing funnel, which is something that often happens, particularly in the world of e-commerce. The sales or marketing funnel only concerns itself with the path to purchase for the purpose of generating maximum turnover with the least possible use of resources. It investigates where and why customers defect and how these thresholds can be overcome. Sometimes greater attention is also devoted to the customer experience, but usually with a finality based on the retailer's perspective. If customers in a webshop repeatedly search for a telephone number and leave the site because they can't find it, the webshop manager will soon add the number in a prominent position on his home page. But he doesn't do this to make his customers' lives easier. He does it because he knows it will yield more revenue.

Of course, mapping the sales funnel is still highly relevant and has an immediate impact on financial results. But it will not help you to develop the out-of-the-box thinking you need to devise your ideal customer journey. Its exclusive focus on sales and marketing is much too narrow for that purpose. What's more, the emphasis is placed too heavily on small improvements that can be tested and implemented with minimum delay.

The use of terminology often makes clear when we are dealing with a sales or marketing funnel dressed up as a customer journey. The different phases are not named from the perspective of the customer, but from the perspective of the seller: the origin of the need is referred to as 'awareness'; investigation becomes 'consideration'; choice is 'interest', 'desire' or 'engagement'; and purchase is nearly always 'conversion'...

It is often a good idea to translate the generic terms given above into something more industry specific:

» In the telecom sector, the Dutch provider KPN makes a distinction between three main phases: (1) from discovery to purchase; (2) from receipt to use and payment; and (3) from giving help and making changes to final termination.
» In the travel sector, the standard phases are early preparations, concrete planning, choosing hotels and transport, booking your choices, the pre-journey period, the actual journey, and the post-journey period.
» At Vlerick Business School, you don't 'buy' a training course but register to take part in one. This registration is followed by a confirmation, the actual course, and after-care.

When you are developing your ideal customer journey, it is necessary to list all the different steps the customer takes.

For example, your weekly visit to the supermarket to do your grocery shopping usually begins with making a list of what you want. And you begin your next list for the following week the day after your visit, starting with the products that were sold out or otherwise not available. In the course of the week you add lots of other things that the different members of your family need. Husband Peter fancies some Camembert. Son Jacob has finished off the last pot of Nutella. Lady of the house Brigit has run out of hairspray... And so the list gradually builds up.

On Friday evening, Peter and Brigit plan what they are going to eat during the next few days. The necessary ingredients are added to the list. At the same time, they have a look through the publicity folder of special offers they have received from the supermarket. These offers not only help them to decide what they will eat, but also what they will buy to store for a later date. For example, this week there is a 'buy one get one free' offer for washing powder, so they add this to the list as well. On Saturday, before he sets off for the supermarket, Peter checks what snacks are still available for the kids in the cupboard and what's left in the fridge to put on next week's sandwiches. He adds 'crisps', 'ham', 'cheese' and 'spreads' to the list. At last, he sets off for the supermarket and parks his car – which is not as easy as it sounds: the parking spaces are narrow and Peter's Lexus SUV is a big car. He eventually manages it and walks over to get a shopping trolley, only to find that he doesn't have the necessary coin to put into the release slot. Fortunately, he has one of those plastic tokens back in the car that will do the job, so he goes back to fetch it. Once Peter is finally in the supermarket, he works his way through his shopping list. He takes the Nutella almost automatically from the shelf: he buys it almost weekly and he knows exactly where it is. At the meat and cheese counter he picks out what he needs. He wants to check the sell-by date on the pre-packed ham, but the letters are so small that he needs to get his reading glasses. When everything is in the trolley, Peter makes his way to the check-out. He no longer uses his old plastic customer loyalty card. Peter has scanned it onto his smartphone, using the supermarket's clever app. The only snag is that this time the cashier's scanner doesn't seem to be able to read the barcode, so that she has to type in the long number. Hopefully, his phone won't switch into 'sleep' mode before she has finished! Fortunately not, but he now discovers he has forgotten to bring the reusable plastic bags he bought last week. Damn! He'll have to buy some more...

All these different actions are part of the customer journey. They help us to translate the generic steps into specific steps relating to the process of groceries shopping. Because in this instance the purchases are routine, there is no real 'investigation' involved. The supermarket therefore defines the phases of its path to purchase as follows: making a list (in your head or on paper); choosing in the store; paying; taking your purchases home and putting them away. If they want to look beyond the path to purchase, they would need to add things like cooking, cleaning, taking a shower, etc. It is only then, for example, that you can arrive at concepts like the Hello Fresh meal box.

The relevant level of detail is dependent on the objective. If we want to draw up our ideal customer journey from A to Z, then the description of groceries shopping as given above for Peter and Brigit is too complex. Instead, it would be better to work at a more aggregated level, since this will better allow us to determine the main priorities for improvement. The level of detail can then be increased for the high priority areas for improvement. More about this later.

The following matrix demonstrates this more aggregated approach for the customer journey for a family holiday. The different actions are now placed in separate columns for each of the main phases.

MAIN PHASES	preparation		concrete plans		choosing			booking	before holiday	holiday	after holiday
WHAT?	choose holiday type	choose destination	determine activities	determine route and duration of stay	choose transport there/back local	choose-hotel	other choices	make reser-vation	read make lists buy things	journey and stay	print photos write review

THE REASONS FOR THE INDIVIDUAL ACTIONS

The next step is to try and understand why the customer takes each of these actions. We make a shopping list because we don't want to forget anything. We look in the supermarket folder because we want to save money. Some products we only choose in the store because we are in search of inspiration. We pay at the check-out because we are obliged to. We take things home because otherwise we would not be able to use them. We put them away because we want to keep our house neat and tidy. We do this with some degree of system because we want to be able to find everything easily when we need it. And we put fresh products in the fridge because that is the best way to keep them for longer.

Drawing up a list of objectives – the whys and the becauses – can often lead to useful insights. Why do we need a coin for the trolley? Because that is what the supermarket wants. Why does the supermarket want that? Because that way the trolleys are properly returned.

Why do we need our reading glasses? Because the letters on the packaging are often tiny. Why do we want to read a sell-by date? Because the shelf life of some products is relatively short.

In the matrix for the customer journey for a family holiday we can now add a list of similar reasons for the things people do. Even though you first need to identify these things (the 'whats') before you can assess the reasons for doing them (the 'whys'), in the matrix it is customary to put the explanations before the actions:

MAIN PHASES	preparation		concrete plans		choosing			booking	before holiday	holiday	after holiday
WHY?	to seek inspiration	inspiration within type	miss nothing good mix	to make booking possible	to avoid paying too much to get what best suits you			obligatory	to dream of what is to come to forget nothing	to enjoy	to reminisce
WHAT?	choose holiday type	choose destination	determine activities	determine route and duration of stay	choose transport there/back local	choose hotel	other choices	make reservation	read make lists buy things	journey and stay	print photos write review

It is important to remember that the customer journey is never as linear as this kind of matrix might (misleadingly) suggest. However, there is no other way to depict the customer journey as clearly. So we will just have to live with it.

Another practical tip? Spreadsheets are ideal for helping to visualize the customer journey.

THE CHANNELS AND TOUCHPOINTS IN THE CUSTOMER JOURNEY

Each different way that a customer comes into contact with your company is known as a 'touchpoint': a customer loyalty card, a plastic bag, your shop staff, your promotion folder, your advert in Google Shopping, your banner advertising on the internet, the signposts leading to your car park, your page on Facebook, your webpage with the store's hours of opening, your app, etc., etc. The list, if not endless, is at least long.

Most of these touchpoints can be grouped into sales and communication channels. A first cluster amalgamates all your digital channels: your website, app, e-mails, social media and various forms of digital advertising. The most important analogue channels are the store itself and other analogue communication channels. If necessary, the latter can be sub-divided on the basis of medium (print, TV, radio, etc.). The contact center (if you have one) should be treated as a separate entity.

The customer not only comes into contact with your touchpoints and, consequently, your channels, but also with the touchpoints and channels of others. Perhaps he makes use of the touchpoints and channels of your competitors, which are often a reflection of your own. Not that all of these third-party touchpoints are rivals. Some of them will support your own activities. For a retailer, this might mean the website of the manufacturer whose products he sells. Conversely, for the manufacturer, it might be the touchpoints of the retailers who sell his brands.

In addition, there are also countless other touchpoints and channels outside your own distribution column. Some of these can also be influencers, like TripAdvisor in the travel sector, organic search results on Google or editorial pages in the media. Your customer travels to your city center store by car? Perhaps he has checked the local authority website to find the location and cost of the nearest car park. This is also a touchpoint.

In the matrix, channels are placed as labels in the first column. The touchpoints are added – where relevant – under the individual actions. The specific pages of your website are touchpoints, whereas the website itself is a channel. Similarly, your Facebook page is a touchpoint in your social media channel.

This means that the first main phase for our family holiday matrix will now look something like this:

MAIN PHASES	preparation	
WHY?	to seek inspiration	inspiration within type
WHAT?	choose holiday type	choose destination
CHANNELS?		
online		
▪influencers	Tripadvisor	Tripadvisor tourist info
▪travel agents	TUI, … Booking.com	TUI, … Booking.com
▪search engines	Google	Google
▪hotels, etc		"what to see"
▪social media		
offline		
▪media		travel guides
▪friends		

Research conducted by ComScore has shown, for example, that 95% of all holiday-goers search online before they make a booking. As many as 73% start with a generic search task, without mentioning any specific destination: 'adventure holiday', 'beach holiday' and 'cheap holiday' are typical search terms of this kind. Only 2% of searchers add a destination right from the very beginning.[65]

Using a relatively high degree of detail for the touchpoints can help to find insights that will allow the customer journey to be further refined. In contrast, using too much detail in the channels is often at the expense of overall clarity. This explains why some companies will make a distinction between their ordinary website and their mobile site, whereas others will not. The creation of a residual category – 'other channels' – can also be useful.

DOING, THINKING AND FEELING

The 'Holy Trinity' of the customer journey consists of describing what the customer does, what he thinks while doing it, and what he feels while doing it.

We have already set down what he does: this is our list of individual actions. But we now need to add a list of what he thinks while doing all these things. These thoughts typically take the form of questions. 'What are we going to eat next week?' 'Have we got enough of everything?' But also: 'Where is the nearest car park?' 'Where is the entrance to the store?' 'Where is the sell-by date on the packaging?' 'Is there a deposit on the packaging?' 'Where can I find the Camembert?' 'Is there a difference between the three different kinds of Camembert?' 'Which check-out has the shortest queue?'

To this we need to add yet another list, this time indicating how the customer feels while performing each of these actions. Does he find it annoying to have to think in advance about what he is going to eat next week? Is he irritated because the car park is too small and nearly always full? Does it bother him that he needs to use a coin to get a shopping trolley? Does he enjoy searching through the range of fine cheeses? Or is he exasperated when he needs to decide if there is a difference between three kinds of Camembert?

In our family holiday example, the consumer asks the following questions, which may result in the feelings listed below:

MAIN PHASES	preparation	
WHY?	to seek inspiration	inspiration within type
WHAT?	choose holiday type	choose destination
CHANNELS?		
online		
▪influencers	Tripadvisor	Tripadvisor tourist info
▪travel agents	TUI, ... Booking.com	TUI, ... Booking.com
▪search engines	Google	Google
▪hotels, etc		"what to see"
▪social media		
offline		
▪media		travel guides
▪friends		
THINK?	Europe or elsewhere? Where haven't we been? What is the weather like? Will the kids enjoy it? Do they have good food? Is it peak season or not? Is it an expensive destination?	
FEEL?	It is difficult to choose... There is lots of info about individual destinations... ... but nothing to compare them with. All the info reads like an advertising folder: where can I find real information?	

CUSTOMER SATISFACTION AND THE ARC OF TENSION

In most customer journeys 'customer satisfaction' is depicted separately from 'feeling'. If the focus is on the various touchpoints, a differentiating color code or symbol is sometimes used. After all, a single action can make use of different touchpoints – for example, making a shopping list based on a paper promo-folder from your store, your online folder or the folder of one of your competitors. The level of satisfaction can be different for each of these touchpoints.

Even when a color code or symbol is used, it is still customary to add a separate line for customer satisfaction, which is used to indicate in each cell just how satisfied the customer is (or isn't) about each specific action.

Finally, it can sometimes be useful to draw an arc of tension to depict the 'highs' and 'lows' of the customer journey. This usually takes the form of a graphic and requires a level of excitement to be assessed for each individual action. A high value implies plenty of excitement; a low value suggests rest or indifference – sometimes known as the 'thrill' and 'chill' factors. Whether or not thrill or chill are 'ideal' expressions of customer satisfaction will depend on the context. If you are sitting on a roller coaster ride, you want as much excitement as you can get. If you are queuing up for a ticket for the ride, you will want things to be a little calmer.

TOWARDS A PRACTICAL AND WORKABLE CONCLUSION

At the very bottom of the customer journey matrix we leave a blank section that can be used to make a synthesis and record our conclusions. The first line should highlight possible opportunities for improvement. The second line should outline possible ideas to exploit those opportunities. This is sometimes supplemented with an additional line to sketch the possible implications for your internal organization. Which departments, technologies, processes and systems are involved with the relevant customer actions and will therefore need to contribute to their further refinement?

HOW DO YOU FINALLY ARRIVE AT THE IDEAL CUSTOMER JOURNEY?

Many of today's companies make use of the customer journey to outline their strategy, but the emphasis is usually on the short and medium term.
The aim of this approach is to develop conclusions and ideas that are practical and immediately usable:

» We are operating well within the existing customer journey.
» We search for incremental improvements.
» We place the emphasis on a single phase of the customer journey, on which we must then focus in more depth.

The objective of my matrix approach is more ambitious: instead of seeking to improve the existing customer journey, I want to help you to draw up the *ideal* customer journey, ignoring for the time being any potential objections. This means that we need to be able to free ourselves to a much greater extent from the current situation.

SURPRISE ME!

A thorough analysis of the customer journey for holiday-goers provides the insight that many of them suffer from a significant degree of choice stress. As a result, the phases from the preparation to the booking can often take quite a long time to complete. On average, there is a gap of roughly 100 days between the first exploratory online search and making the final reservations. Finding and booking the right flight and airline takes an average of two and a half hours. Finding and booking the right hotel can take as much as three hours.[66]

Of course, you can save yourself time and effort by booking an 'all-in' package holiday. But even then you still need to choose your destination and pick a hotel from the travel agent's long list. What's more, you have the feeling of being caught up in the web of mass tourism, which is not everyone's cup of tea.

These factors have been seen as an opportunity by several start-ups. Kiddotravel,[67] for example, offers individual holidays to long-haul destinations like Florida, Thailand and South Africa, specifically for families with children. All you need to do is select your destination, duration of stay and your preference for any of the child-friendly activities on offer. Once you have done that, the company puts together a made-to-measure 'package' that is ready in no time at all. The target group is two-earner families who are prepared to pay something extra for a an exceptional travel experience with none of the usual hassle.

SurpriseMe,[68] a Dutch company specializing in city trips, takes things even further. All you need to say is whether you want a trip in southern Europe or northern Europe, what level of comfort you require and when you want to travel. Once you confirm your booking, you are sent information about what you need to take with you. You are also given a scratch card to open when you arrive at the airport. It is only then that you discover your destination! In short, you pay for a combination of ease of organization with the emotional experience of a surprise!

You can draw up the ideal customer journey by using the following step-by-step plan:

Step 1: formulating a hypothesis

The aim of this step is to prepare a first design for your ideal customer journey, focused on priorities for improvement in the long term. You should make this design by organizing a one-day workshop:

1. Start by choosing the scope of your customer journey. In the initial phase it is a good idea to keep things fairly general, so that you can easily run through the entire trajectory followed by the customer from A to Z. At this stage, it is important not to get lost in too much detail about the individual customer actions. The scope must also take account of the target market: do you sketch a customer journey for all target segments or do you confine yourself to the most important one? The same applies to the buying occasion and the product categories. Once again: keep things simple and avoid too much detail.

2. Decide who you want to participate in the workshop. It is important to include functions from across the company, so that you can benefit from a wide range of different perspectives. Also arrange a good mix of young and old, men and women, and different hierarchical levels. This will enrich your discussions. At the same time, also ensure that the voice of the customer is properly heard. This means you should avoid having too many people who have no direct contact with or feeling for the behavior of customers. The personality of the participants also requires some thought. Once again you need a good mix: this time between creative and analytical minds, who have a good and practical understanding of customer actions and wishes, and who know what is possible and what not. Junior members of staff must be sufficiently assertive to express their opinions in the presence of their seniors, while the seniors must accept that in the context of the workshop their hierarchical position plays no role. Make sure that you have the right number of participants: too few means too little input; too many means that people will be less inclined to contribute actively. The minimum will depend on the complexity of your company and its customer journey, but should never be less than four people. At the other end of the scale, regard twelve as a maximum.

3. Provide a good briefing and make careful preparations. Collect relevant information relating to the customer journey; for example, based on market research and data about actual customer behavior. Send this background information in advance to all the workshop participants. Also give them guidance about the methodology of the customer journey matrix and set clear guidelines for both objectives and scope. Select a good venue, where people can think undisturbed for a whole day.

4. The first part of the workshop should be devoted to generating ideas about the different individual actions that make up the customer journey. The most usual method nowadays is to give all the participants a pack of post-it notes. Once they have an idea, they write down the relevant action on one of the notes. These are then stuck on a board in the order in which they appear in the customer journey, until the journey is complete. Once again, it is important to achieve the right level of detail. At this stage, it is now better to have too many rather than too few ideas. When compiling the trajectory of the journey, detailed actions that are similar in nature can be positioned under each other, so that they are effectively combined into groups. In this way, the underlying background information does not get lost.

5. The next step involves the translation of the generic main phase headings into headings that are more appropriate for your own particular target market.

6. The following step is to discover the reasons why customers take the actions you have identified. This allows you to establish the customer's objectives.

7. It is likely that most of the touchpoints will already have been named on the post-its. Even so, it is recommended to check at this point that none of them have been overlooked.

8. The fifth step normally involves the touchpoints being grouped together in relevant channels. However, this can also be deferred to a later stage, if desired, since it is not strictly speaking necessary to involve all the workshop participants in this process.

9. Next, you need to analyze what the customer thinks and feels for each of the touchpoints. If relevant, you can also draw an arc of tension.

10. The results of the previous step are now used as input to evaluate the level of customer satisfaction for each action and each touchpoint.

11. Running parallel with the above steps, it is necessary to note down all
     the opportunities for improvements and other possible actions. In this
     first workshop it is important not to be tied down by potential objections,
     practical or otherwise. For this reason, you should avoid listing the way
     the various improvements and actions may affect your internal depart-
     ments, systems and processes.

12. The most important task of this workshop is to identify the main short-
     comings in the customer journey and therefore the areas that offer the
     biggest scope for improvement. In essence, you can do this by asking
     two simple questions: can you simplify the action in question or can you
     enrich it in some way? At the end of this exercise, you should have a list
     that will show you where you can most improve and least improve your
     customer satisfaction. Once again, it is essential at this stage not to look
     at this list from the perspective of practical feasibility. For the moment,
     your thinking must be purely 'out of the box'.

13. As a final step in this first workshop, you need to double-check that your
     previously defined scope was not too general. Do you perhaps need to
     repeat this exercise for specific customer segments, product groups or
     buying occasions?

Step 2: testing the hypothesis

In step 1 the customer was not involved in any way, shape or form. Instead, you attempted to estimate for yourself what he does, why he does
it, which questions he asks when he does it, how this makes him feel and
what level of satisfaction he experiences at the end of his journey. At the
same time, you also formed your own view about the priorities for the
customer.

That being said – and bearing in mind the strategic importance of this
exercise – it is vital not to regard the outcome of step 1 as being anything
more than a hypothesis. And like all hypotheses, it needs to be tested.
The most obvious way to do this is to now make use of actual customers
to match your suppositions against their realities. Setting up a number of

focus groups will allow you to check to what extent they agree with your analysis.

Be careful, however: it should not be your intention to question customers about possible solutions. They can certainly contribute towards incremental improvements in the short and medium term, but don't ask their advice about your ideal customer journey in the long term.

As well as questioning customers, it is also useful to present your hypothesis for comment to other colleagues in the organization (who were not involved in the workshop) and to external experts in the sector.

Step 3: in-depth analysis

Once you are convinced that your hypothesis has identified the correct problems in the current customer journey and has prioritized them accordingly, the moment is ripe to conduct a more in-depth analysis. For this, you should organize a second workshop, but this time with a narrower scope. You must now zoom in on the phase(s) or aspects where you can see most room and the greatest need for improvement. You can also opt to focus on a particular context or target group. Repeat exactly what you did in step 1.

The participants in this second workshop must be chosen in function of your focus. If your focus is delivery and installation, you will need different people than you would for a session concentrating on customer choice processes.

Step 4: the creative phase

The most difficult but also the most fascinating phase is the phase in which you switch from analysis to creation. Leaving aside for the moment all practical objections, you draw up an alternative plan for your priority improvements. This task is carried out by a dedicated work group; a work group where creativity is central. As far as the group members are concerned, selecting people with a good mix of experience both inside and outside your sector gives you the best chance of success. They need to be able to detach themselves completely from your current way of working. Only then will they be able to sketch a brand new customer journey that approaches the ideal.

The outcome of this phase is another new hypothesis. But this time you cannot test it against a reality. The customer does not know what he wants until he sees it. What's more, the customer journey that you now propose will only be possible in the future. And because you cannot predict the future, you will need to adjust this 'ideal' journey several times before it can finally make the leap from theory to practice.

Even so, the result of this theoretical exercise now gives a clear direction towards which you can work for the future.

Step 5: the planning phase and the technology scan

You now have a blueprint for your ideal customer journey. This is the point at which you need to make an inventory of all the practical objections to your plan. Bearing in mind technical, budgetary and organizational feasibility, draw up a step-by-step plan with action points and milestones for the short and medium term that will allow you to overcome these objections. The closer the milestones, the more concrete your action points will need to be.

An essential step in this process is the requirement to carry out a technology scan. The speed of change in the retail market is a direct consequence of the speed at which technology evolves. Things that were impossible yesterday become a reality today. For years, we were all content to tick in a code to gain access to our smartphone. Now we all expect to be able to do this by fingerprint. And soon we will only be happy with facial recognition!

At the same time, we are continually bombarded with new technological developments, which consultants predict will disrupt our sector from top to bottom. Do you remember how 3D-printing was 'destined' to lead to a situation where shops would no longer need to keep stocks? In the most extreme version of this scenario, we would all have a printer at home where we could print off everything we buy: e-commerce would no longer mean delivering a product to your doorstep, but downloading a design and hitting the print button… So far, very little of this has come to pass.

If you want to move beyond the digital hysteria, it is essential that you try to assess: (1) which future technological developments will occur that are likely to have an effect on your company; (2) how these developments can contribute towards your ideal customer journey; and (3) how likely it is and with what timing that these developments can be implemented commercially. These three factors will determine the speed at which you can put your ideal customer journey into practice.

The same technology scan should also be used as standard input for your 'normal' strategic planning in the form of a SWOT analysis. In this context, technological evolution can be both an opportunity and a threat. However, in the context of the ideal customer journey it is better to only use the technology scan as input once the creative phase has been completed: it is important to take the needs of the customer – not the company – as your starting point. In that way, you can use technology to better respond to those needs. In other words, technology is a means to facilitate change, but certainly not an end in itself.

You can use various sources to carry out your technology scan:

» There are specialized bureaus that follow the evolution of technological developments and publish reports. One of the most well-known is the Gartner Hype Cycle, which each year gives a summary of emerging technologies and how far they are from likely commercialization. You can find a graphic display of their general findings for free on the internet, but all further reports are only available on a paying basis. Forrester is another well-known name in the field of technology monitoring. The big advantage of using one of these companies is that they have no direct interest in the technologies they investigate, so that their findings are relatively objective.

» Next, there are the consultants, the technology suppliers and the trend-watchers. Major players, such as the 'big five' in consultancy, specialist retail consultants, software companies and other influencers also monitor technological evolution. The difference with the specialist bureaus is that these sources have a (not so) hidden agenda: they live from technological change. Their objective is to sell advice in the form of technological workshops. With this in mind, they publish white papers and free research reports, as well as deliver presentations in public fora, in the hope of attracting paying customers. For example, it is standard practice nowadays to invite technology suppliers to give internal presentations in your company. But these sources are not quite so reliable when it comes to making the crucial distinction between a hype and a trend, because they have much to gain from feeding the digital hysteria from which they hope to benefit. Even so, they remain a good way to get some idea of the likely impact of particular technological developments.

» A third relevant source of information is participation in congresses and study trips. The annual Big Retail Show organized by the NRF, the American National Retail Federation, brings together tens of thousands of retailers, consultants and suppliers. It is a place where you can almost sense the trends: consultants and suppliers feed the hype, while participants from the retail sector network and consult with each other about what to believe and what not. Study trips to Silicon Valley and China can also be useful to get a glimpse of what might be possible in the distant future. Visits to trendsetting shopping cities like Shanghai, London and New York demonstrate what is more likely to happen in the medium term.

Step 6: annual follow-up and revision

Your competition, your technology, your own internal organization, your customers: these are all things that change at lightning speed. As a result, you need to evaluate them annually and, where appropriate, make necessary changes:

1. Do you still believe in your vision for your ideal customer journey? What adjustments, if any, are needed?
2. Do you stick by the order of priorities you have made or do these priorities need to be amended?
3. Have the technological possibilities changed since your last review and, if so, what effect does this have on your ideal customer journey?
4. What results have you already achieved in the short term? What steps have you already taken towards your medium- and long-term objectives?
5. How should you update your step-by-step plan? Which action plans and milestones should you now program for the short and long term?

In the fourth and final part of this book we will devote more attention to the broader implementation of an optichannel strategy, with a particular emphasis on strategic adaptability and organizational flexibility.

THE IDEAL CUSTOMER JOURNEY

1. How well have you mapped out your ideal customer journey? Do you need to make a distinction between specific customer groups, buying occasions and product categories?

2. Ignoring practical objections at this stage, which aspects should be dealt with as priorities to make the biggest possible impact on customer satisfaction?

3. On the basis of the above analysis, do you now have a clear vision for your ideal customer journey?

4. What does your technology scan tell you about possibilities for the short, medium and long term? How can technology help you to transform your ideal customer journey into a reality?

5. What are the milestones on the way to your ideal customer journey?

6. Which initiatives will you need to take in the short term to move you in the direction of your ideal customer journey?

7. Are you being sufficiently flexible in your approach? Do you challenge your vision from time to time? Do you update your technology scan, action plans and milestones regularly enough?

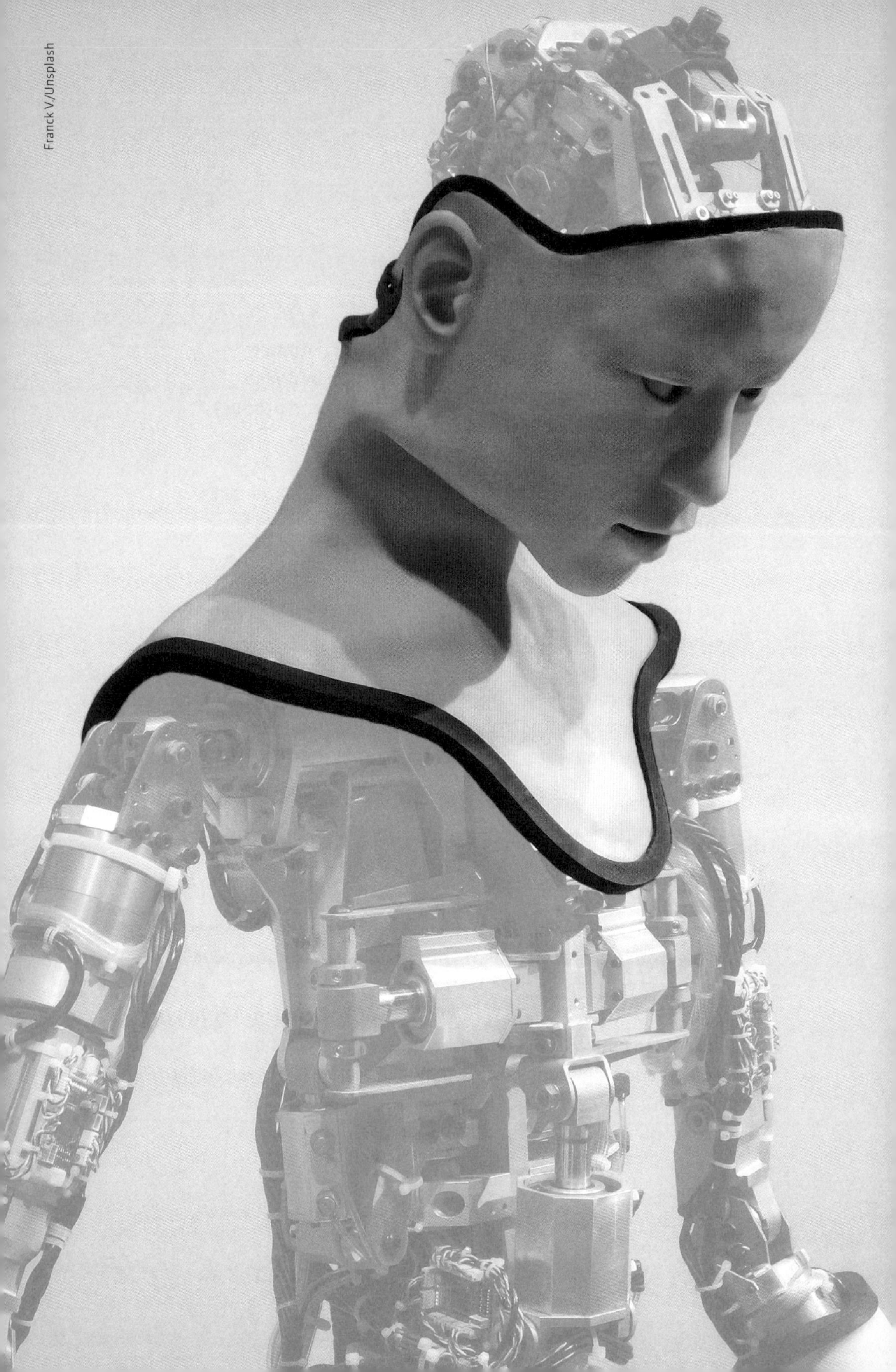
Franck V./Unsplash

CHAPTER 7
A BUTLER FOR EVERYONE!

'Companies may be armed with indescribable amounts of data, but they need to learn how to behave like a butler, not a stalker.'

Ana Andjelic (Chief Brand Officer for Rebecca Minkoff)

The chance that a reader of this book will ever have had a butler is pretty small. However, thanks to films, TV series, books and comics we all know what a butler looks like – and what he does. Perhaps it is improper to say so in these politically correct times, but a butler is always a man. His name is James and he is discreet, preferring to remain constantly in the background. He is completely devoted to his master, like the character played by Anthony Hopkins in *The Remains of the Day*, who continued to perform his duties even as his father lay dying. A good butler knows his master through and through, and can anticipate his every need. In the richest families, he is also the head of a whole team of household staff. He introduces arriving guests, but expects a more junior member to open the front door. And when the guests depart, he will hand them their hat and coat, but again expects that others will first fetch them from the cloakroom. Of course, it is the master of the house who decides what menu will be served for formal dinners, but the butler knows in advance what his master likes and what he finds appropriate on such occasions. As a result, his suggestions are usually accepted.

A BUTLER FOR EVERYONE?

Ten or so years ago, when our three children were still very small, I once considered employing an au pair. All young parents will be familiar with the challenge of combining the care of their children with a busy professional career. Even the simple task of delivering them to the nursery or school in the morning and collecting them again in the evening requires careful planning, which can easily be disrupted by a thousand and one unforeseen eventualities that send our stress levels soaring through the roof.

Even so, in the end we decided against the au pair. Why? Because convenience only comes at the expense of privacy. You have someone – effectively a stranger – living permanently in your house. What's more, this someone can walk in on you at every moment of the day or night – even when you are in your pajamas or relaxing semi-clothed in front of the television on your favorite couch. And as the success of Pockies[69], the boxer shorts with pockets, clearly shows, many men do indeed like sitting around trouserless in their homes – but they don't all like to be disturbed by a young (and usually female) au pair while they are doing it!

This is essentially the same problem rich people face when they think about employing a butler: to what extent are they willing to give up their privacy in return for greater convenience?

In future, it will also be the dilemma increasingly faced by consumers. Because nowadays there are butlers available that every middle-class family can already afford. These butlers will not be real flesh-and-blood people, but will be virtual personal assistants. And they will no longer be called James. Instead, they will answer to names like Alexa or Siri. But just like the traditional butlers of the past, they will know who visits us, what we like to do, what we like to eat – and whether or not we sit around the house half naked...

ALEXA, WHAT DO YOU KNOW ABOUT ME?

Much has already been written about Amazon Echo, Alexa and other rival systems. If these developments have passed you by in recent years, a quick read of the box below will bring you up to speed. After that, we will look at the strategic consequences of these in-house assistants.

THE BATTLE OF THE DIGITAL PERSONAL ASSISTANTS

In November 2014, Amazon launched an intelligent loudspeaker known as Echo, which consumers can activate simply by addressing it as Alexa. Echo comes with a number of different functionalities as standard. For example – and perhaps not so unusual for a loudspeaker – you can listen to music. This can be music from the Amazon music service, but also from Spotify or various radio channels. Via your smartphone, you can also listen to iTunes or

Apple Music. In addition, you can ask Alexa all kinds of questions; for example, about the latest weather forecast. She – yes, this is a female butler – can also carry out web searches for you. And it doesn't stop there. Alexa can operate most of your household domotics and – last but very definitely not least – can help you to make purchases via Amazon. What's more, Amazon continues to add new functionalities, in part through software updates for Echo but increasingly through additions in the cloud. As a consumer, you can even add 'skills' of your choice. These are more or less equivalent to apps. Via the Starbucks skill, for example (and as you might expect), you can place orders with Starbucks.

In the meantime, the original Echo has been joined by a number of brothers and sisters. The Dot is the size of an ice hockey puck and offers the same functionalities, but only has a tiny loudspeaker. You can use it in your bedroom or bathroom, but also connect it to an external speaker system. The Dot, which only costs half as much as the Echo, is currently the best-selling model in the 'personal assistant' range. In part, this is due to some very aggressive marketing by Amazon. On Black Friday 2017 the Dot was offered for sale at a price of just 30 dollars![70] In April 2018, the company offered a discount of 20 dollars on the basic Echo package and the Dot, so that it was again effectively possible to buy the Dot for 30 dollars. And for people who are mad about Dots and want one in every room, Amazon now sells them in packs of six and twelve. Meanwhile, a variant specifically for children has also been launched...

Perhaps more interesting are the Echo Show and the Echo Look. The Show has a screen, so that Alexa can now not only tell you lots of things but also show you lots of things as well. This is a big selling plus: when you want to buy something, it is often easier if you can see it first. Show has already been followed up by Spot, which is essentially Dot with a viewer.

Echo Look takes things another stage further. Because it is fitted with a camera, Alexa can now see you as well as hear you and talk to you. For this reason, Look is marketed as being particularly suitable for the bedroom: you can also take photographs of yourself and ask for style advice. [71]

In November 2016, Google finally launched its answer to Amazon's Echo. This was Google Home, for which numerous further variants have since been developed. The functionalities are comparable with Echo and the virtual assistant is named – somewhat uninspiringly – Google Assistant.

With the launching of HomePod in February 2018, Apple also entered the intelligent loudspeaker arena. The Apple assistant is called Siri, whose help had already been available for some time on other Apple devices such as the iPhone, Apple Watch, iPod and iPad.

Microsoft only invests in software and with Cortana has developed its own virtual assistant, initially for the Microsoft Phone, Xbox and Windows 10. In the meantime, however, Cortana has also become available for Android. Moreover, the company concluded an alliance with loudspeaker manufacturer Harman Kardon, resulting in November 2017 in the launch of the intelligent Invoke speaker, which only works with Cortana.

From a strategic perspective, the virtual assistant is much more important than the hardware. This assistant will effectively become the consumer's gateway to the internet. In other words, there will be a battle between Alexa, Google Assistant, Siri and Cortana for our hearts and minds. And just as you can use Google as a search engine on all your hardware or install Android on most makes of smartphone, it is likely in future that hardware suppliers will allow their customers to decide which virtual assistant they want to install. Sonos is already marketing intelligent loudspeakers that are compatible with both Alexa and Google Assistant. Not surprisingly, Apple has made a different choice: Siri (for the time being, at least) is only available on Apple devices.

The penetration of these systems in the United States is progressing rapidly: by the end of 2017 some 16% of families already
had an intelligent loudspeaker in their homes – twice as many as
the previous year. Amazon Echo led the way (11%), followed by
Google Home (4%).[72] But the figures for the first quarter of 2018
suggest that Google is catching up fast: for the first time more
Google Homes were sold than Amazon Echos. Why? Because retailers increasingly prefer to sell Google products rather than the
products of Amazon, a company that is not exactly the retailer's
friend.[73] What's more, on a worldwide scale Google Assistant
has the advantage that it will be more quickly available in more
languages.

By 2022 penetration is expected to rise to 55%.[74] For what purposes? Current research shows that 74% of Echo owners have
used it at least once to listen to music, 40% to turn their lights
on and off, 25% to add products to a shopping list, 20% to order
products and 6% to make a booking on Uber.[75]

Via their virtual assistants Amazon, Google, Apple and Microsoft are battling
to gain maximum insight into consumer behavior. This is a battle where
Google has the most to lose. As a result of the consolidation that took place
during the first wave of e-commerce (see chapter 1), more and more consumers are starting their search for products directly in a webshop or marketplace, rather than in Google. In the United States, Amazon is now the starting
point for more than 50% of all product searches, whereas the figure for search
engines has fallen to under 30% in just a few years' time.[76]

So far, however, Amazon's impact has remained confined to 'product searches'. If we want to know how to build a soapbox car or start a herb garden,
we still turn first and foremost to Google. At least for now. From now on, of
course, we can ask the same questions to Alexa – but this is a field where
Amazon still has a lot of work to do. The company does not currently have its
own search engine and a collaboration with Google seems highly unlikely, so
that Alexa's functionality in this domain is limited. For this reason, many peo-

ple expect Amazon to seek an alliance with Microsoft for access to the Bing search engine. The announcement by both companies that Alexa and Cortana are already capable of communicating with each other seems to point in this direction.[77]

Of course, these intelligent loudspeakers are capable of much more than simply capturing data from search tasks. Via Echo, Amazon listens to everything that takes place in your home. In fact, with Echo Look Amazon even goes so far as to invite us to install a camera in our bedroom. The images it makes may initially be intended to give us fashion advice, but they also show whether we are overweight, are suffering from acne or urgently need a new interior!

A good example of the levels to which this kind of thing can be taken was provided by Amazon's recent collaboration with (and subsequent acquisition of) Ring, a company that makes smart locks. The principle is very simple: Ring allows you to open your front door with a code. This code is also linked to an app, so that you can easily activate and de-activate different codes, either temporarily or permanently. The doorbell is equipped with a digital camera, so that no matter where you are you can use your smartphone to see who is standing outside your front door. There is also an option to extend the network by installing other cameras to film your interior, so that Ring serves as a kind of all-round security system.

Smart locks have been a matter of interest for some time in e-commerce circles, primarily because of the role they can play in the delivery of parcels. If the consumer is not at home, couriers can be issued with a temporary code, which gives them one-time access during a limited and pre-determined time period to the customer's home, so that the package can be delivered without the need to make a return visit. In Antwerp, Parcify (since taken over by bpost)[78] has already conducted tests with smart lock deliveries of this kind.[79] In the United States, Walmart has taken things even a stage further: with the customer's permission, the courier actually takes the ordered groceries through to the kitchen and puts the perishables away in the fridge! Of course, the customer can follow the whole process via an app on his smartphone.[80] Since October 2018, the British Waitrose chain of supermarkets has been carrying out similar trials.[81]

But let's return to Amazon. When the company launched its Echo Show, it also made approaches to a number of smart lock manufacturers, including Ring, but also Nest.[82] By downloading the right skill, it is possible via Show to see exactly who is knocking at your door. But if you can see it, so can Amazon. What's more, they can also see what is happening on every other camera installed in your home. This takes insight into customer behavior to a new and unprecedented level. It also explains why Amazon opted to collaborate with Ring rather than Nest. Nest is owned by Google – and Amazon has no intention of sharing its valuable customer data with one of its biggest rivals. As a result, the company was prepared to pay an estimated billion dollars to acquire Ring lock, stock and barrel. Not the kind of investment you make without very good reason...[83]

The first strategic consequence of these developments is obvious: thanks to their digital personal assistants, the tech giants are gaining ever greater insight into everything we do. This means that the competitive gulf between these giants and other companies is getting bigger all the time. In the first instance, retailers quite rightly point the finger at Amazon, because Echo is unquestionably strengthening the market dominance of the e-commerce mastodon. Figures show that since purchasing Echo its owners buy 10% more at Amazon than they did previously.[84] Similarly, research on behalf of Google has shown that 58% of owners use their loudspeakers to draw up their shopping lists, while 44% regularly order products.

THE RAPID GROWTH OF VOICE SEARCH

But intelligent loudspeakers also have a second important strategic consequence: they boost the extent to which we talk with our devices.

Even though Siri has been fully integrated into iOS 5 since 2011, its use has remained relatively limited.[85] No fewer than 98% of iPhone owners admit to having tried Siri at some point, but of these 70% say that their use is 'occasional or seldom'.[86]

We sometimes refer to this as a 'hands free' method of communicating, which implies that we wouldn't do it if our hands were free. Or to put it another way: we regard talking to technology as something unnatural and therefore we don't like doing it in public. This explains why 62% of those questioned said that if they use Siri they prefer to do so in the privacy of their car, where no-one can overhear them. To some extent, this is a generational thing. Young people, who are much less inhibited by change, are coming to terms with the idea of voice search much more rapidly. As far back as 2014, 55% of American teenagers admitted to carrying out online searches with voice command on a daily basis.[87] It is a form of behavior I can recognize in my own children.

But the tide is beginning to turn – and turn fast. Voice search has exploded in recent years, thanks to the improved quality of the talking assistants and the related rapid rise of sales in Echo and Google Home. Some 53% of respondents now say that it feels natural to talk to a loudspeaker; 41% say that it is like talking to a friend or another person; for 72% talking to an intelligent loudspeaker is part of their daily routine.[88]

Voice search already represents about 20% of the total search volume. ComScore predicts that by 2020 this figure will have risen to 50%.[89] This is the result of a kind of 'snowball' effect: because we see other people doing it, our reluctance to do the same weakens, until we eventually give it a try ourselves – in public. But there is still a long way to go. For the moment, most voice searches are still done at home (43%), followed by the car (36%), with just 19% 'on the move'.[90] This last category will undoubtedly increase in the years ahead. 'Hands free' remains the main reason for speaking to a device, but the gap with other reasons is also set to get smaller.

Consumers are increasingly discovering that talking to a device is quicker and easier, because you don't need to bother with any tedious and complex menus on a tiny and often hard to use screen. This is why Amazon has integrated Alexa into the Amazon app, so that the personal assistant can also be used via your smartphone.

As a result of all this, people are starting to realize that spoken search behavior is something very different:

1.   We use spoken language instead of keywords.[91] If we want to know what the weather is like in Ibiza, in Google we simply type in 'weather Ibiza'. But for a voice search we would probably ask the question in full 'What's the weather like in Ibiza'. In other words, a longer formulation. Consumers typically make use of interrogative words like who, what, where, how and when.

2.   Voice search generally reveals much more about the intention of the customer. 'What is the difference between a Maxi-Cosi AxissFix and the 2WayPearl?' is a very different question from 'How much does a Maxi-Cosi AxissFix cost?' and 'Where can I buy a Maxi-Cosi AxissFix?' Questions beginning with 'where' are usually closest to the moment of sale, whereas 'what' and 'how' questions are more likely to belong to the orientation phase.

3.   Voice searches often have a more local dimension, which can only increase when the amount of 'on the move' vocal interaction with smartphones likewise increases.

The use of other search terms means that we will have to fundamentally rethink our efforts in the field of Search Engine Optimization (SEO). In turn, this also means that we will be able to match content much more closely to intention.

Some search tasks will continue to produce largely visual results, because the consumer will continue to be seated at his PC or will be looking at the screen of his smartphone, tablet or Echo Look. But an increasing number of results will be 100% spoken. Gartner expects that by 2020 roughly 30% of all browsing sessions will be fully auditive.[92] This can only work if the content is written in spoken language, requires no visual support and is sufficiently succinct. In short, we need to radically revise our websites. Responsive and adaptive design will have to take account of the need for 'voice only' results.

Finally, Search Engine Advertising (SEA) will also inevitably come in for the same kind of 'restructuring'. Google is already experimenting with sound bites as adverts in combination with spoken search results. Some brands are also considering investment in the development of distinctive sounds as part of their brand identity.

As a reader of this book, your company is probably not an Amazon or a Google. So how should you respond to the developments described above? In concrete terms, there are three options:

1. Stick your toe in the water: test things out on a limited scale.
2. Monitor search behavior and try to anticipate expected changes.
3. Try to fully understand the new forms of purchase and advice behavior.

Let's have a look at each of these options in more detail.

STICK YOUR TOE IN THE WATER

Sticking your toe in the water is the only way to test its temperature. The British online supermarket Ocado quickly launched an Echo skill, allowing customers to add products to their shopping lists. This is only a minor intervention but it closely reflects our existing behavior as consumers. If I notice at the breakfast table that we have almost run out of cheese, I ask my daughter Jasmine to write it down on the shopping list that is pinned to the notice board hanging above our fridge. From now on, I can ask Alexa to do it.

Alexa's software will then search for the right product among the range of the 15,000 most frequently sold Ocado items (about one-third of their total assortment). This search also reflects your standard behavior. If you usually buy 250-gram packs of mature Cheddar, this is what Alexa will suggest. If these packs are currently not in stock, Alexa will suggest a suitable alternative. The skill also allows you to ask Alexa whether or not cheese might already be listed on your shopping list (you don't want to buy too much!). In this way, you can gradually compile your shopping list as the week progresses.[93]

I imagine that, like me, most Ocado shoppers would probably want to see the full list again before confirming the order. But I am only guessing. Ocado doesn't need to guess. They already know. By setting up this test, they have quickly learnt how consumer behavior is evolving and in what direction: how many people make use of the Echo skill, for what percentage of their shopping list, for what kinds of products, via which of the functionalities, etc. Of course, it would be even better if they could make their full assortment available via Alexa, but Ocado wanted to go ahead with its trial as quickly as possible – and 15,000 items is not bad for starters. It is certainly what the jargon refers to as a 'minimum viable product'.

The collaboration with Amazon was a carefully considered choice. However, it is a choice that works both ways. Ocado does it because it wants to learn and wants to serve its consumers better. But at the same time it also stimulates the further use of Amazon Echo and gives Amazon – a retail competitor – access to the ordering behavior of Ocado customers. What's more, Ocado makes use of the artificial intelligence (AI) of AWS (Amazon Web Services) to search for products in its assortment and suggest possible alternatives, which not only provides Amazon with extra turnover but also helps to make their AI software even smarter.

The Dutch supermarket chain Albert Heijn decided to opt for integration with Siri in its app. Using Siri, customers can add or delete products on their Appie shopping list and can ask for a summary of its total contents. To do this, it is not even necessary to open the app. They can access it directly by pressing the 'home' button on their iPhone or iPad and starting up Siri. They are also at liberty to shop in the manner that best suits them: in the supermarket, with home delivery or via collection at a pick-up point.[94]

The choice of Albert Heijn for collaboration via Siri raises a second interesting point that merits our attention: the speed of adoption for voice search is dependent on the quality of the speech technology in the mother language of the consumer. This is the key factor in achieving rapid penetration. Alexa is dominant in the Anglo-Saxon lands, and variants already exist for American, Canadian, Indian, Australian and British English. Meanwhile, she also speaks German, Italian, Japanese and Spanish.

By the end of 2017, Amazon had launched a so-called 'international' version of Echo in almost 30 countries. This version only speaks English and does not allow the full range of skills to be downloaded, nor is it possible to listen to music on Spotify.[95]

France was absent from the list of countries covered, as are all the Spanish-speaking lands. That being said, Amazon is highly active in both these regions. At the time of writing, some skills are currently being developed in French.[96] This suggests that Amazon is planning to launch a French version of Alexa in the not too distant future. But this would also mean that all the other countries where the 'international' Echo has been launched are likely to be deprived of an Alexa in their mother tongue for quite some time to come. This explains, for example, why in Belgium you can only use the international version to buy products from Amazon.de and not from Amazon.fr: the target group is very clearly the Dutch speaking consumers! Since iOS 8.3, Siri can speak 14 languages, including both Dutch and French. Google Assistant speaks ten languages, although the company had announced that by the end of 2018 this number would increase to 30.[97]

Companies that are only active in countries where Alexa does not currently speak the language can afford to adopt a 'wait-and-see' attitude for a little while longer. In the meantime, they can experiment with Siri and Google Assistant, neither of which is a direct competitor in the same sense as Amazon.

The brand manufacturers have also been experimenting with spoken interaction. Most of the examples are situated in the United States, where brands make uses of Alexa skills to learn more about the 'spoken' search process. P&G brought a skill onto the market for its 'Tide' brand of washing powder, which made it possible for consumers to ask for advice about the best way to remove 200 different kinds of stains.[98] Campbell's used its Kitchen skill to suggest recipes, which involved the use of spoken instructions as a cooking aid.[99]

At the same time, the number of other devices that you can operate through Alexa is also systematically increasing. You can ask Alexa when your Miele washing machine has finished its program or she can activate your LG robot lawn mower, Bosch robot vacuum cleaner or Toshiba television. You can even connect your Yamaha Disklavier piano to Alexa.[100]

MONITOR SEARCH BEHAVIOR AND ANTICIPATE

In addition to experimenting with voice search, it is also important to monitor the search terms that people are using in connection with your own company, brands and products. For the moment, Google makes no distinction in its reports between spoken and typed search requests, but sooner or later this is bound to happen. But this should not prevent you from already looking at the ways consumer search behavior is changing.

Try using benchmarks to estimate the extent to which your target market is subject to these evolutions to a greater or lesser degree than average. Is adoption taking place faster than you anticipated? Are search responses increasingly 100% auditive or do the majority of people still look at search results on a screen? For which type of search tasks is the shift to voice-activation taking place most quickly? You can find a list of benchmarks of this kind in the generic research into voice search available online and in relevant publications. Make sure that any bureaus you work with are sufficiently alert to these important matters.

Depending on the findings of your monitoring, you will probably need to amend your website. Develop relevant content in the right format, appropriate to your new forms of interaction.

You will also need to test new forms of spoken SEA. Don't be afraid to experiment and don't be afraid to learn!

UNDERSTAND THE NEW PURCHASE AND ADVICE BEHAVIOR

In the years ahead, the consumer will ask his butler with ever greater frequency to book flights for him, to add cheese to his shopping list or even to order the most recent management book. This means that the butler will have a bigger say in what is bought and, above all, where.

This is the following step in what has been a long evolution. In the distant past, brand manufacturers were able to use retailers as a kind of middleman for their products. The consumer was loyal to these brands and the alternative private label products offered by the retailers seldom amounted to much. However, this brand loyalty gradually began to wane and the consumer increasingly went to the shop to decide what he wanted to buy. When he arrived there, he found the private label products presented at eye level. The manufacturer brands now had to pay for their place on the shelves or near the check-outs and B brands were delisted from the range altogether. But now it is the butler who has taken over the role of filter for consumer choice from the retailers. And the butler is no longer called James, but goes by the name of Alexa, Siri or Google.

The digital doom-mongers paint a picture in which Alexa will systematically promote the Amazon private label to the number one position and will thereby break the power of the other brands. But is that really the case?

In an interesting study conducted by the L2 research centre, Alexa was asked to buy some 400 products. The researchers portrayed themselves as non-customers, so that Amazon was unable to take account of any past purchases. The results shed a fascinating light on the algorithms used by Alexa:[101]

» In each case, Alexa only suggested two product alternatives, which is obviously far fewer than you would get with a typed search request online and also far fewer than you would see in an average shop or supermarket. In other words, the butler clearly applies a filter to the offer.
» In only 16% of cases was the preferred of the two alternatives the product that would have occupied first position in a typed online search via the Amazon webshop. In contrast, Alexa puts forward the 'Amazon choice' in 59% of cases, a choice based on turnover, rating and reviews, and on the fact that it is eligible for Amazon Prime delivery. Finally, Alexa suggests the best-selling product in first place in 25% of cases.
» Over a period of three weeks the recommendations remained relatively stable. In only 13% of cases was there a change to the product recommended in first place.

» It is also worth noting that, depending on the product category, ordering via Alexa was between an average of 0.6% to 5.5% more expensive.
» Alexa gives serious discounts in order to promote the Amazon private label products.

With repeat purchases, Alexa naturally consults your past purchase history. Paradoxically enough, this results in more rather than less loyalty to your preferred brands!

The conclusions are clear. On the one hand, Alexa applies a far more highly selective filter to consumer choice than is the case with the average webshop. On the other hand, Alexa promotes the brands that most closely reflect the 'best practices' of Amazon. This is a very customer-oriented approach. Amazon certainly promotes its private label products, but does not systematically recommend them in first place. In other words, whoever wants to score well with Alexa must first score well in the Amazon webshop!

A BUTLER FOR EVERYONE!

1. How quickly is the adoption and penetration of virtual digital assistants progressing in your target market? Do your customers, products and buying occasions vary from the average in the market and, if so, how?

2. To what extent are digital assistants already available in the mother languages of your customers?

3. How can you exploit this trend:

    a. Can you just stick your toe in the water?
    b. Can you just monitor the situation and see how search behavior develops?
    c. Can you try to fully understand how purchasing and advice behavior is changing? What are the likely consequences for your company? How can you make best use of the opportunities this presents?

4. What impact does this have on your (progress towards) your ideal customer journey?

    a. In terms of speech technology in general?
    b. In terms of digital assistants in particular?

CHAPTER 8

THE NEW CUSTOMER RELATIONSHIP

'You don't need a big idea.

You need a little idea you can make big.'

Jeremy Gutsche (Founder/CEO of Trendhunter)

Even though the butler will henceforth be a first point of contact for his master, he can't run the entire household on his own. What would he be without a good cook, chauffeur, housekeeper and gardener alongside him? These lesser-known figures often work more in the shadow, but enjoy the thanks and appreciation of the master every bit as much as the butler. In the same way, there are still many opportunities for today's retailers and brand manufacturers who remain in the shadow of the tech giants and their virtual butlers; opportunities to develop a more focused relationship with the consumer.

NOTHING NEW UNDER THE SUN?

In 1994, Don Peppers and Martha Rogers had huge success with their best-selling book *The One to One Future*.[102] Their prophetic vision brought about a revolution in the world of marketing. They argued that the way forward was to develop relationships with individual customers, so that you could win their loyalty and over time sell them more. The theory of 'the segment of one' was born (see box).

THE 5 I'S

In their book *The One to One Future* Peppers and Rogers introduced the 5 I's, which still have a surprising topicality about them today:

1. *Identification*: you need to collect as much information as you can about your individual customers.
2. *Individualization*: customers differ from each other, both in terms of their needs and in terms of the way they represent value for your company; you must respond to those individual needs (what we now call personalization) in relation to the value that the individual in question can potentially mean for the company.

3. *Interaction*: you must engage in constant dialogue with the customer, so that you can better understand his needs; every interaction must be registered to avoid the customer being asked the same question twice.

4. *Integration*: the individual relationship with the customer must be evident in all elements of the marketing mix; your business organization must be based around the customer and not around a product or business unit; the value of the customer is the yardstick for everything.

5. *Integrity*: developing a relationship based on the collection of data can only work if you have the customer's full trust; this means that you must deal with all customer data with integrity.

It is ironic (to say the least) that this adagio should now be put forward 25 years later as the future of marketing. So what has been going on during the past quarter of a century? Is there really nothing new under the sun? To understand what is happening we need to look deeper at the concept of personalization.

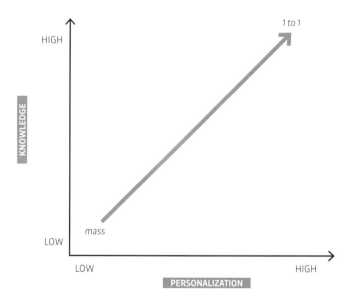

A one-to-one customer relationship demands that we know the customer sufficiently well. This knowledge is derived from two key factors: the number of data we are able to collect about the customer and the extent to which we can convert that data into relevant information.

Companies that wanted to implement the Peppers & Rogers theory 25 years ago were immediately faced with a number of challenges.

Apart from the banks and the telecom operators, most companies in the consumer market did not know their customers by name. For brand manufacturers it was even a difficult task just to collect the address of their customers. Retailers saw possible opportunities with the introduction of the customer loyalty card, but when the frequency of purchase was low the collection of data remained limited.

Moreover, the state of the available technology at the time also imposed further limitations: the companies that were capable of collecting a lot of data – like supermarkets – were unable to save them, because data storage at that time was so expensive.

Similarly, the slow processing speed of late 20th-century computers made it hard to translate the data into usable information. As a result, the all-important 'knowledge' about the customer remained at a generally low level.

Implementing greater personalization was also easier said than done. In personal sales – for example, in business-to-business or in a bank – you can communicate with the customer in a specific 'made-to-measure' manner. But that's where it stops. In the analogue era, most companies were delighted if they were able to work the names of their customers into a standard letter or could send them congratulations on their birthday. For the rest, consumer marketing came not much further than the dispatch of segmented mailings: for example, P&G was able to discover from hospitals the name, date of birth and gender of newborn children, so that they could send the parents a discount voucher for Pampers.

THE SEGMENT OF ONE RE-INVENTED

The first wave of personalization amounted to little more than an elementary form of segmented communication. It was necessary to wait for the internet era before the real breakthrough could be made:

» All behavior on the internet leaves traces. Everything is measurable. Companies can see, for example, not only what you buy, but also what you investigate in depth and decide not to buy. This has led to an explosive growth in the amount of collectable data. To give you some idea: during a five-minute visit to the luxury fashion webshop Farfetch the company collects 15,000 data points about the customer.[103]

» The data storage capacity and processing speed of computers has improved and become cheaper at an exponential rate.

» The possibilities for analysis have also improved spectacularly. Software in the cloud provides everyone with ad hoc access to the most advanced applications in the most flexible form. And thanks to artificial intelligence in the near future we will be able to maximize still further our use of big data to enhance our insights into customers.

» Digital communication media now make it possible to personalize messages at the individual level without any significant increase in cost. In fact, data analysis and personalization have moved beyond the realm of mere communication. They now steer product development and make it possible to gear the assortment to individual customers.

Hence the most trendy new one-liner of recent years: 'data is the new oil' – just like oil was once the new gold...

DATA: THE NEW WIND POWER

This one-liner refers, of course (and correctly), to the value of data for creating more knowledge. But the comparison also contains an explicit flaw in its reasoning: oil reserves are finite, whereas in theory data can be generated endlessly: every visit to a website is equivalent to a new 'well' being tapped!

For this reason, it is probably more accurate to compare data with renewable energy. And since the topic of data comes with an awful lot of wind and hot air, perhaps 'data is the new wind power' is a neat alternative! The art of success consists in setting the right number of wind turbines in the right place to harness this power.

So how do you do this, exactly?

In essence, it all boils down to the fact that we need to forget everything we have ever learnt about statistics. With statistics you attempt to extract the maximum amount of information from the minimum amount of data. The smaller the sample, the lower the costs. That is why you need to keep a careful eye on representativity and the quality of the data. And you need to use complex analytical techniques to discover the relevant causal relationships.

At the end of the day, however, the final objective is a simple one: to test out (and hopefully confirm) a previously formulated hypothesis. This is very definitely not the case with data as the new wind power!

1. To begin with, we need to ditch the standard rules relating to sampling. Sometimes we now use all the available data (n = all). Sometimes smaller quantities of data are sufficient. In Japan, for example, analysts succeeded in proving match-fixing based on a dataset containing all the results of eleven seasons of professional sumo wrestling – in total 'just' 64,000 individual sumo bouts.[104] With language, of course, it is difficult to examine all the different texts in the world. Even so, we no longer need to use relatively small representative samples, but can opt for giant datasets instead. Google has created a databank containing 95 billion English sentences and a trillion different English words. By counting how often different words appear after each other, Google was able to achieve an important breakthrough in speech technology.[105]

2. Secondly, we no longer need to devote as much attention to the quality of our data. Google has not checked to ensure that all 95 billion of those sentences are grammatical and contain no spelling mistakes. It is precisely because we are now dealing with such huge amounts of data that we are able – and willing – to take the bad with the good: it is better to base

our findings on huge amounts of data with some errors than on small amounts of error-free data.

3. The analysis of this data no longer seeks to identify causal relationships but searches instead for correlations. This can sometimes lead to curious insights. Passengers who order a vegetarian meal in advance from their chosen airline are less likely to miss their flight. Orange second-hand cars have fewer defects than cars of other colors.[106] People who correctly use capital letters when filling in a request form for a loan are a better risk.[107] Your response to all these insights might be to ask 'Why?' But that is something the data cannot tell us. We can assume that people who order a personalized meal in advance are more forward-thinking and better organized; or that people who buy a car in an eye-catching color are more concerned to take better care of it; or that people who respect the rules of spelling are more respectful of rules and obligations in general. But we cannot know these things for certain. It is on this basis, for example, that Amazon recommends books for its individual customers, by searching for correlations with other books in its huge databank. It might be fun to know how all these different books relate to each other, but from the company's perspective that insight would do nothing to stimulate increased turnover.

4. In statistics, data is collected in relation to a specific hypothesis that needs to be tested. We try to refine our conclusions via trial and error. Our own insights, intuitions and experience are central to the formulation of the initial hypothesis. We try to understand what happened yesterday and today, so that as managers we can make smarter choices for tomorrow. In the data age, however, it is the data that is central. By collecting together pieces of information on a massive scale, we discover new insights and connections that we would never have been able to discover based on our intuition alone. This means, of course, that our intuition and experience become less important. The purpose of analysis is no longer to understand the past and the present; its purpose is to predict the future.

A DATA TYPOLOGY

Of course, this excess of available data means that it is sometimes difficult to see the wood for the trees. So how can we bring some structure into this mass of information?

A first important dimension is the speed with which data often changes. Some data remain relatively stable, such as customer identity details, the location of shops and their catchment area, insights from market research, the characteristics of the products we sell, etc. Quite a lot of historical big data also falls into this same category; for example, the analysis of the credit-worthiness of customers based on their use of capital letters.

However, other kinds of data can evolve rapidly. Interactions on social media, details relating to customer behavior in a shop or their search behavior online are all highly volatile and unpredictable. Because real-time analysis is more complex and more expensive, you need to assess the extent to which real-time data actually needs to be analyzed in real time. Often, it is enough simply to add this data to your pre-existing historical datasets.

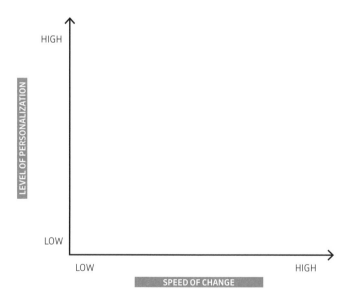

A second dimension is the extent to which the data relates specifically to individuals. For example, we can observe how Mrs Smith navigates her way around our website and we can try to deduce her preferences accordingly. But we can also analyze how all our customers do the same thing, so that we can understand their collective preferences. Via the search terms used in Google or the 'likes' recorded in social media it is even possible to discover trends in the market.

A DATA STRATEGY

In order to make use of the power of data, we need a good data strategy. Sadly, a simple 'copy-paste' of the approach used by Amazon or Google is not possible. Consequently, we need to focus on searching for an alternative method that can contribute to our ideal customer journey, increase our competitive power and improve our financial results.

This strategy must consist of two separate components: data collection and data use. The collection is just a means to an end; the real end is always the use!

We can start by using existing data previously collected but never processed. How much knowledge can we now extract from data of past surfing behavior on our website? Sometimes a little more effort is required to convert existing observations into data suitable for analysis; this applies, for example, to telephone conversations with customers. At the same time, we can also create new sources of data; for instance, by launching an app.

In dealing with all these matters it is important to determine whether we want to gain new insights at the level of the individual customer, the segment or the entire company. The segment of one should not be regarded as some kind of dogma. There are plenty of other intelligent choices we can and should make, depending on the circumstances.

At the end of the day, data collection and analysis must ultimately serve the following purposes:

1. How can we get to know our individual customers better?
2. How can we better detect market trends?
3. How can we work more effectively and thereby increase turnover?
4. How can we work more efficiently and thereby reduce costs?

USING UNUSED DATA

Many companies have a veritable treasure trove of data at their disposal but fail to use it to extract strategically relevant information. More and more companies are now storing data 'for later'. Because storage costs are now affordable and because data analysis techniques are improving all the time, they hope that this data might one day prove to be useful. Perhaps you can compare it with the retention of the urine samples collected from sportsmen and women: competitors who test negative for doping today may test positive in the future, once the methods of detection have improved.

In other words, just because previous attempts at analysis have not worked, this does not necessarily mean that new attempts won't work in the future, once new technological advances have been developed.

Even so, sometimes it can be useful to change course entirely. This is how the product recommendations made by Amazon first came into being. At the end of the 1990s, when Amazon only sold books and artificial intelligence was much less sophisticated than it is today, the company wanted to gain a better understanding of its customers. It decided to make recommendations based on historical purchasing behavior – or 'user-to-user collaborative filtering', to use the jargon.

As a method, it produced very little in terms of new insights: customers only bought a limited number of books, so that the amount of data was also relatively limited. For example, if all you had bought recently was a guidebook for Florida, your next recommendations from Amazon would probably be for other guides to Florida or other American states. Not really what most people would be interested in. In other words, this first attempt at personalization was a failure.

Then someone at Amazon had a bright idea: instead of focusing on the customer, why not focus on the book? What correlations might exist between different books? And so the well-known 'Customers who bought this book also bought this book' was born. From a commercial perspective, it is ideal that you can calculate these correlations in advance. It means that when someone selects a new book, you can show them a correlating book in real time – which significantly increases your chance of cross-selling. But the really smart thing was how Amazon then went on to use this same methodology for other product groups.

Amazon patented this technique as 'item-to-item collaborative filtering'.[108] It turned out to be extremely useful if you have far more customers than items. The dataset with items is smaller and therefore easier to analyze. Moreover, customer data evolves much faster than product data. This means that you constantly need to compare changing customer profiles, which leads to an extremely dynamic – and therefore less stable – model.

DATAFICATION OF EXISTING OBSERVATIONS

Retail professionals like to have an accurate idea about the number of visitors to shopping streets and malls. Using this information, they can calculate the extent to which the variations in the number of visitors to their particular shop reflects the variations in the number of people passing through the shopping streets. Shop owners and managers are interested in these figures, since it is this traffic that determines the rent for the shop premises. Local councils also want to keep their finger on the 'numbers' pulse, so that they can monitor the attractiveness (or otherwise) of their town and city centers.

With this in mind, a number of specialist bureaus now make a living out of quantifying this pedestrian traffic. Not so long ago, this was all done manually by 'field researchers', who simply stood in the streets and counted the number of people per hour passing by on a certain day. Because this was labor (and therefore cost) intensive, it was only possible to compile figures based on samples.

Nowadays, manual counting is a thing of the past. Today, strategically positioned receivers pick up the signals from the cell phones of passers-by: every phone has its own unique MAC – or media access control – code. What's more, measurements are no longer taken periodically but permanently, 24 hours a day, seven days a week. Are there weaknesses? Certainly. Not everyone has a cell phone and not everyone has it switched on. As a result, there are measurement errors. Even so, the huge number of measurements now taken means that the 'new' data is still much more accurate than the 'old' data. It also provides relevant subsidiary information that was not available before. For example, the MAC signals now show how long someone stays in the shopping street. At the same time, the number of receivers has been increased, which not only means more streets are now covered, but also makes it possible, for example, to measure which shops a person visits in a shopping mall. By applying shop-to-shop collaborative filtering to this data, it can be determined which shops attract the same customers and which shops are the mall's real draws.

It should be noted, however, that datification is not the same as digitalization. We can digitally record analogue conversations in a contact center and play them back later. But it is only by means of speech recognition technology that we can apply textual analysis to this recorded data. It is this that makes possible the evaluation of the content for the purpose of identifying trends and patterns that can be used to improve service.

Books are another example. A book can be digitalized, so that it becomes an e-book. The datification of an e-book might, for example, monitor if and how quickly the book was read. If you use a Kindle reader, you already know that Amazon will be watching to see if you finish the latest thriller in a single sitting at half past three in the morning or spread it out over several or more days, or even weeks. In this way, they don't need a review or rating to know whether or not you found it exciting and, consequently, whether or not they should recommend you other titles by the same author.

CREATE NEW SOURCES OF DATA

As a final alternative, you can opt to create new sources of data. In this context, it is noticeable that successful companies increasingly focus on 'end to end' customer journeys. It is no longer the path to purchase alone that is central; the use of the product is now equally important. We are seeing an evolution from purchase brands to usage brands.[109]

Walgreens is an interesting example of this trend. The company is the second largest operator of drugstores and dispensaries in the United States. Like so many retailers, they use a loyalty card to monitor the purchasing behavior of their customers: with each purchase the customer is awarded a number of points and after collecting so many points they are eligible for a discount. The program has 150 million registered customers, of whom 85 million are active users. Impressive, but nothing out of the ordinary.

What makes Walgreens special is the fact that they have added a 'healthy choice' section to the program, which allow customers to earn extra points if they adopt a healthy lifestyle.[110] The company encourages people to add apps like Runkeeper and devices such as the Fitbit activity tracker to their personal program, and is willing to award a considerable number of loyalty points to those who are willing to try. Points can also be earned every time you take exercise, record your sleep patterns, measure your blood pressure or blood sugar, register your weight... There are even points for participating in a program to stop smoking.

There is one other interesting functionality that Walgreens has added to its app: the 'pill reminder' alerts people when it is time to take their medication. What's more, they also need to tick a box to confirm they have done it. This is clever of Walgreens, but not wholly altruistic. The aid is mainly used by the chronically sick, who just happen to be the customer category with the highest expenditure levels in drugstores…

It is clear that Walgreens wishes to use this innovative approach to create and tap an almost inexhaustible source of data that will allow them to gain even deeper insights into the lives and health of their customers.

What's more, it seems to be working. Customers who sign up for the 'healthy choices' module remain faithful to the concept and to Walgreens: 70% of new connectees are still registering activities twelve months later.[111] They are also more conscientious about taking their medicines and more frequently reach their sport and weight-loss targets.[112]

The less good news is that not enough customers are sharing their data. In absolute figures we are still talking about 800,000 people and 250,000 registered devices and apps, but in relative terms this means that the company only manages to activate 1% of its total customer base as recorded in its loyalty program. It is also noticeable that the profile of this 1% differs significantly from the average Walgreens customer: the 'healthy choice' participants are 82% female (as opposed to 60% for average customers) and are more likely to be white, well-educated, and slightly younger.[113] No figures are available for the use of the pill reminder.

A final point worthy of consideration in this section is the way in which brand manufacturers are increasingly turning their attention to servitization and the internet of things. A good example is the way some industrial companies have begun to fit sensors to their products that can monitor performance. Any deviation from standard parameters gives early warning of a potential defect or malfunction.

At the service management center of Vlerick Business School, we were already exploring these avenues before the turn of the century, amongst others with ABB (the machine manufacturer) and Schindler (the lift company).[114] The latter is a good case in point. In the pre-internet era lifts were fitted with a cell phone that was used to transmit the collected data automatically. Nowadays, this is done much quicker and more efficiently via the internet. Developments of this kind open up the possibility to invoice customers for use rather than selling them products. For example, you no longer pay to buy a photo-copier and its supply of paper and print toner; instead you pay for each copy you make. All necessary maintenance costs are also included in the price. In this way, products become services – which is what we mean by servitization.

Today, the popularity of both these approaches is increasing rapidly. Technological advancement means that data transfer can be conducted with ever-greater efficiency. The latest analysis techniques also make the monitoring of machines more effective than ever before. As a result, we are now seeing consumer brands enter this arena for the first time. Printers already automatically order their own toner refills; later, we will all end up paying per print. In both scenarios, the producers tap new sources of data.

IT'S ALL ABOUT THE USE

This is all very interesting, but don't let the above section deflect you from the real priority: collecting data is all well and good, but the most important thing is to do something with it! Sometimes this can be ultra-sophisticated – but it doesn't need to be.

The Belgian bpost postal service invites all its customers to register their delivery preferences in the event of their not being at home; the options include delivering to a neighbor, leaving the package in a hidden location (for example, a garden shed), or collecting it from a post office. This kind of data is simple and changes only very slowly, but still allows a degree of personalization.

More elaborate is the 'Your Selection' program run by the Belgian food discounter Colruyt. Since 2010, customers have been receiving a folder in a sealed envelope. The four-page folder contains thirty week-long special offers for the products that most closely match the customer's past purchasing behavior. In the supermarket, the customer can, of course, make use of all 400 of that week's special offers, on condition that he does so using his registered customer loyalty card. No card, no discount. And if registration is made using a fictitious address, no personalized folder. Not that this is usually a problem. Most customers are delighted to receive a personalized advertising folder that only contains products they regularly buy.

For Colruyt this means processing a lot of data, but at least it is data that remains relatively stable: most customer profiles only change slowly. But the resulting clear increase in customer satisfaction is translated into greater customer loyalty and a significant uplift in promotional sales. It is only the brand manufacturers who have mixed feelings about the scheme: they finance the discounts, which are given to customers who are already buying the brand and not to potential new customers. In other words, Coca Cola customers get no special offers for Pepsi and vice versa.

In a different vein, Lincherie, a chain of Dutch lingerie stores owned by the Belgian Van de Velde Group, has been experimenting with a new Styling Center in Amsterdam.[115] A 3D-scan is made of each customer's torso, on the basis of which they are then given personalized advice by a stylist to establish their preferences in terms of look (lots of lace, minimalist, etc), color (always black, matching with the outer garments, etc.) and model (balcony or push-up). There are about one thousand bras that can be tried on in the store, but they can only be purchased through ordering for home delivery.

The level of conversion and the average ticket price are both considerably higher than in the ordinary Lincherie stores, which suggests that the majority of consumers are happy with the concept. But just as important for the company's success is the valuable data it captures. The 3D-scan provides precise information about the ideal size and fit of each customer. The additional knowledge from the advisory conversation with the stylist is also added to the overall database via a tablet. This makes choosing the right model much easier – now and in the future. True, collecting the data is fairly labor intensive, but this is more than compensated by additional sales in the Styling Center.

Even though the female body – and therefore the ideal size and fit – can change, on the whole the data is relatively stable. What's more, the analysis doesn't have to take place in real time. There are several advantages to this way of working. Customers who register can be helped in a more personal manner both online and in other Lincherie stores. Online, the landing page is automatically adjusted to reflect each customer's recorded preferences. In addition, the customer can also enjoy the benefits of curated commerce and is pleased with the fewer returns this involves. In exchange, Lincherie is able to generate increased turnover as a result of higher conversion and improved customer loyalty and also has lower costs thanks to the lower rate of returns.

The fashion sector is also making increasing use of publicly available big data that can change quickly and is therefore less stable. Which search terms are trending on Google? If you suddenly see lots of people using 'bomber jacket' as their search term, you can reasonably conclude that this is a new trend. Visual searching on social media can be used in the same way; for example, by monitoring which items receive most likes in a short period on Instagram or Pinterest. You can even check out the products getting the highest ratings at your competitors.[116] Of course, this information has little value unless you are able to respond to it with the necessary speed. If you have already fixed your collection for the full season, you probably have little room for maneuver. This is why more and more fashion players are following the example of Zara and commit only part of their collection before the season starts. This allows you more latitude to cash in on short-term trends.

Picking up trends of this kind may seem particularly relevant for the fashion sector, where one season's collection runs quickly into another. But other sectors are also keen to benefit from comparable insights. For example, Heineken has recently set up Beerwulf, a niche webshop dedicated to the sale of craft and other special beers.[117] Beerwulf operates independently from Heineken, although the Dutch beer giant is the sole owner.

In a similar vein, in 2016 AB InBev – the world's largest brewer – acquired the French webshop Saveur Bière.[118] The shop now delivers to seven different European countries. Two years ago, the brewing mastodon also took a non-specified minority stake in RateBeer, the most popular beer review site in the world. Known as 'the TripAdvisor of beer', the site records what beer-lovers of all ages from all over the planet think about a huge variety of brews, both specialist and otherwise. AB Inbev's most recent acquisition is the Israeli Weissbeerger, a company whose baseline is 'turning drinks into data'.[119] By installing measuring units in bars and cafes, Weissbeerger is able to record how much of which beer is sold, when and where. And the good thing about catering is that in this particular context 'selling' and 'using' go hand in hand.

For both Heineken and AB InBev, the emphasis is not on getting to know each individual customer better. They are more concerned with identifying up-and-coming trends before they become mainstream, so that they can gear their own product development to the next new hype before it has even started.

EVERYONE A STALKER?

Whenever I reach the theme of personalization during my many keynotes and presentations, I can see the participants mentally lining up to ask questions on the same contentious subject: 'So what about our privacy?' It is a reasonable question and one that is being heard ever more loudly in public debate. The risk is that we get caught up in slogans and clichés, instead of conducting an honest intellectual discussion with an open mind.

With only a little simplification, it is possible to divide the critics into three groups. A first cluster is worried about the tech giants. Google and Facebook are typical companies that you love to hate. Politicians understand this and are often ready to join the bandwagon. I am writing this section on the very day that Facebook CEO Mark Zuckerberg was called before the American Senate to explain how the Cambridge Analytica scandal could possibly happen.

The second group contains people who think that all multinationals and big companies are 'dirty' and not to be trusted. After all, they pay almost no tax, scrap jobs to earn even more money and now they are even infringing our privacy! They believe that AB InBev is not a brewer but a banker and their toes curl when they read that RateBeer has been taken over by the beer giant.

The third group has an aversion to all companies and the marketing practices they use. For them, all advertising is misleading, deliberately so. For this reason, they are against the collection of data as a matter of principle, since this serves simply to increase the manipulation of consumers.

It is important to conduct the privacy debate without these preconceived ideas. In this respect, I would like to put forward the following arguments for consideration.

First and foremost, there is nothing 'wrong' in itself with the collection of data. On the contrary. More data can lead to new insights. As long as the details remain anonymous, there is no question of a breach of privacy – at least, not in my opinion. No-one has a problem if someone stands on a street corner to count the number of people passing by, but the moment cameras and cell phone signals are used people are up in arms. Similarly, I have no problem if an intelligent screen makes publicity for Gillette or Tampax, based on the intervention of a smart camera that can see whether a man or woman is watching. The resistance to this kind of advertising is irrational. As long as this data is not registered, I can see no breach of privacy whatsoever.

In addition, companies also collect personal details about their customers, primarily through interactions with those customers. Of course, this must only be possible with the permission of the customers. The data must also be sufficiently well protected. The new European GDPR regulations seek to ensure that this is the case. As far as I am concerned, a shopping mall can measure without my approval how often my telephone comes into their shop (as a 'unique visitor'), but not how often Gino Van Ossel, living in Brussels, enters their premises. For me, that is comparable with what AB InBev is doing via RateBeer: it should be allowed as long as the intention is simply to collect market insights and not to establish the preferences of individual consumers.

It is clear that most consumers understand what is at stake. When discounter Colruyt introduced its customer loyalty card and personalized folders, some of the customers expressed concerns about their privacy. But once the mechanisms were explained to them, almost no-one withdrew from the scheme: 'data in exchange for discount and a personalized folder' seemed like a good deal to the vast majority of people.

At Albert Heijn you also need a bonus card to benefit from discounts, but there is no obligation to register. And because AH distributes its folders door to door, there is no compelling reason to do so. True, this does mean that you will be denied the additional benefit of personalized communication, which is usually conducted digitally. For this reason, some customers opt to register voluntarily, while others prefer to continue using their card anonymously: either consciously or because they think the benefits do not outweigh the bother.

In this respect, Walgreens has taken things much further. Is it right that a company can use data from health apps to make commercial propositions to consumers? And is it acceptable that it subsequently gives access to that data to the suppliers of its health products? This is an area where legislation currently provides no real solution. True, the new European GDPR regulations would require the customer to give the company explicit permission to do this, but we know that the vast majority of people give their approval for such things without reading through the relevant texts, so that they don't really know what they are doing.

Viewed from an ethical standpoint, I would argue for the use of clearer communication and simpler language that everyone can understand. Many companies could do worse than follow the example set by the Dutch webshop Coolblue. They explain clearly and transparently what they do and why: 'You can contact us by phone, e-mail, Twitter, Facebook or chat. To avoid the need for you to tell your story twice, we will remember what you tell

us first time. Okay, this means we will have to note it down –
but after all, we're only human! To make our service a little bit
better each day, we will analyze all our contact moments. They
can teach us a lot. And if we record telephone conversations for
training purposes, we will let you know in advance.'[120]

Of course, the biggest area of concern is when our data is im-
properly used. Should Walgreens be able to sell my health details
to an insurance company to assess my level of risk? For me, that
is taking things a step too far. It's effectively the same as if a
bank would analyze your payments or your telecom operator
would listen to your calls! This is the kind of area where the government needs to protect consumers against themselves.

And so we come to the tech giants. Do we think it is okay for
Facebook Messenger to analyze our messages or for Google to
screen our agendas and Gmail? Should Apple be able to monitor where we all are? Are we happy that Alexa can listen to
everything being said in our homes?

So far, the Cambridge Analytica scandal has not persuaded many
people to ditch Facebook. But it has given both the company
and society a serious wake-up call. Yet in some ways not serious
enough. One newspaper warned its readers to be extra-careful
when logging in on apps with Facebook, because those apps get
access to all the data on your Facebook account. But on the same
day the same paper's online site explained that it was possible to
read an article behind a paywall for free via a Facebook log-in...
In other words, there is still a lot of work to be done.

The ultimate example is WeChat, sometimes referred to as the
'national operating system of China'. WeChat is like Facebook,
WhatsApp, Twitter and Instagram all rolled into a single app.
You pay with it, keep your agenda on it, log-in free to wifi with it,
keep your boarding pass for your next flight on it, etc., etc.

In China, everyone is on WeChat – and only on WeChat. For digital gurus, this is a dream, because everything is so much easier and so much quicker.[121] But the impact on privacy is dramatic. I hope that in our own societies we would not accept such a high level of integration. This would bring us just a little bit too close to a Big Brother scenario, especially since the Chinese government has announced that from 2020 onwards it intends to give a 'social credit score' to all its citizens – which effectively means a state seal of approval for what constitutes good citizenship.[122]

At the end of the day, I find myself siding with the vision of Peppers and Rogers: the only correct way to deal with privacy matters is for companies to display sufficient voluntary honesty and integrity in respect of their collection, storage and use of our data. Of course, developing a concrete approach remains difficult. On the one hand, the matter is too important to be to be left to self-regulation. On the other hand, it is difficult to impose a concept like integrity within a legal framework. Perhaps we need to set up a college of experts at the European level: a Jury for Ethical Practices in Data Collection and Use that can offer advice and make binding judgments?

Let the discussion begin!

NOTHING NEW UNDER THE SUN?

At the start of this chapter we saw how the idea of the 'segment of one' is nothing new. But we now know that in some respects the current version goes much further than in the past and in other respects not as far.

It goes further because the concept no longer looks simply at communication. Nowadays, we can also gear products to customers. The most modest form of this process is curated commerce, where we select products from a standard assortment that we think best meet the needs of the individual customer.

Think back, for instance, to our Lincherie example. A more intermediary form – and one that is not really data-driven – is made-to-measure products. It is now possible to order your jeans tailor-made from Levi's, complete with trendy tears. The next step is mass made-to-measure, but even this is not really new: NIKEiD has been available for some time. What is new is that all these products can now be delivered much faster than in years gone by. Adidas has taken this trend to the next level with their 'Knit for you' pop-up in Berlin: here it is not only possible to design your own jersey on the spot, but you can actually watch it being woven to the perfect size based on a 3D-scan of your body. It is literally ready in minutes.[123][124] Last but not least, there is also data-driven made-to-measure. In this sense, Acusto goes a stage further than Lincherie, by using a full body scan to make complete outfits of personalized suits and shirts that fit like a glove...

But also in some ways not as far. If we can succeed in identifying trends more quickly, it should also be possible to mass produce products that better match the needs of all our customers or a specific customer segment – and that's great as well!

The segment of one must not become a dogma.

THE NEW CUSTOMER RELATIONSHIP

1. **Data typology:**

    a. Which data do you want to collect at the level of the customer, your segments, the company as a whole and/ or the market?
    b. How quickly do the data change?

2. **Data collection:**

    a. Can you make better use of the data you already collect?
    b. Can you transform observations that you already make into data suitable for analysis (datafication)?
    c. Can you create new sources of data, which connect in a meaningful way with your information needs? In this context, do you think about the entire customer journey (both purchase and use)?
    d. Do you keep enough data, even if you don't know at this stage what you will be able to do with it?

3. **Data analysis:**

    a. Do you have sufficient in-house expertise to do this? What do you want to do yourself? What do you want to outsource?
    b. What methods do you use? Are these the right methods? Are you fully aware of the most recent developments? Are you experimenting with artificial intelligence?
    c. Have you carefully assessed which analyses need to happen in real time and which can wait until later?

4. **Use of data: what do you want to achieve**

   a. How can you get to know your individual customers better?
   b. How can you better detect market trends?
   c. How can you work more effectively, so that you generate more turnover?
   d. How can you work more efficiently, so that you can reduce costs?

5. **Respect for privacy:**

   a. Are you fully complying with legal requirements?
   b. Are you dealing with data honestly and with integrity?
      - Do you ask the customer permission in a sufficiently clear manner, so that he really understands the choice he is making?
      - Do you make it sufficiently simple for the customer to consult your privacy policy and to check what data you hold about him?

6. **How do data, AI and personalization contribute to the ideal customer journey?**

CHAPTER 9

THE STORE OF
THE FUTURE

'Our competition is not Netflix. It's not the internet.

It is sporting events, it is bowling, it is nightclubs.'

Tim Richards (CEO of Venue Cinemas)

Why should you make the effort of going to the cinema if you can also watch a film at home? Digital TV in high resolution, ever bigger screens, 3D-glasses, surround sound in your own living room and (with Netflix) a whole film catalogue at your disposal. You must be barmy to fight your way through the wind and the rain to pay 10 euros for the privilege of watching the same film in someone else's building! Mustn't you?

Even so, the cinema is holding its own,[125] but only because it has been able to reinvent itself. The level of comfort is greater than ever, we are buying more popcorn and drinks than ever, and the legendary 'back row of the movies' is now specially designed without arm rests to make things cozier – and easier – for budding lovebirds. You can even watch live relays of opera, concerts or football instead of a film.

But that's only the start! There are now some cinemas where you can watch films from under the comfort of a duvet in a double bed. The serving of alcohol and gastronomic finger food in auditoria is also becoming more common.[126] Inevitably, technological innovation – for example, the use of ceiling speakers – also plays a role. The result is a totally different cinema experience in comparison with just a decade ago.

This shows that physical channels and touchpoints also have their place in the customer journey of tomorrow. In this chapter we will focus on the future role of the shop and the showroom.

THE BATTLE FOR TIME

We are all busy. Very busy. Too busy. For kids and teenagers, it's because they have to do their homework but still want to spend hours gaming, chatting or just chilling on the sofa. For young couples, it's because they want to have time for each other but also for their 'old' friends. For parents, it's because they need to combine care of their children with a career. For pensioners, it's because they're off for a month in Benidorm next week but still need to get the garden ready for the winter before they go.

All these people need to carefully weigh up how they can best use their time and, if possible, save a few precious minutes or hours here and there. This means that when retailers are drawing up their ideal customer journey, it is vital to take account of this non-stop battle for time.

In essence, there are two kinds of customer journey. Consumers follow a functional customer journey when they need something. They follow a hedonistic customer journey because they want to. The nature of the customer journey is dependent on the target market; in other words, the customer himself, the product and the context (See chapter 5: 'Choose your target market). The fashionista wants shoes but needs a new PC; the nerd wants a new PC but needs shoes. One day you would like a leisurely meal out with your partner; the next day you need a quick snack before the concert starts.

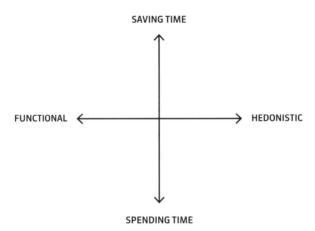

Having said that, every hedonistic customer journey nearly always contains functional elements: the fashionista loves looking at shoes, trying shoes and choosing shoes, but even she eventually has to get in the row at the check-out or else order and pay for them online.

SAVING TIME

The first wave of e-commerce was largely driven by the customer's desire to save time. It is only a mild exaggeration to see Amazon as the ultimate time-saving machine. This was the company that 20 years ago patented the 'one-click buy'. Now you can ask their Alexa to order everything you need and have it delivered to your home, leaving you time to spend the evening watching a film from the comfort of a double bed (with finger food, of course!) at your local cinema. And your courier? No problem! Once he arrives at your house, you let him in with your smart lock.

This compulsion to save time will continue to feed the further growth of e-commerce and put pressure on the share of turnover earned by physical stores. But this does not mean that the role of the physical store is played out. Far from it.

The first reason, as we have already seen, is that shopping can be hedonistic as well as functional. When questioned, two-thirds of consumers say they enjoy shopping and almost half admit to shopping even when they don't specifically need anything.[127] More about this later.

The second reason is that e-commerce is not always easier or quicker. If you are returning from a business trip and suddenly remember you haven't brought a present for the kids, the small Hamleys toy shop at Heathrow or St. Pancras will come to your rescue.[128] And if you want to grab a quick snack before catching your evening train home, you are not going to order it online but will simply pop in to a Tesco Express or Carrefour Express.

The tech giants also understand this. We saw in chapter 1 how JD.com plans to open a million local supermarkets in mainland China in just five years' time. Amazon also surprised people when it opened its Amazon Go store in Seattle. At just 170 m², the shop is about the size of a Tesco Express. Of course, people are super-impressed when they can leave the premises without the need to scan in their items at a check-out, but Amazon by no means has a monopoly when it comes to till-free shopping (see box).

Finally, it is important to remember that the location of a store can be a decisive factor. Under our Vlerick campus in Brussels there is a Proxy Delhaize convenience store. Just across the other side of the busy inner ring road there is a Carrefour Express. Very few shoppers make the effort to cross from one side of the road to the other out of preference for one or other of these stores.

THE TILL-FREE STORE

In recent years we have become familiar with self-scanners and the self-scan check-out, first in supermarkets and later in non-food stores like Ikea, Decathlon, Zara and Zeb. The advantage for the customer is obvious: you don't have to spend half an hour queuing at a till and so you save time. The advantage for the store is equally obvious: they can operate more tills in the same space with fewer staff. Some staff will always be necessary to keep an eye on things, in part because of the greater risk of theft and in part because no technology is completely idiot-proof.

At Decathlon, Zeb and Zara all the items are fitted with a RFID tag. These can be read automatically by the till, so that they don't need to be physically scanned. Decathlon and Zeb also use the tags as a form of anti-theft protection. As soon as you have paid, the tag is automatically de-activated, so that you can leave the store without problem.[129] The big disadvantage of the system is that the tags can easily be cut out with just an ordinary pair of scissors. This is why Zara has decided to use a different kind of anti-theft device, which is fitted to the actual product. Customers can also remove these devices themselves at the self-scan check-out, but always under the watchful eye of a Zara member of staff!

Till-free shopping clearly makes things easier for customers. As a result, the number of experiments and tests now run into the hundreds, if not thousands. Equally, the risk of theft increases, because there is no direct supervision by personnel. This explains why most of these initiatives have been confined to smaller stores; so far at least, because (among others) Amazon and MediaMarkt have announced pilots in bigger stores.

The simplest method is to allow the customer to use his smartphone as a scanner, which he then also uses to make payment. This avoids the need to queue up at a separate payment terminal. For example, MediaMarkt Saturn has run a successful test with a till-free store in which they only sell a number of their smaller items, such as earphones and chargers. Customers scan and pay for their products with their smartphone. The payment de-activates the RFID tag, which still also serves a security function but is now placed inside the product packaging, making it more difficult to remove.[130] In supermarkets, where the value of individual products is much lower, Spar is also testing the smartphone scan-and-pay system.[131][132]

Albert Heijn has taken things a stage further. In their AH to go stores it is possible to enjoy till-free shopping without the need to either physically scan or pay. This system also makes use of tags, but they are fitted to digital shelf cards and not to the individual products. You hold your smartphone in front of the shelf card and the product is automatically added to your bill. If you don't remove it within ten minutes, you are automatically charged for it. This, again, is a reason why such a system is harder to implement in bigger stores, where the bigger area means that you realistically need more than ten minutes' thinking time. Even so, the system does allow AH to go customers to walk freely in and out of the store without physically paying, just like in Amazon Go. According to Albert Heijn, the test at the pilot store in Zaandam has shown that faster transaction speed encourages shoppers to come to the store more often and to buy more when they do.[133] The company is rolling out the system nationally.

Elsewhere, other experiments are being carried out with faster methods of payment, which no longer require customers to remove their bank card from wallet or purse. Contactless payment via NFC is gaining ground in the United States, while in Asia the scanning of QR-codes is on the increase. The use of both methods is also becoming more common in Belgian stores. In China they are even testing methods with sound waves, voice recognition and other biometric characteristics as a way to increase the speed and convenience of the payment process.

Increasing convenience and speed is also a priority in the foodservice sector. At Starbucks and McDonalds you can use an app to order and pay 'on the move', following which your coffee or burger will be waiting for you to pick up when you arrive. Just as clever is the zero-click app from Domino's, which we saw in chapter 1.

SPENDING TIME

As we have already seen, two-thirds of consumers say that they like shopping. However, this strikes me as being an underestimation, because people tend to narrow down their definition of shopping to 'shopping in a shopping street or mall'.

But shopping can be so much more than that. No holiday to the south of France or Italy is complete without a visit to the local market. In the Provence, hotels and tourist offices deliberately exploit this by distributing folders with details of all the local market days on a large scale. In Barcelona, the Mercat de la Boqueria is rightly regarded as one of the city's top ten 'things to see'. And in my own home town of Brussels the weekly *Marché du Midi* attracts as many tourists and visitors out for a stroll as it does local shoppers with a list of things to buy. The dozens of brightly colored stalls, many of them run by migrants, gives the market an exotic feel…

Some years ago I had the good fortune to be able to watch a football match at Old Trafford, the home of Manchester United. After the match, we had a tour of the stadium, followed by the obligatory visit to the fan shop. Other men in our group who had told me on the way to the ground that they hated shopping now stood just half an hour later with a full basket of United memorabilia, queuing up to pay and complaining that the tour actually left them with too little time to do the shop visit properly!

Of course, this does not detract from the fact that recreational or fun shopping is also under increasing pressure. Shopping now has to compete with the binge watching of TV series on Netflix, a visit to the cinema, doing some sport of your own, city trips, and a whole host of other options. The range of choice in leisure activities has boomed in recent decades.

The wider context is also unfavorable: the ageing of the population puts pressure on consumption, while young people prefer to spend their money on Tomorrowland and their iPhone than on fashion and shopping. At the same time, the physical stores will continue to experience increasing competition from webshops, also for recreational shopping: the second wave of e-commerce (see chapter 3) will further nibble away at store turnover.

FEWER STORES?

The conclusion is clear: the continuing growth of e-commerce will inevitably lead to fewer shops and stores. Today in the Netherlands there are some 96,000 stores, in comparison with 106,000 a decade ago: a fall of 10% in just ten years. During a recent meeting of the Dutch Council of Shopping Centers, a group of property professionals were asked to outline their vision of the physical retail future: 37% expected a further decline of 20% during the next ten years, with 54% saying that another fall of 10% was more likely; only 5% thought that the status quo could be maintained, with a further 5% of optimists believing that there might even be a return to growth.[134]

In spite of these gloomy predictions, there will always be a need for shops. But what kind of shops? What will they look like? How big will they be? What will be their future role? Where will they be located? How many of them can we support? These are difficult questions to answer.

You often hear it said that 'we must give the customers a reason to keep on coming to our shops and stores'. For me, this approaches the problem from the wrong direction – unless you are a property investor or a city center manager for a local council. The ideal customer journey does not take as its starting point the needs of the shop, but the needs of the customer. And once we have established these needs, we then decide which touchpoints can best serve them within the context of our target market. Are physical stores the best way to do it? Great! But if it is a showroom, a webshop, a customer contact center, or an app... that's great as well!

In the rest of this chapter we will look first at functional and then at hedonistic shopping, assessing what role the physical stores can play in each domain.

FUNCTIONAL SHOPPING

What do you do if you have a customer service question for your telecom provider? Do you pick up the phone or surf to their website? A research study by McKinsey involving 2,000 West European consumers revealed that more than half (54%) now use the digital option.[135] But the same study also revealed that all too often these digital consumers are disappointed by what they find. And because they are unable to find an answer to their questions online, in the end they need to resort to the phone anyway...

The remaining 46% of consumers prefer either to phone immediately or to call in at one of the provider's stores. Perhaps they know from experience that the online option won't give them the answers they need, or maybe they feel more comfortable putting their questions to a real flesh-and-blood person. But whatever their reason, all these customers are less satisfied than the digital-only customers: people who search for and find solutions online are significantly more satisfied than all other types of customer!

With a little bit of willingness, it is possible to regard a customer service journey as an example of functional shopping. We do it because it is necessary, not because we want to. For this reason, we look for the line of least resistance and opt for the solution that will cost us the least time. In other words, 'convenience' is always a basic need in functional shopping.

In most cases, it is a digital solution that offers the greatest convenience, so that the functional customer journey will also become increasingly digital. And, as the McKinsey study demonstrated, this leads to a high level of satisfaction in the digitally-oriented customer. These are the customer journeys that we prefer to delegate integrally to Alexa or Siri – which is what colleague Steven Van Belleghem means when he says that 'convenience is the new loyalty': the customer becomes loyal to the interface.[136]

But if this is true, why aren't all functional customer journeys digital? And why – at least in my opinion – is that never going to happen? It all comes back to customer needs. Saving time might be a core need inherent in functional shopping, but it is not the only need and not necessarily the most important one. This becomes clear if we zoom in on the different building blocks of the target market.

The profile of the customer

My barber is an entrepreneur without personnel. A one-man business. He works by appointment only, appointments you can make by telephone but not via the internet. While I am sitting in his barber's chair customers sometimes pop in to make an appointment in person. I estimate that about a third of his appointments are made in this way. To me, that's strange. I can't ever imagine myself doing it. At the same time, it doesn't surprise me. You have probably already guessed that my barber is not exactly the trendiest in town and his customers – like me – tend to be on the wrong side of fifty.

It is a simple fact that not all customers are digitally minded – and never will be. The need for personal contact will always remain. Of course, this segment will continue to shrink, but I don't believe it will ever disappear entirely.

The context

If I want to book a restaurant, I usually do it by phone, because it is quicker than doing it online. Even if you already have an account on a booking interface, I find it cumbersome to scroll through a menu on my smartphone, tick in the time I want to eat, the number of people, etc. It's just so much easier to say it.

But what if the restaurant is closed when I call? Then, of course, I do make use of the software option. And a very handy option it is, too! Or at least it is, providing I can see immediately that they still have a table free and my reservation has been confirmed. This is the case with most booking interfaces, but by no means all. What's more, there are some restaurants that only take bookings outside their normal opening hours by e-mail. If you are looking at lunchtime for a restaurant for the same evening, nothing is quite so irritating as when you fail to get an immediate confirmation for your request. Have they got a table or haven't they? I usually end up going somewhere else or phone as soon as I think there might be somebody there to answer.

This example illustrates that I have a preference for a digital option, but only if it is the most user-friendly option. My ideal 'booking journey' might therefore look something like this: I ask Siri to make a booking. Siri contacts the restaurant's Alexa and receives an immediate reply. Unfortunately, all the tables are already reserved, so Siri suggests other restaurants that still have tables free. Clever Siri not only knows my favorite restaurants, but on the basis of item-to-item collaborative filtering also helps me to sort through the other restaurant options until I find what I am looking for... Perhaps this scenario is still a little way off for most of us, but in the meantime I ask myself why restaurateurs don't take the trouble to make their booking interfaces easier to use, also for cell phones. If that was the case, I probably wouldn't need to bother them with my telephone calls anymore...

The product

I recently bought a foldable bike. After surfing to look at the reviews and the ratings, I was sufficiently convinced that it was worth paying a little extra for a Brompton. Having said that, the reviews made clear that the cycling experience of a foldable model is very different from an ordinary bike and that for some people the folding process is not easy. As a result, I wanted to have a go myself before making the purchase and, consequently, I went to my nearest supplier for a test ride. The test went well, they had one in stock and so I bought it on the spot.

For some types of products certain customers always want to have physical contact with it – a sensory experience – before they commit to a purchase. Of course, companies like Zalando have proven that this does not necessarily need to happen in a shop. It can just as easily be done in your own living room. Having said that, not every customer is happy with this method. Returning the products you don't want can also be a nuisance. And sometimes 'a nuisance' is putting it mildly. Imagine you want to choose between a TV with a flat screen and a curved screen. Getting them out of the box to compare them is no problem. But getting the one you don't want back in again? That can be a nightmare. And for bicycles it is even worse. The delivery is seldom for free and return costs are also often charged to the customer. If that is the case, I much prefer to drive to my nearest physical store for advice. For now. But what if delivery and returns were free? And what if webshops were willing to collect returns from your home?

These three examples demonstrate why physical stores still have a role to play in terms of functional purchases:

- Not all customers are digitally oriented. A (probably) shrinking segment will always prefer physical stores.
- The digital solution is not always the easiest – remember the Tesco Express in the station or the Hamleys toy store in the airport.
- Some customers will always want to touch and feel certain products before they buy them. Service advice can be given at distance, but physical contact is generally more effective.

VIRTUAL OR MIXED REALITY?

One of the most 'fashionable' discussions at the moment relates to the extent that virtual reality will have a role to play in the shops and stores of the future. In the short term, there are certainly plenty of possibilities. For example, the American home improvement retailer Lowe's is currently testing the Holoroom How To, a virtual reality application that takes do-it-yourselfers step by step through various technical processes. You can feel the virtual test drill shaking in your hand, but without all the dust and the mess.[137]

The point is, of course, that virtual reality can be used just as easily in the customer's home as in the physical shop. This makes it even more relevant for the consumer, but less interesting for the future of the shop. The same is true of augmented reality. With the Samsung TV Size Assistant App you can immediately see on your cell phone or your tablet how a TV screen of a certain size will look on your wall.

For the physical store, mixed reality offers better perspectives. This allows you to integrate a physical and virtual experience. For example, you are sitting in a potential new car at your car dealer's showroom and a pair of mixed reality glasses will show you the interior in various different colors. The same technique can be used in a furniture store, where the glasses will allow you to see a new sofa in blue, green, beige, etc. This is something that can't be done at home, because that's not where the new car and sofa are located...

This allows us to formulate the following general rules:

» E-commerce will become the most important sales channel:
  ▪ for replenishment; in other words, functional repeat purchases, where the customer knows exactly what he wants (Nutella) or where the nature of the product means that the brand is not so important (he just wants new batteries and the brand is irrelevant);
  ▪ for one-off functional purchases where the choice can be made easily online.

» The physical store will remain the most important sales channel:
  ▪ for customers who are less digitally oriented;
  ▪ for functional purchases where the customer feels it is difficult to make a choice online or feels that the option of order-and-return is too much of an inconvenience;
  ▪ for functional purchases where the store is quicker or easier;
  ▪ for functional purchases for which the level of convenience offered online is too expensive.

» Products and their packaging:
  ▪ the products for which the customer needs to go to a physical store to make his choice must be displayed out of their packaging;
  ▪ the products for which the customer goes to a physical store simply because it is more convenient need not be displayed out of their packaging.

» Service & advice:
  ▪ for some customers the provision of personal advice can be a reason to go to a physical store for certain functional purchases;
  ▪ in some instances advice can be digitalized – for example, via Skype or by means of video clips – as a result of which this role of the physical store is likely to diminish in the future.

FRUSTRATION-FREE PACKAGING

Many retailers and brand manufacturers call themselves 'customer-oriented', whereas in reality they are still very much shop-oriented. Their ideas about packaging are symptomatic of this tendency. Packaging traditionally serves two functions: (1) it needs to protect the product during transport; and (2) it is an aid to help sell the product.

A good example of the problem is the Little People pirate ship by Fisher-Price. The ship is packed in a cardboard box with a transparent plastic front. This allows you to actually see the ship, and not just a photo on the box. There is also an opening in the plastic with an adjacent arrow marked: 'Try me'. If you press the button, the boat makes a sound.

The same ship can also be bought online. Of course, then the packed ship needs to be put inside another cardboard box before it can be sent off to your home.

The current packaging has three main disadvantages. First, it takes an average of eleven minutes to unbox the ship. Second, in addition to cardboard it also contains plastic and metal, which complicates the recycling. Third, for selling it online we use additional packaging: not only the extra box for shipment, but also an environmentally unfriendly sheet of bubble plastic.

So why not design an alternative packaging specifically for e-commerce sales? This would only need to serve a single aim: the safe transit of the product. The marketing function falls away, since the product is chosen in the webshop (or in the physical store). This makes it possible to have non-transparent packaging that consists of cardboard only. No need for plastic or metal. It also makes it possible to get the ship out of the packaging in one minute instead of eleven. If the pack is sufficiently strong to be shipped, you can sticker it with the customer's address, eliminating the need for secondary packaging and the bubble wrap. This is easier for the customer, better for the environment, cheaper to manufacture and ship (less handling).

With this in mind, Fisher-Price has now indeed created a second packaging for the pirate ship: the traditional packaging has now been given a 'frustration-free' companion, developed in collaboration with Amazon.

Of course, this increases the complexity for Fisher-Price. In time, we need to work towards a solution that allows the same packaging to be used in both the physical store and e-commerce. I don't need to go to the store to look at a packed product – I can do that online. The role of the store should be to have the product out of the packaging, so that I can see it, and then take home the e-commerce packaging once I have decided to buy it.

This principle is already applied for some products. Shoes, for example, are always presented out of the box. The role of the box in the in-store buying process is limited to helping you find the right size. The ultimate example of this approach is Ikea. You first pass through an experience world, where you can see a series of fully equipped rooms. At the end of your route through the store, you find the products that you want to buy, in cheap and simple packaging that is designed exclusively with transport in mind!

AND WHAT ABOUT INNOVATIONS?

Innovations present a specific problem. In chapter 5 (Choose your target market) we looked at the example of vacuum cleaners. This is a functional purchase, for which an increasing number of customers are opting for the convenience of online shopping in preference to a physical product experience in a store. Ratings and reviews make it possible to choose the right vacuum cleaner without ever having seen it. In comparison, the exact color and shape are of much less importance.

However, a sensory experience can still be necessary to convince consumers to buy new innovations. People who have never tried a Dyson cordless vacuum cleaner will probably only see its high price. Will they be willing to pay that extra cost simply because someone online says that the new vacuum is the best thing since sliced bread? Probably not. They are going to want to see it first. If the shops of tomorrow have less and less space to display things like vacuum cleaners, innovations will find it harder and harder to break through with customers. Because in this context customers often need a product experience, even if they don't realize it. For this reason, it is wise to familiarize them with the new technology before their purchasing need arises.

To achieve this, Dyson can, for example, give demonstrations away from the vacuum cleaner department, in a zone where more customers pass. They can even give demonstrations in a completely different location, including a more hedonistic shopping environment. With this in mind – and in addition to two flagship stores in the heart of London and New York – the brand has also opened shop-in-shops in department stores, so that a wider range of consumers can be surprised and seduced by their new technological wizardry.

HEDONISTIC SHOPPING

I can still remember well that in the 1970s, when I was a child, the decision whether or not to broadcast European football matches on television was only taken on the day of the game. If, say, Anderlecht or Club Bruges was playing at home in the European Champions Club Cup, there was a fear that live TV transmission would keep supporters away from the ground. And because we are talking about the days before the payment of lucrative broadcasting rights, the clubs often decided to ban the cameras from their stadiums, rather than risk losing income.

Nowadays, there is football everywhere on TV. If you are a paying subscriber to a sports channel, you can watch football seven days a week. Even so, more people now go to watch live football matches than ever before. During the 2017-2018 season, every game in the Dutch Premier League was attended by an average of just under 19,000 supporters, an increase of almost 50% in comparison with 20 years ago and a doubling in comparison with 40 years ago.[138] During the same period, ticket prices have gone through the roof and many games are still sold out.

If we replace football with shopping, we can see that the same pattern emerges. Nowadays, you can shop online 24/7. But you can also go 'live' shopping in the high street. Some shopping streets are so crowded they almost seem like football matches; others are (much too) quiet. At some locations, retailers have to queue up before they can rent suitable premises; at others, the number of empty properties increases week by week.

As we have already mentioned, recreational shopping is under increasing pressure: e-commerce, the ageing of the population and the changing uses of people's time – and therefore money – are all having an impact. There is shrinkage, but this shrinkage is not being evenly distributed across the board. In fact, physical retail seems to be moving towards a 'winner takes all' model.

WHERE DO WE DO OUR RECREATIONAL SHOPPING?

Which football matches and clubs attract the most spectators? The best! These tend to be the tradition clubs, like Barcelona, Manchester United or Bayern Munich. That is why the Champions League is now so important for clubs from smaller competitions: if Austria Vienna or Anderlecht are drawn against one of these top names, they know they are guaranteed a full stadium.

You can also see the same phenomenon in national competitions: leading clubs like Ajax have more spectators than the lesser footballing gods. Ajax has an average crowd of around 50,000, which is twice the average for other clubs in the Dutch Premier League. The clubs in the sub-top are also doing fairly well, but the smaller ones – especially in the lower divisions – are often struggling to keep their head above water.

And it's no different with recreational shopping. We do it less often than in the past, but if we do 'go shopping' for a day we expect it to be something special. For example, the big city centers like London, Paris, Berlin and Brussels are all booming. This creates a kind of self-perpetuating cascade effect: because more people are going shopping there, all the different kinds of shop formulas want to get in on the act. And because there are more shopping formulas, even more people find their way to the top high streets and malls. There is a clear analogy with what we saw about online marketplaces in chapter 2. At the same time, an increasing number of retailers are deciding to limit the size of their shop network. They close down branches in smaller towns and focus instead on the big cities. As a result, these cities become ever more attractive for shoppers: there is an increasing number of shops that you can now find there but nowhere else.

Just below these top cities, there is a tier of thriving regional centers. They play at a slightly lower level: not in the Champion's League, perhaps, but doing very nicely in the Premier League. In the Netherlands, these are typically cities with a population of more than 100,000 (or 75,000 in Belgium). Large malls and outlet centers away from the cities also fulfill a similar role.

But elsewhere, recreational shopping is steadily fading away. What's more, this decline seems to be irreversible. Clothes shops in these smaller centers will need to focus on a more functional approach based on proximity if they want to survive – but even then this is by no means certain. Viability is getting harder and harder to achieve.

The future direction of physical retail is therefore clear: fewer but better shops and stores. And just so that there is no misunderstanding: better shops and stores not only means that we can enrich the hedonistic customer journey to an unprecedented degree, but also that we can simplify the functional steps involved in fun shopping to the maximum possible extent!

THE PULLING POWER OF CITIES

Investors in the property market are following all these evolutions closely. They tailor their investment policy to the attractiveness of the various shopping areas. Retail property specialist Redevco has developed an interesting methodology to assess these matters, the outcome of which closely matches the above analysis.[139]

Their model has classified 825 European cities in order of attractiveness as shopping centers. Redevco only invests in cities in the top 20% of their list.

The main parameters of the model are:

- the population: size, catchment area, evolution;
- the economy: income, unemployment, shop turnover per resident...;
- the retail property market: empty shops, rents, return, current portfolio of retailers...;
- the quality of the city: creative professions, tourism, average age, other assets and attractions.

This final parameter – the quality of the city – illustrates that recreational shopping cannot be viewed in isolation from the entirety of the urban environment. Cities that are attractive for shopping are also attractive for other reasons – whether you live there, work there or are just visiting.

EVERY SHOP AN AMUSEMENT PARK?

What do shops and amusement parks have in common? Well, in this analogy they are both places where you go to have a good time. In other words, shopping as an end in itself. I also like the comparison with a casino. A casino isn't interested initially in whether a customer wins money or loses money. The most important thing is that the customer has a good time – because then he is likely to come back for more. In that way, the casino always wins in the end... But for now, let's stick with the amusement park analogy – which at least has the virtue of perhaps being a bit more politically correct!

What makes an amusement park successful?

» The overall experience
» The attractions
» The revenue model
» The visitor frequency

Let's have a look at each of these aspects in a little more detail.

THE OVERALL EXPERIENCE

One of the things that makes a visit to a Disney park so special is the general atmosphere of the place. Every detail is designed to give visitors the feeling that they are stepping into a magical world. All our senses are stimulated. The staff – or cast members, if you prefer – are an integral part of the performance. Because each park is precisely that – a carefully staged performance. Of course, Disney has its lovers and its haters. But the concept works because its target group are nearly all lovers.

The best shopping concepts do exactly the same. Superdry, Niketown, Ikea, Lush or Hamleys: they all create a pleasing atmosphere throughout their shops and stores. Of course, a good match with the brand is also essential: good brand positioning and a great shopping experience go hand in hand. For example, the experience at Lush is completely different from the experience at Sephora. In brand stores the match between shop and brand is even closer. The Apple Store embodies the brand. And in a Niketown you experience sport 'the Nike way'.

THE ATTRACTIONS

An amusement park without attractions would be pretty boring. There has to be something to do. The roller coasters and merry-go-rounds, which you actively experience, are central. But the parks also organize parades, fireworks and photo-moments with Disney figures, which you experience more passively.

In shops, it is the products that are the attractions. You can test them actively. In their flagship store in Soho, Nike has installed a basketball court on the top floor, where customers can play, if they want.[140] Cameras register what you do, so that you can share the images with family and friends on social media.

Lululemon, the Canadian brand for yoga-inspired athletic apparel, is another company that places a strong focus in their shops on how its products are used. At their flagship store in London's Regent Street, the racks of clothes (deliberately set on wheels) are regularly pushed to one side so that customers can take part in yoga sessions. In similar fashion, the Belgian Veritas chain gives in-house sewing lessons to promote its range of textiles and fashion accessories. In New York, Sephora has opened Beauty TIP Workshop stores, where TIP stands for Teach, Inspire and Play. Customers can take part in individual or group sessions, where they are given beauty advice by cosmetics professionals with the help of Sephora's augmented reality application, Virtual Artist.[141]

The Lego flagship store in London has Lego models of famous London landmarks, like the London underground and the typical red telephone boxes, with the explicit intention of encouraging people to take photographs and share them with their online community. Nowadays, a good hedonistic store needs to be 'instagrammable'.

THE DEPARTMENT STORE OF THE FUTURE

With its new department store in London's White City (Westfield), the British John Lewis chain – which hopes to derive half of its turnover from e-commerce by 2020 – offers us a glimpse into the future of retail.[142] Customers at the new store can not only shop, but also do things and even learn things!

For example, there are stylists who (on appointment) can give you styling advice either individually or in-group about your outfit and make-up. You are free to pick the stylist of your choice and it is also possible – if you so wish – for you to be kept up to date by the stylist about new collections of your favorite brands and other things that might interest you. In the various 'lifestyle' departments you can get similar free advice about your home interior. Another eye-catching 'first' in Europe is the Apple Smart Home space, where you can try out the Apple Home app and see how Siri can run all your home domotics. The store even has its own demo-kitchen, where you can follow cooking lessons. And if you don't know where to look first, the staff at the concierge desks will be happy to explain all the different services on offer. They will also make any appointments you need with special advisors or register you for the events the store regularly organizes.

To ensure service of the highest possible standard, the company has devoted a lot of time, effort and money to staff training. All its personnel have followed a performance course at the National Theatre, while the stylists have all received instruction at the London College of Style from a former editor of Vogue Fashion.

THE REVENUE MODEL

An amusement park lives from its parking fees, entrance fees, catering, the sale of souvenirs and, in some cases, sponsoring and advertising.

Not all of these are possible for shops and stores. Asking customers to pay an entrance fee would be taking things too far. True, the Livraria Lello bookstore in Porto does charge people for admittance, with the ticket then serving as a discount voucher for the purchase of a book. So how does the store manage to get away with this? Are the Portuguese such avid book readers? Or is it tourists who are willing to pay to admire the remarkable Art Nouveau interior. Or is it because the store is reputedly the place where author J.K. Rowling first got the idea for her Harry Potter books?

Some stores are now more a medium of communication than a sales channel. As a result, they are also a cost center, where the store turnover is not immediately intended to cover its running expenses. Instead, these stores must serve to encourage greater sales in the company's other sales channels, so that the overall earning model remains viable. This can only work if the operator of the store is also the owner of the brand:

» In the most extreme version of this scenario, the store is no longer a store at all; it is just a showroom, where it is not possible to actually buy anything. A good example of this is the Miele Experience Center near Utrecht in the Netherlands. Here, you can test out Miele products and receive expert advice. You can even follow cooking lessons and companies can hire the complex for their business events. But nothing is for sale. Similarly, the Gazelle brand of bicycles has a showroom where you can test ride the different models without necessarily buying them, while the Dyson flagship stores in London and New York we mentioned earlier also come close to this 'showroom' concept.

» A pop-up is an alternative to a permanent showroom and is also a much cheaper way to turn the spotlight on your brand and products at a specific location for a temporary period. For example, the American Krazy Glue demonstrated the bonding power of its adhesives during the Christmas season by sticking a pool table, a television and other potential gifts to the ceiling of their pop-up store in Manhattan.[143] In this way, they were able to turn a functional product into an attraction in a hedonistic day's shopping. The pop-up was only open for a single afternoon, but the resulting media attention – carefully stimulated by the company – lasted for weeks.

» Some brand stores serve a dual purpose for both brand promotion and sales. To the outside world, it is not always clear whether these stores are profit or cost centers. For example, Bosch has recently opened its first store in the heart of Vienna with a floor space of just 400 m². [144] Generally, it is more common for stores of this kind to be large flagships, such as the stores of Tommy Hilfiger, Lululemon and ASICS on Regent Street in London. In this context, the Apple Stores once again lead the way. Although fundamentally a communication channel, they are so profitable that they do much more than simply cover their costs!

Self-evidently, stores that intend to be profit centers must, like the Apple Stores, generate sufficient turnover to more than meet their operating expenses. Since it is not feasible for them to charge admittance, this turnover can only come from the sale of products. In this respect, multi-brand retailers, such as John Lewis, Macy's or Best Buy, are faced with a specific challenge: they need to avoid becoming showrooms for consumers who then buy the branded products elsewhere. One solution is to ask the brands who 'advertise' products in their stores to pay a 'sponsorship' fee – which is effectively a kind of commission on the brand's own sales. More about this in part 3, when we look at future business models for retail.

VISITOR FREQUENCY

One of the main challenges for amusement parks is to maintain visitor numbers at the same – and sufficiently profitable – high levels. Most visitors probably think that Disney World is great, but once they have seen it they may prefer to try something else. So how can you convince the customers to visit your park again and again? One way to do it is with subscriptions, nocturnes, themed events and new attractions.

This need to constantly re-invent yourself is also faced by shops and stores. However, shops and stores have the added advantage over amusement parks that they can change their range of 'attractions' – in other words, their products – more quickly. This helps to explain the success of so-called 'fast fashion', which sees new collections being presented on an almost weekly basis. Events, themed displays and the possibility to follow courses of various kinds are also interesting options to keep your customers coming back for more.

CHECKLIST
THE STORE OF THE FUTURE

1. **The customer:**

   a. What percentage of your customers are digitally oriented?
   b. How will this evolve in the coming three, five and ten years?

2. **The product:**

   a. Is your assortment for your target group primarily functional or hedonistic? Is it possible to quantify this in percentages?
   b. Functional
      - What proportion of your assortment is replenishment?
      - What proportion of your assortment is available to the customer online?
      - For what proportion of your assortment does the customer first prefer to physically experience the product in the store?
      - For what proportion of the assortment does the customer first need advice?
   c. Hedonistic
      - How successful are webshops in creating a 'fun shopping' experience around these products (second wave of e-commerce)?
      - How successfully are you able to do this with your own website and webshop?

3. **Context:**

   a. For what percentage of your turnover do different buying occasions play an important role?
   b. To what extent do these buying occasions generate different needs?

4. **Specifically for the retailer:**

   a. What percentage of your turnover is still generated today by physical stores?
   b. Which products do you need to physically display on the shop floor (product experience)?
   c. How can you add value to those products on the shop floor?
   d. Should you provide personal advice for these products or can this be arranged in a self-service format?
   e. What shop experience is needed and how can you provide it?
   f. What brand experience is needed and how can you provide it?
   g. How can you best show the full range of your assortment (products that you are not able to display physically on the shop floor)?
   h. What does this mean for your shop format? Will you need to have different formats?
   i. How many shops will you need in each format? What will this mean in terms of the respective turnover per square meter? Is this profitable?
   j. How will the answers to all these questions change over the next three, five and ten years?
   k. How will you monitor these evolutions?

5. **Specifically for brand manufacturers:**

   a. What percentage of your turnover is still generated today via traditional retailers (and their webshops)?
   b. Which products do you physically need to display to your customers? With what added value? Should this added value include personal advice?
   c. Can you reach the customer in this way via your existing retailers? Should you be looking for new retailers?
   d. To what extent do you wish to create physical touchpoints in your retail outlets to enhance your brand experience?
   e. Can you reach the customer in this way via your existing retailers? Should you be looking for new retailers?
   f. Can your retailers still earn money in this way? What will they expect from you in return?
   g. Do you want to set up your own physical touchpoints? If so, which, how many and where?
   h. How will the answers to all these questions change over the next three, five and ten years?
   i. How will you monitor these evolutions?

PART 3

TOWARDS A NEW BUSINESS MODEL

CHAPTER 10
THE NEW REALITY

'A desk is a dangerous place from which

to view the world.'

John le Carré (British writer)

The theory of Charles Darwin is often used as a metaphor to describe the digital disruption of the retail sector. To be honest, it's something I am guilty of as well. You know, 'the survival of the fittest', and all that... Ultimately, however, the comparison is a false one. Survival in evolution theory is largely a question of luck. Animals were not able to adjust consciously to their changing environment. The genetic mutations that led to success were largely created by chance.

In this sense, developments in the retail sector are following an entirely different pattern. It is a market with very clear winners and losers. For this reason, a metaphor like a 'flock of animals' is more appropriate, with the weakest ones being eaten by the circling predators, waiting to pounce.

In the previous part of the book, we saw how we need to go in search of the ideal customer journey. The role of the physical store in this journey will be more limited and different. But, in fact, it is the entire retail business model that needs to be revamped – and this will be the subject of the following chapters. First, we will analyze the new reality, before focusing on competitive power and how you can create value both for the customer and yourself.

THE OSTRICH SYNDROME

A classic retailer buys goods and tries to sell them at a profit. The difference between the purchase price and the sale price is his mark-up or net margin. From this, he still needs to pay all his other costs. Before they can be sold, the goods need to be brought to the store and displayed on racks and shelves. This doesn't happen by magic. It requires people to do it – and personnel costs are one of the heaviest charges on the margins of brick-and-mortar retailers, followed by the costs associated with the store itself: rent, fitting out, other operating costs, etc.

To say that the distribution model of e-commerce companies is different is like kicking at an open door: you deliver the product to the consumer in his home and he can send it back if he doesn't like it. Getting the products ready for delivery is mostly done by the company operating the webshop itself; the actual delivery is usually farmed out to logistics specialists.

For many people, it seems counter-intuitive that the e-commerce distribution model is cheaper than the traditional retail model. Even so, in my previous book I proved this black-on-white, by showing how in the fashion sector H&M and Zara spend more money as a percentage of their turnover on their store network than ASOS and Zalando on home delivery and returns, even with a return rate as high as 50%.

Of course, the distribution cost is only a part of the total cost picture. For ASOS and Zalando, the webshop is their store, and investments in ICT can be astronomically expensive. These are costs that a retailer without a webshop does not have.

Once you have a store, you need to make sure that it attracts the customers. Ten years ago, Zara – whose stores are all in prime locations – hardly spent a eurocent on media advertising. The visibility of these stores – which admittedly cost a fortune to rent – was deemed to be sufficient to get passing consumers through the doors. In this sense, you can see the rent as a kind of marketing cost. In contrast, webshops have no passers-by: they actually need to go and find their customers. This explains why Zalando spent nearly 27% of its turnover on marketing in 2011.

If you add the distribution and marketing costs together, it often transpires that the total for physical retailers is lower than for the e-commerce pure players. And it is precisely for this reason that so many retailers have continued to stick their heads in the sand for so long. By claiming that there is no real money to be made in e-commerce, they convince themselves that the digital storm will soon blow over...

THE NEW REALITY

THE NEW REALITY

Be that as it may, there is no denying that it was hard for the retailers to wake up to the new reality. This reality is the outcome of other developments that have affected both the brick-and-mortar retailers and the e-commerce pure players during the past ten years.

In chapter 1, we described the wave of consolidation that has taken place in e-commerce. Let's now have a look at what this means in concrete commercial terms for a company like Zalando, the European market leader in online fashion:

» The number of active Zalando customers has more than quadrupled, from just under five million in 2011 to more than twenty million in 2017. But during this same period their turnover has actually increased ninefold, from half a billion euros in 2001 to 4.5 billion euros in 2017. In other words, turnover per customer has increased by more than 200%.

» Existing customers are ordering more frequently via the Zalando app or by surfing directly to the webshop, without the need for Zalando to invest in advertising on search engines.

» This creates a lever effect: more turnover per customer and lower marketing costs per order. In the annual profit and loss account, we can see that this translates into a fall in marketing costs as a percentage of turnover from 27% in 2011 to less than 8% in 2017.

» The same economies of scale also apply to Zalando's other fixed costs, such as investments in technology.

» A noticeable exception to this trend are the distribution costs, which have not really fallen as a percentage of turnover. This is because such costs are (to a large extent) variable costs: you pay for each package sent. The efficiency gains in terms of making the packages ready for delivery is currently still being offset by the cost of necessary investments in extra capacity. Zalando continues to build new distributions centers ever closer to its customers, so that delivery can be made even faster. In other words, the customer gets a better service for the same price.

The result is that Zalando – like all the other major players in e-commerce – is performing better in financial terms than ten years ago. Its profitability has increased significantly.

THE BRICK-AND-MORTAR RETAILER: THE OTHER SIDE OF THE COIN

In contrast, the average traditional retailer operating physical stores has moved in the opposite direction during the past decade. Retail profitability has come under increasing pressure:

» The growth of e-commerce has weighed heavily on store turnover, so that distribution costs as a percentage of turnover have risen. Irrespective of the level of your turnover, you still need to pay the rent each month. Personnel costs also remain relatively fixed. True, you can cut your number of staff if you have fewer customers and less work, but you will always need to keep a minimum complement.

» As we saw in the previous chapter, shops are having the hardest time in medium-sized towns and cities. As a result, the fall in overall retail turnover is not evenly distributed. In the short term, you can try to compensate for this by negotiating lower rents, but in the long term the closure of loss-making stores is unavoidable.

» Store closures simply accelerate the speed at which turnover continues to decline. Before you know it, the cost of the company's central activities also becomes too expensive in relation to this falling income. If, for example, you attempt to maintain your level of marketing expenditure while income is decreasing, it will inevitably eat up an ever-bigger proportion of your shrinking revenues.

» At the same time as all this has been happening, traditional retailers have also been trying to develop their own e-commerce activities. But promoting these new activities required even more marketing expenditure, on top of which – the poisoned icing on the cake, as it were – the extra cost of home deliveries also needed to be met. As a result, both marketing and distribution costs continued to spiral.

» But it didn't stop there. In addition to operating costs, investments also shot through the roof. Creating a webshop in an omnichannel context not only demands significant investment in new ICT applications, but also further costly investment in the store network, in the shape of screens, electronic shelf labeling, tablets for staff, etc.

In a first phase, retailers came to the conclusion that their profitable store turnover was being increasingly replaced by less profitable online turnover.

The advent of the gigantic marketplaces simply added insult to injury. Companies like H&M and Zara had no previous experience of wholesale activities and were therefore used to keeping the entirety of their gross margin for themselves. Selling via a marketplace immediately implied the need to pay a commission to a third party. In turn, this meant earning less per product in comparison with sales in their own webshops. Not nice, of course, but if you want to go where the shoppers are, this nowadays inevitably involves doing a deal with the marketplaces. There is simply no viable way of avoiding them. This explains why even a giant retailer like Ikea has announced its intention to sell on Amazon and Alibaba.[145]

THE PARADOX OF DISTRIBUTION COSTS

You can prove with figures that Zalando's distribution costs are lower than those of H&M and Zara. But that's not the way store-based retailers see things. For example, the British department store chain John Lewis has calculated that shipping a product to a customer's home actually costs three times more than shipping the same product to one of its stores.

So where does this difference come from?

It all depends on how you allocate your costs. Of course, John Lewis is right when it says that it is cheaper to deliver a lorry load of a product to a single store and display it on a shelf than to pack each product individually and then ship it to individual consumers each living at different addresses.

But getting your products onto your shelves is only one element of the distribution cost: the store in which the shelves are located and the people manning the store also need to be paid for. If you add these elements to the equation, you get a very different picture! And this is where the real problem lies for brick-and-mortar retailers: in omnichannel you incur costs for both home delivery and your store network. As long as your e-commerce growth is not made at the expense of store turnover, there is no problem. But if store turnover falls, your store costs become proportionally heavier and heavier!

THE FALL GUYS

The biggest challenges are faced by the multi-brand retailers. If you want to buy Ikea or Zara products, you have no option but to buy from them, be it in a physical store or in their webshop. They have a unique assortment. But if you want a Samsung television, you can find it not only at MediaMarkt but also at Amazon and many other online and offline competitors.

During the first wave of e-commerce, when consumers systematically compared prices online before making a purchase, the margins of the multi-brand retailers began to come under increasing pressure. Part of the problem was that it is precisely this kind of brand product that is most ideal for showrooming. Customers came to the stores to look at things and then went away to buy them more cheaply elsewhere.

Falling turnover, lower unit margins, increasing marketing and distribution costs, and soaring investments in e-commerce and omnichannel: for many, it proved to be an impossible combination. The list of retailers who have been forced to throw in the towel in recent years is a long one!

To make matters worse, the arrival of the marketplaces poses yet another new dilemma for the multi-brand retailers. They have a lower gross margin than the integrated retailers, who only sell their own private brands. This means that the commission paid to marketplaces weighs more heavily on the multi-brand retailers. What's more, you probably won't be the only seller of Samsung TVs on Amazon. So why should a consumer buy from you?

Because you are cheaper? There goes your margin again! At the same time, you also run the risk that the owner of the marketplace will eventually add your best-selling products to his own assortment, so that he can keep the full trade margin for himself. This will leave you with just a series of slow rotating products with (at best) modest margins... It hardly sounds promising, does it? In short, the multi-brand retailers look set to become the fall guys in this new commercial configuration.

THE THIRD DOG?

Like the third dog in the famous proverb, the branded goods manufacturers have been able to watch these developments from the side lines. But will they be able to run away with the bone? It is certainly true that their business model is less directly threatened: it is their distribution channels that are currently being hammered the hardest. Of course, this situation is not without danger for the manufacturers as well. If, for example, as a toy manufacturer you decide not to sell on Amazon because you don't want to risk upsetting your current top distributors – Toys"R"Us or Blokker Holding – you may discover in a few years time that you have opted for the past rather than the future. Conversely, if you throw yourself too enthusiastically into the arms of Amazon, you may indeed find yourself sanctioned in the short term by today's retail market leaders, accounting for the bulk of your turnover!

This dilemma has prompted most brand manufacturers to make what might be called a logical transition. In keeping with the basic rule of thumb that a brand needs to follow its customers, most companies now sell their products via all channels. They deliver not only to the e-commerce pure players, but also to the omnichannel retailers and the brick-and-mortar retailers without webshops. A significant number have also decided to move into direct selling, either via their own webshop or brand store, or even a combination of both.

The marketplaces are also managing to attract more and more brand manufacturers. The financial advantages for the manufacturers are obvious: the commission they need to pay to the marketplaces is just a fraction of the margins they need to concede to the multi-brand retailers. Even if the manufacturer is required to pay for the distribution costs on the marketplace, he may still end up earning more!

Sounds good? It is – up to a point. But this does not necessarily mean that the horizon is trouble-free for the brand manufacturers. They have their problems to face as well. Market transparency has sent the prices of many brands spiraling downwards, while over-large discounts are in danger of damaging brand image. What's more, some of the large retail players like MediaMarkt and Fnac Darty are trying to compensate for their own shrinking margins by putting the screws on the margins of their suppliers. Consolidation is leading to a new balance of market power. Last but not least, the temptation to solve these problems by moving into direct sales also has serious financial implications, since the cost of keeping the stock must then be borne by the manufacturer rather than the distributor!

TOWARDS A NEW BALANCE

Companies like Amazon, who resolutely play the price card in their attempt to gain market dominance, feel happiest when there is a race to the bottom. Everyone else thinks that this is a game that can benefit no-one in the end. Online price transparency presses down so hard on margins that it threatens the financial viability of entire sectors. At the same time, visual search makes showrooming that much easier for consumers. To find the product that you want online, all you now need to do is take a photograph of it with your smartphone in the physical store. Upload the photo into the relevant Amazon or Ali Express app and you will automatically get all the information you require.

That being said, markets always have a tendency to find a new balance that avoids total dominance. And the retail market is no different. The main strands of this new balance are already clearly evident. The different market players are making strategic choices and adjusting their business models accordingly. The most important tendencies are:

» Verticalization: the end of the multi-brand store.
» Greater selectivity in distribution: the brand manufacturers take the lead.
» Vertical collaboration: collaboration 2.0.
» The survival of the traditional multi-brand store.

VERTICALIZATION: THE END OF THE MULTI-BRAND STORE

Verticalization means that brand manufacturers are increasingly opting for forward integration and direct sales to consumers, while retailers are switching to backwards integration and exclusive reliance on their own private brands. As we saw in chapter 4 when we discussed optichannel, everyone is becoming both retailer and brand manufacturer/supplier.

The advantages of this model are obvious. Where, for example, can you buy the Billy bookcase by Ikea the cheapest? The answer will always be: 'from Ikea'. Because Ikea is the only vendor of Ikea products, even in the marketplaces. Verticalization gives a company complete control over its distribution and price setting. But it is not just about price. The manufacturer can now also decide how his products are presented and how the brand is positioned. He is no longer dependent on third parties.

In these circumstances, there is no reason to prevent a brand from building its own showroom, where consumers only come to look, but not buy. This is now a risk-free option. Why? Because when the consumer has finally made up his mind, the only place he can buy the product of his choice is from the brand manufacturer. And it doesn't matter whether he does it online or offline!

Multi-brand retailers can verticalize by focusing increasingly on their own private brands, so that they become less reliant on manufacturer brands. An extreme example of this is Decathlon. In the sporting goods market, which is dominated by strong brands like Adidas and Nike, this company has developed its own range of relatively low-cost products, using in each category a different private brand – and with success. In some markets, the turnover share of private label products and brands can reach as high as 80%.

In a similar vein to Decathlon, the British department chain John Lewis has the ambition to ultimately develop an assortment that consists of 50% of either its own brands or third-party branded products sold exclusively at John Lewis.[146]

The same trend can also be seen in a number of the e-commerce players. The British ASOS now generates 40% of its turnover from its own brands and another 20% from products that can only be purchased exclusively from them.[147] Bonobos, Boohoo and Warby Parker are all examples of successful e-commerce companies where 100% vertical integration has been implemented.

Vertical integration always demands a minimal scale, which varies from sector to sector. For example, small production ranges are more feasible for clothing than for bicycles or shoes. Moreover, there is a fundamental difference between designing your own products and having them made, which is what Ikea, Zara and Decathlon do, and purchasing existing products that you then market under your own brand name, which is a common practice in the worlds of supermarkets, building supplies and consumer electronics.

Brand manufacturers are moving in the opposite direction and are systematically increasing their share of turnover from direct sales, not in the least by setting up their own webshops. For example, Esprit has a long tradition of direct sales to consumers. Ignoring their webshop for a moment, sales from their own stores account for 57% of their turnover, while their wholesale customers are good for just 43%. However, their webshop now generates more than a quarter of their total turnover, which means that in overall terms direct sales are responsible for almost 70% of their revenues.[148]

Marketplaces are helping to accelerate this trend: sales to Zalando or Amazon are indirect sales, but sales on the Zalando or Amazon marketplaces are direct sales.

These various developments ultimately lead to a self-perpetuating phenomenon. As we have already seen, the multi-brand distributors are under pressure. Price competition is causing many of them to shrink and a significant number to fall. The survivors opt for verticalization, which gives the brand manufacturers less room for their products in physical stores. This inevitably leads to a fall in indirect sales, as a result of which the brand manufacturers are forced to switch to more direct sales, which puts the multi-branders under yet more pressure – and so the dance continues…

Even so, we must be careful not to generalize too much: not all brand manufacturers are able to make this choice:

» If your brand is not sufficiently strong, your chances of success in a direct sales environment are much smaller. Your stores and webshop will not generate enough traffic to be viable. An inability to verticalize successfully is usually a symptom of a more fundamental underlying problem. The weakness of your brand means that you risk becoming the plaything of your dealers.
» Your assortment must be sufficiently large to make an attractive offer to consumers. For example, Adidas markets a wide range of articles, including shoes and clothing, which covers an equally wide range of sports. In contrast, Yonex – which focuses on just three sports, namely badminton, golf and tennis – will find it more difficult to develop a viable store network. This also explains why there are more brand stores for clothes than for shoes.
» Not all categories of products are equally suitable for direct sales. When the consumer wants to buy a variety of products during a single visit – as is the case, for example, during the weekly visit to the supermarket – convenience becomes the most important element in the customer journey. You don't want to go to a Nestlé store for your coffee, a Unilever store for your washing powder, etc.

GREATER SELECTIVITY: THE BRAND MANUFACTURER TAKES THE LEAD

As long as the brand manufacturer is not vertically integrated to the maximum possible extent, he will not have 100% control over his distribution and prices. Once again, Esprit can serve as an example. Esprit regards its franchise holders as wholesale customers. As a brand, you usually have control over your franchise holders (which is why some companies count them as direct sales). In the case of Esprit, these franchise holders represent just 18% of the total number of points of sale in their European wholesale turnover, while they are good for 48% of the total number of square meters of floor space. This means, of course, that the remaining 82% of points of sale are run by 'pure' wholesale customers, who also sell other brands and are therefore subject to only minimal or even no control by Esprit. If a small retailer in Southampton, Dortmund or Gothenburg wants to slash Esprit prices in his webshop, there is nothing to stop him – with all the negative consequences this implies for the brand...

The digital disruption in the retail sector primarily affects smaller entrepreneurs, who have only a single or at best a handful of stores. They do not have the resources to invest sufficiently in a digital presence or to afford the rents for top locations in major cities. As a result, owner managed multi-brand retailers find it hard to survive; they are pushed out by the big chains, resulting in a consolidation wave among the multi-brand retailers.

This is another reason for brand manufacturers to control their indirect distribution channels more closely than ever before. In a shrinking channel with fewer but larger players, there are more opportunities for smart brands to make increasingly advantageous deals.

With this in mind, in recent times there has been a veritable flood of examples where companies have re-examined their distribution policy. One of the most striking developments was the news in June 2017 that Nike had unilaterally decided to end its 20-year collaboration with the Bristol shoe chain for the sale of its sneakers. The reason: the discount image of Bristol no longer matched the brand image that Nike wants to achieve.[149]

But the real bombshell was dropped in October of the same year, when Nike unveiled its new distribution policy during its Investors' Day. Central to this policy is a more personal relationship with the consumer through the Nike Plus membership program. This is linked in turn to Nike Direct, which encompasses direct sales from the seven thousand Nike stores (both those operated by Nike itself and its franchising outlets). In addition, Nike also has indirect sales from some 30,000 retailers with more than 110,000 different points of sale. However, Nike now announced that it intended to select just forty retailers as its strategic partners for the future; in other words, just 0.13% of its wholesale customer base! These partners were chosen because they were deemed to create a Nike branded experience in the manner that the company wishes and are willing/able to participate in the digital strategy that Nike henceforth intends to pursue: 'With our strategic partners, we will move resources away from undifferentiated retail and towards environments where we can better control with distinct consumer experiences.'[150] In due course, two-thirds of the Nike range will be reserved exclusively for these partners.

This does not mean, of course, that Nike plans to ditch its other 29,960 wholesale customers, as some pundits have temptingly suggested. At the same time, the company is also negotiating to sell its products in the Amazon marketplace. They have already been doing it on the Zalando platform for quite a while.

One of the characteristics of the Zalando marketplace is that it guarantees that there is just a single seller for each product. This makes Zalando an attractive proposition for brand manufacturers, since it means that the manufacturers have control over the crucial price setting. In practice, this also means that Zalando no longer offers the product itself. What's more, the manufacturer's multi-brand distributors are also excluded from the platform. This further strengthens the brand's control over its own distribution and reinforces the process of verticalization.

In this sense, Zalando is perhaps the exception rather than the rule. In general, there is much uncertainty about whether the marketplaces will be willing to offer exclusivity to brand manufacturers (see the box about the situation at Amazon). The current feeling is that some marketplaces may be open to this idea for their largest partners. Others are clearly less enthusiastic. In my opinion, the importance of such arrangements is likely to increase in the years ahead.

SELECTIVE AND EXCLUSIVE DISTRIBUTION ON MARKETPLACES: THE AMAZON CASE

Many brand manufacturers would like to have full control over the sale of their brand products via marketplaces, but most of the marketplace owners are not really open to this idea, at least not officially. However, there are signals that they can sometimes be persuaded to think differently.

This double standard can be most clearly seen at Amazon. In their official communication, they offer brand manufacturers the possibility to check that their brand rights are being properly respected. Whoever registers as the holder of brand rights in the Amazon Brand Registry,[151] can see which companies are selling their brands on Amazon and how those brands are presented to the public. You can then further check that no counterfeit products are being sold and also that your brand logo and images are displayed correctly. In other words, in cases of selective distribution you can see if there are sellers active on Amazon who shouldn't be selling your products.

It is worth noting, however, that in such matters Amazon washes its hands of all responsibility: it is up to the brand holder to monitor that his brand is not being misused. If abuses are discovered, at best Amazon will – at the request of the brand – intervene reactively; at worst, the brand will be expected to take its own measures against the offenders. In short, the system is better than nothing, but it is still a cumbersome and potentially slow procedure. In theory, that is!

If, however, you look at what happens in practice, it soon becomes clear that Amazon can react proactively – if it wants to. In the fora where the sellers of products on Amazon communicate, you can see numerous posts which show that it is not possible to sell this or that product via the marketplace:

'Trying to sell a Microsoft headset, but can't add because I need approval?'[152]

The answers from other sellers are crystal clear:

'Microsoft has worked with Amazon to restrict many of their products. There are hundreds of brands that are now restricted – regardless of condition you wish to sell in. For example, Bose, Logitech, Apple, Beats, etc.'[153]

A further brief check reveals the following fascinating insight: the Bose Bluetooth Color Soundlink II is sold on Amazon.de, Amazon.co.uk and Amazon.fr exclusively by Amazon itself! No other third party is allowed to sell this product. In other words, Amazon is acting as a Bose-authorized dealer.

On Amazon.com it is the same story: if I want to order the same loudspeaker for delivery to an address in America, Amazon is again the only available vendor. For delivery to an address in Belgium, this time the purchase is not made via Amazon but through the sole dealer available on the marketplace. And if I want to order my speaker from the Dutch bol.com platform, it soon becomes evident that it is now bol.com who is acting as the exclusive distributor! In other words, Bose has clearly made a number of selective distribution deals, both with Amazon and with other dealers, to the effect that its products cannot be sold randomly via marketplaces.

I am happy to leave the last word on this matter to one of the sellers on the Amazon Services Seller Forum:

'In addition to Amazon having a restriction, many other brands (those that are not large enough to get Amazon to put a restriction) have now started self-policing their products and reporting IP/Trademark restrictions on unauthorized sellers.

For sellers that are not sourcing from distributors and/or without reseller agreements, Amazon is becoming more and more hostile. Unless you can supply a reseller letter and/or provide distributor invoicing to prove your source, you will simply have to sell it elsewhere.'[154]

VERTICAL COLLABORATION: THE MULTI-BRAND RETAILER 2.0

As brands exert more and more control over their price-setting and distribution, more and more opportunities arise for smart multi-brand retailers. In particular, the future will see more and closer collaboration between the brand and the dealer.

If the shop becomes a showroom for the brand, it is only natural that the brand will want a degree of control over the brand product experience in the store. But it is equally natural that the shop will expect to benefit financially from this arrangement. Exclusive products and additional compensations potentially offer a mutually acceptable solution.

In the Nike example mentioned above, the strategic partners will continue to sell other brands than Nike, but they will deepen their special relationship with the sportswear giant to a much greater extent. An example? One of the partners is Nordstrom, an American department store, which plans to combine sneakers and fashion in a collaboration that will focus on the Nike lifestyle collection. At Footlocker, another strategic partner, a special Nike zone will be created in each of its stores, complete with Nike apps, an exclusive assortment and personnel trained by Nike.

In similar vein, we have already seen how John Lewis has created an Apple Smart Home shop-in-shop. In the field of consumer electronics, the displays of both Samsung and Apple are well-known examples.

This inevitably means additional costs for the manufacturer, which again increases the need for greater selectivity. In this context, Adidas speaks of fewer but better stores.[155]

THE FUTURE OF FRANCHISING?

What is the role of franchising in the distribution model of the future? In the first instance, it is (and in some circumstances will likely remain) a useful instrument for brands to create brand stores with a high degree of control, but without the need to invest in infrastructure and to carry the entrepreneurial risk.

At the same time, there are several factors putting the franchise option under increasing pressure. At prime locations, the franchisors increasingly prefer to open their own stores, confining the use of franchisees to secondary locations. The current trend for fun shopping to migrate towards the larger cities and the resulting high vacancy rates in less popular shopping areas also has a bigger impact on the turnover of franchise stores than on self-managed brand outlets. The shift to online purchasing is another complication, since franchisees generally regard webshops as competitors. A combination of these factors has already convinced many franchisees to throw in the towel.

And even if the franchisee survives, the relationship with the franchisor is likely to become more difficult. In an omnichannel approach, the store must be an ambassador for the webshop. But why would the franchisee want to promote an online shop it regards as a rival? For packages ordered online and collected from the store the franchisee usually only receives a fixed fee, which is seldom equivalent to the full trade margin.

Most existing franchise agreements date from before the e-commerce era and are difficult to re-negotiate within the framework of the new business context. New contracts present fewer problems in this respect, because the mutual rights and obligations are made clear right from the start.

Where a stable revenue model is possible, franchising still has a future. This is the case, for example, where proximity is more important than the convenience of online purchasing, which is certainly true for neighborhood supermarkets and fast-food restaurants. The same also applies for functional purchases where it is difficult for the customer to choose online, such as when buying a new kitchen or bathroom.

Opinions differ as to whether franchising is best classified as direct sales (like Nike) or indirect sales (like Esprit). The most important question in this respect is what level of control you (want to) have over the channel. Hard franchising provides more control than soft franchising. Control over price-setting and brand experience is also more important than control over the assortment: as a franchisor, your main concern is that your franchisee respects your recommended prices and product presentation. Allowing the franchisee as an independent entrepreneur a degree of freedom (within limits) to decide which products from your collection are best for his target market is a matter of subsidiary importance.

THE SURVIVAL OF THE TRADITIONAL MULTI-BRAND RETAILER

Finally, we need to remember that in many sectors there is a limit to the amount of verticalization that can be achieved. The supermarket channel, the builders' merchants and do-it-yourself market, consumer electronics and the shoe industry are all examples that will continue to be dominated by multi-brand retailers in the years to come, notwithstanding the possible increase of their own private brands in share of turnover. Even without vertical collaboration, multi-brand stores will also be able to benefit from the greater control that the brand manufacturers will have over their distribution, so that price competition will play less and less of a role.

This trend is already strongly in evidence in the higher price segment. A good example is De Bijenkorf, which is part of the Selfridges Group. Five years ago, this Dutch department store correctly assessed that the mass market in the middle segment would soon come under intense pressure, amongst other things as a result of online price transparency. It decided to take the bold step of repositioning itself higher in the market. One of the results was, of course, that the target market became smaller and that some of its stores in smaller cities like Arnhem and Breda priced themselves out of the market. The subsequent restructuring saw the closure of five of De Bijenkorf's twelve stores. On the plus side, this meant that the company could concentrate the investments needed for its digital transformation on fewer outlets. Its new omnichannel strategy was so successful that its turnover (including online sales) remained the same as in the past, notwithstanding the disappearance of almost half its physical stores.

CHECKLIST
THE NEW REALITY

1. **The multi-brand retailer:**

   a. To what extent is your sector suitable for verticalization? Do you have sufficient scale to design your own products successfully?

   b. Do your current suppliers have sufficient control over their distribution and price-setting to ensure that margins will remain healthy?

   c. Are you sufficiently important for your existing suppliers to be chosen by them for vertical collaboration?

   d. How vulnerable are you to online competition? To what extent are you also able work viably in omnichannel and e-commerce?

   e. In view of the answers to the above questions, is your company still viable today, in the medium and in the long term?

2. **The vertically integrated retailer:**

   a. Do you have sufficient scale to be successful in omnichannel?

   b. Do you invest sufficiently in online turnover? Do you sufficiently monitor the performance of your store network (also see the previous chapter)?

   c. Do you invest sufficiently in the strengths of your brand?

   d. Are you present on the right marketplaces?

3. **The brand manufacturer:**

   a. Is your brand sufficiently strong, both in terms of possible verticalization and to maintain your position in multi-brand distribution?
   b. To what extent is your sector suitable for verticalization? Is your assortment sufficiently large to make possible the development of your own stores? Is franchising an interesting option?
   c. To what extent do you have sufficient control over your indirect sales channels? How can you increase that control? How do you see your accounts evolving?
   d. Can you move towards vertical collaboration with a number of strategic partners? How many? What would this involve?

CHAPTER 11
COMPETITIVE STRENGTH

'We never know the worth of water

till the well is dry.'

Thomas Fuller (British writer)

The further we look into the future, the more we focus one-sidedly on the customer. But if we look instead at a shorter time horizon, the more relevant our current competitive strength becomes. It is this strength that determines how successful we are today and therefore the level of resources we can accumulate to tackle the challenges of tomorrow.

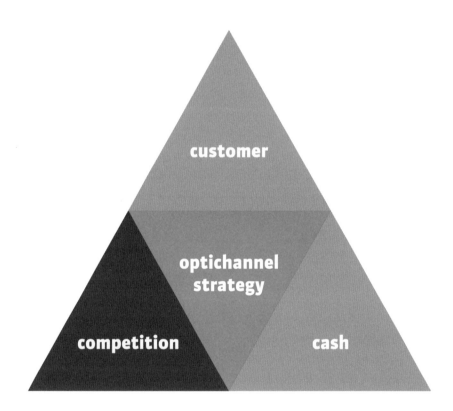

COMPETITIVE ADVANTAGES AND CONDITIONS TO COMPETE

In chapter 4 on optichannel retail, we already saw that we need to make a distinction between advantages and conditions, when assessing our competitive strength. A condition to compete can be regarded as an Olympic minimum. If you drop below this minimum level, you will no longer be competitive. But achieving the minimum does not guarantee that you will win a medal.

To be truly successful, you need to have a competitive advantage. These are the dimensions that can really make the difference between you and your rivals. But be careful. Your competitors will not be standing still. On the contrary, they will constantly be trying to overtake you, so that your advantage will lose its force. Hence the saying: the competitive advantages of today are the conditions to compete of tomorrow.

Even in the new digital era, both concepts are as relevant as they have ever been. The only difference is the speed at which they now change. Advantages can be downgraded to conditions much more quickly than in the past. What's more, indirect competitors now also play a role in raising customer expectations: if Zalando and Amazon deliver for free, customers automatically expect Ikea to do the same. This means that the bar is set much higher for everyone in the field. As a result, the changes we are experiencing today feel more like a revolution than an evolution.

It is precisely this speed of change that makes the distinction between conditions and advantages of such vital relevance. As a company, you need to make choices. It is impossible for you to do everything. By setting priorities, you can commit your limited resources to the things you feel will bring the biggest rewards. Timing is crucial. Some investments that are expensive today may become a lot cheaper tomorrow.

As part of the current digital hysteria, it is often suggested that this is a field where the pure players are racing ahead, while the brick-and-mortar retailers are hopelessly lagging behind. Of course, this is nonsense. It was not until 2017 that Coolblue, the Dutch online market leader in consumer electronics, launched an app, and even then only for iPhone users.[156] An Android version only followed in October 2018 – some nineteen years after the company had first been founded! In contrast, the online supermarket Picnic has done precisely the opposite: their 'mobile first' strategy goes so far that it is only possible to place orders via their app. They don't even have a webshop! Making clear choices like this is certainly something to be applauded. Except: if traditional retailers make similar choices, they are inevitably mocked by the digital gurus: 'They haven't got an app!' or 'They haven't got a transactional site!'

Competition is something that takes place in all dimensions of the business model. We have already discussed target groups in detail in chapter 5. In this chapter, we will confine ourselves to the value proposition. In the next chapter, we will look at the value chain, the profit model and the financial perspective.

THE VALUE PROPOSITION

The value proposition answers the question about why customers choose to buy from you rather than one of your competitors. The following model was central in my previous book about omnichannel, where you can read much more about this subject.

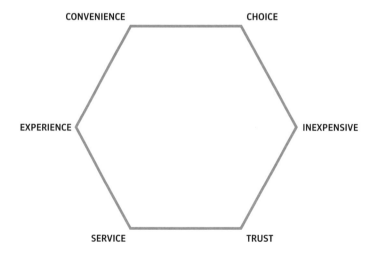

In essence, the value proposition consists of six dimensions:

1. Convenience: how easy is it to buy things from you?
2. Experience: how good is your store, brand and product experience?
3. Service: how good is your advice and the contact between customers and your staff?
4. Trust: to what extent can people buy things from you with confidence?
5. Inexpensive: how price competitive are you?
6. Choice: can you offer customers the right products?

All these questions are formulated in such a way that you can give them a score. You can give yourself a score in comparison with your competitors as a whole. Or you can give an absolute score to yourself and your most important rivals, where you can then compare one against the other. Whichever method you choose and whatever conclusions you reach, one thing is certain: you must ensure that your value proposition seamlessly matches the needs of your target market. In other words, you need to develop a competitive advantage in the dimensions that enjoy the highest priority for that market.

So let's now take a look at each of these questions in turn and identify which concrete developments we can see in each dimension of today's markets.

CONVENIENCE

In chapter 9, when we discussed the role of the store, we saw that convenience is one of the core needs for all aspects of functional purchases. For fun shopping, it is only a need at certain steps in the customer journey. The advent and rise of the digital virtual assistant and the trend towards greater personalization mean that customers in future will become more loyal to their interface than to individual stores and companies. And as the further shift of functional purchases towards e-commerce continues, so the role of these interfaces is destined to become bigger and bigger.

It would be a mistake to underestimate the impact that this development can also have on offline sales. Whoever asks Siri during a city trip for a recommendation about the nearest place to buy a micro-USB charger cable is allowing his offline behavior to be influenced by his voice assistant.

Another good example of the same thing is the digital shopping list. Whoever measures the importance of such lists simply in terms of the market share of e-groceries is making two basic errors in reasoning. Firstly, penetration is much more important than market share: no fewer than 40% of Britons regularly shop for groceries online, but the share of total sales is just 8%. Secondly, it needs to be remembered that a digital list can also be used to go shopping at a physical supermarket. And whoever compiles their list using the Tesco or Walmart app and makes specific choices for specific promotions and products (which store brand products, what size of packaging, etc.) will also be more inclined to go to a Tesco or Walmart store than to a Sainsbury's or Kroger's.

In the meantime, it has also become clear that Amazon intends to pin all its hopes on Alexa, so that the so-called 'Dash' buttons will disappear into the background. The Dash buttons were designed for the purpose of allowing consumers to order a product with just the single press of a button. If, for example, you have a Dash button for Tide washing power alongside your washing machine, you can just hit the button when you see your powder is running low and it will be automatically reordered. A number of brand manufacturers invested in Dash buttons for their products, largely to generate goodwill with Amazon, who was the main beneficiary of the public attention generated by the buttons. Fortunately, consumers soon decided that it is not very convenient to order and have your grocery needs delivered product by product. As well as being harmful to the environment, it is unnecessarily time-consuming. Alexa offers far more convenience and ease than ten individual brand-specific Dash buttons: she allows you to order all brands and products, simply by adding things to your list for future collective delivery at a time of your choosing, rather than immediate and separate delivery.

DELIVERY

This brings us neatly on to a second key aspect of convenience: delivery. If ease of ordering is important, ease of delivery is often more so. Free delivery for orders above a minimum amount is a condition to compete in most sectors, although there are some exceptions – for example, groceries, bicycles and furniture – where paying for delivery is still the norm.

In general, however, it is a smart idea not to charge your customers for delivery. If you do, you risk driving them into the arms of your competitors for their online purchases. People who order toys or books for a first time with Amazon and make an account usually end up by gradually transferring all their online toy and book purchases to the e-commerce giant. A consumer may perhaps remain loyal to his favorite physical toy shop or bookstore, but the retailer will almost certainly lose out in the fast-growing online channel.

The biggest danger is that this loss of turnover is only modest – in the beginning. At first, you may just notice that you have started losing a few customers. But then you notice that orders per customer are falling across the board. You notice equally that many of your remaining customers increasingly order from you online, but with the option of free collection from the store. Even so, you still fail to recognize the danger signs. But then suddenly there comes a tipping point, when your loss of turnover begins to accelerate. You try to win back your lost online custom but things have already gone too far...

In terms of speed, 'ordered today, delivered tomorrow' is now the new normal. Marketplaces have discovered that there is a huge difference in conversion rates for sellers and products with long delivery times. So important has delivery become that often 'same day delivery' is now the only way to gain a competitive advantage. In fact, in major cities delivery within two hours is already commonplace. In the Netherlands, the Albert Heijn supermarket chain calls this its 'lightning delivery service' and is conducting trials with products delivered from its AH to go stores by bike courier.[157] In China, customers at Alibaba's Hema supermarkets can even expect to have their groceries delivered to their homes within 30 minutes, providing they live within a radius of three kilometers of the store (where, thanks to China's high density of population, as many as 300,000 people can live!).[158] In Paris,

Monoprix offers a comparable service, but for shoppers who have already done their shopping in the store. All you need to do is leave your shopping bag at a special reception desk and Monoprix arranges to have it delivered to your door two hours later, so that you don't need to carry everything on the bus or metro. The company has also recently announced a new collaboration with Amazon to introduce Amazon Prime Now in the French capital.[159]

For the moment, fast service of this kind is usually on payment, but more and more companies are turning to the idea of a subscription system, in imitation of Amazon Prime. At bol.com in the Netherlands, for example, you only need to pay € 9.99 to become a 'Select' customer for a full year, which entitles you to free same day delivery, irrespective of the amount of your order, with options for evening or Sunday delivery, or even delivery by appointment. Order just four times a year and you have already recouped your annual fee! Since October 2018, bol.com has also been trying to develop synergies with its mother company, Albert Heijn: 'Select' customers are automatically registered in AH's own subscription formula, and vice versa. Not wishing to be left behind, Zalando has launched Zalando Plus in Germany. For just €19 per annum, returns can be collected from your home and you also have preferential treatment for other extra services, such as early access to special offers and the possibility to chat with expert stylists.[160] These programs are all designed to generate a high level of customer loyalty: if you pay the fee, you want to win back your investment by ordering frequently. On top of that, you receive a faster and more flexible service. Of course, the companies benefit as well: subscribers to Amazon Prime spend roughly two and a half times as much as non-subscribers. And if you realize that Amazon has more than one hundred million Prime customers worldwide...[161]

In today's market, this approach undoubtedly yields a competitive advantage. Of course, the problem starts when everyone in the market tries to do the same thing: customers won't be prepared to pay all their suppliers €10 for these special 'privileges'. This means that first-movers are ahead of the game. But you can only cement this advantage if your customers place orders with sufficient frequency. In this respect, generalists score better than specialists, simply because their assortment is so much wider. But whatever your positioning, you can improve the situation by focusing on the real fans of your store. It can also help if you link additional 'soft' benefits to your program, which are often more applicable in the user phase than in the purchase phase.

In addition to the competitive advantage of fast delivery, the subscription formulas also seek to make an advantage of free delivery for all orders, regardless of order value. In the fashion sector, it is Zalando that has set the market norm. This is not a problem for brands that are positioned in the higher price segment: almost every order is above the value that entitles free delivery. It is only the customers who order accessories or basics that may be required to pay. But for cheaper brands, like H&M, things are not quite so easy.

In the Netherlands, the online supermarket Picnic has shown that speed is not the only advantageous criterion for the delivery of the weekly groceries. Picnic's customers can only choose from a limited number of fixed time windows, since the company's deliveries are made on the basis of pre-determined delivery rounds. You can only receive a delivery when a delivery van is somewhere in your area. This may seem less customer-friendly, but it is certainly more cost efficient. This also makes it possible for Picnic – in contrast to its competitors – to offer free home delivery. At the same time, it makes the system palatable for customers by keeping the time windows as narrow as possible: just a single hour. And on the day of the delivery, it even sends a text message to say during which twenty-minute period within that hour the delivery will take place. The Picnic app allows you to track the progress of the delivery van in real time.

The success of Picnic shows that its target group prefers free and predictable delivery to speed! This translates into a weekly ordering frequency that is much higher than the frequency of its competitors.[162]

In this context, it is also worth noting that more and more consumers are starting to ask questions about the societal and environmental impact of fast deliveries and narrow time windows. Research has shown that it is possible to motivate customers to choose an environmentally-friendly delivery option. The British online supermarket Ocado marks its time windows as 'green' on the basis of the orders that have already been placed, so that the delivery can be carried out more efficiently. In the Netherlands, Albert Heijn adds a green leaf to delivery slots of six rather than two hours.[163]

Similarly, the increase in night work is also being viewed with a more critical eye. It was for this reason that the Dutch barrister Margreet de Boer proposed the introduction of a 'no hurry' button as part of the ordering options. This means that your delivery would be prepared the next day, instead of during the middle of the night.[164]

Of course, considerable attention is also being devoted in the offline world to increasing consumer convenience. We have already looked at the till-free store, but the rapid growth of 'click and collect' means that queues can still develop. To overcome this, various retailers, including Walmart and Zara, are carrying out tests with automated dispensers, where customers can pick up their own orders without the need for help or waiting.[165]

EXPERIENCE

You can find the Palazzo della Mercanzia near to the Palazzo Vecchio in the Italian city of Florence. Since 2018, this 14th-century jewel now plays host to the Gucci Garden. On the ground floor, there is a new restaurant – the Osteria Gucci – run by the Michelin-star chef Massimo Bottura. Elsewhere in the building you can visit a Gucci 'souvenir shop', where you can buy a special selection of products from the high-end fashion icon, which has its roots in Florence. The shop's assortment also includes books, ceramic items and other gadgets that are cheaper than the normal Gucci products.

The palace's top floor houses the Gucci Museum, for entrance to which you need to buy a ticket costing eight euros. Gucci donates half of this fee to a fund for the restoration of other historic buildings in Florence.[166][167]

The Gucci Garden is the latest in a long line of projects by manufacturers to create an experience around their brand. From the Heineken Experience in Amsterdam to the World of Coca-Cola in Atlanta and the Harley-Davidson Museum in Milwaukee, strong brands are able to convince hordes of tourists to pay good money to visit their modern-day temples. Lego has even gone so far as to build its own theme parks.

The big limitation to this concept is, of course, that you can't build a museum everywhere. What's more, it is usually only people who were already fans of the brand that can be persuaded to part with their hard-earned cash. With this in mind, Jack Daniel's – which also has its own museum – has developed a travelling pop-up around its whiskey that can be visited free of charge.[168]

It is taking things a bit too far to claim that having your own museum or pop-up is a competitive advantage. But as we have already seen in the previous chapter, creating an experience around your brand is of supreme importance. In the domain of fun shopping, the bar is being set higher and higher all the time. Fewer but better shops mean that in key shopping centers the public's expectations are continually on the increase. As a result, competition is intense. If you offer a poorer experience than the shop next door, you are going to be in trouble! As far as functional shopping is concerned, we saw in chapter 9 that customers are now keen to try out products before they buy them. Stores that only display products in packaging are not only going to lose out – they are going to lose the reason for their very existence.

Leaving aside museums and pop-ups, great product experience can give you a competitive advantage. The American b8ta is a physical store for technological gadgets.[169] Under the title 'Retail designed for discovery', they offer makers a showroom for their products. The company started in 2015 with just a single showroom, where they were only able to display about 80 articles. This was a showroom in the purest sense: nothing was for immediate sale, everything had to be ordered. Today, b8ta has nine showrooms and a dozen or so shop-in-shops under the name Smartspot in the stores of Lowe's, one of America's leading builders' merchants. The products on display are now kept in stock, so that you can buy them and take them home without delay.

The revenue model of b8ta is 'retail as a service'. They do not take a commission on turnover; instead, the makers pay a fee for their presence in the showroom and for the information they receive about the way in which consumers respond to their products.[170]

SERVICE

In the United States, Amazon has repeatedly been crowned as the store with the best service. The strength of their customer relations is based on the premise that the customer is always right. If you let them know that you have been sent the wrong product, you are sometimes told: 'Keep it; we will send you the right one today!' Likewise if your package is not delivered: there is no discussion about whose fault it is; a second package is dispatched immediately. The customer is king!

In this way, outstanding customer service becomes the norm: avoid making mistakes and correct them quickly if they happen.

Even so, this vision on customer service is relatively narrow. There are lots of other things you can also do with service. For example, you can use it to add value. The Belgian shoe retailer Torfs creates a competitive advantage through the remarkable friendliness and helpfulness of its staff. What's more, Torfs has succeeded in extending this same level of service to its webshop. This is a direct consequence of their personnel policy – which perhaps explains why the company wins Belgium's 'Great Place to Work' competition year after year. This is also a field where the online supermarket Picnic scores better than its rivals. By working with fixed delivery rounds, customers are often served by the same driver, whose name is listed in the company's app. In this way, it is possible for customer and driver to develop a more personal kind of relationship, which reflects positively on the Picnic brand image.

Other companies prefer to focus on the superior provision of advice. There can be different ways to do this successfully, even within the same sector. Coolblue, for example, targets customers who like to find things out for themselves. Online, you can find all the information you need to make your choice of product: YouTube films, a help menu, clear product descriptions and plenty of reviews and ratings. And if you are still having problems to make up your mind, you are encouraged to chat with or phone one of their product specialists. On the basis of these conversations, the content of the website is amended, so that in future new customers won't have to make the same calls. Of course, if all else fails, you still have the option of visiting a Coolblue store... In essence, everything that Coolblue does is geared to helping people choose the right product by themselves, which is also effectively what happens for the majority of the sales they make. Customers love this feeling of being in control and from Coolblue's perspective it is highly efficient. What's more, the extensive information provided by Coolblue also yields them a further advantage: the company scores well in organic search results. For example, if you type in (in Dutch, of course!) 'how to drill through a tile', you will be offered the Coolblue webshop as your third result.[171]

But Coolblue hasn't stopped there. In order to control all phases of the customer journey, the company has now taken over the delivery of its products. They started by providing their own two-man teams for the delivery of washing machines, not just to the door (like many delivery services) but to the actual point of installation – even if that is on the fifth floor. They have since rolled out a delivery network of Coolblue bike couriers for the delivery of smaller packages in major cities.

Expert is a buying group that operates in the same market and also focuses on service and advice. The big difference is that Expert gives independent entrepreneurs and shops the central place in its business model. You don't buy from Expert but from a specific store, even in their webshop. Of course, smaller purchases in the webshop are delivered from a central distribution center, but if you buy a washing machine online, you will be phoned by a local store. He will check that you have made the right choice and, once this is confirmed, will make arrangements for the delivery and installation. The system also works in the opposite direction: if you can't immediately make up your mind online, Expert will put you in touch with a local store to help you. Last but not least, Expert also has an outstanding repair service. In a difficult sector, where many companies have gone under in recent years, Expert Netherlands has managed to achieve growth that is faster than the growth of the market as a whole. While Coolblue scores with self-service advice, Expert concentrates on personal contact. Both companies sell the same products with success – but to different target groups.

TRUST

In today's markets, trust has become a generic condition to compete. The average customer now trusts webshops every bit as much (or as little) as he trusts a physical store. As a result, this is a dimension where it is no longer possible to make a difference.

INEXPENSIVE

We have already discussed (repeatedly) the effects of online price transparency and the race to the bottom. The resulting price sensitivity of modern consumers means that being perceived as inexpensive is often an absolute condition to compete. People are not prepared to pay (much) more simply because your staff are super-friendly, your advice is first-class and they can try out products in your store (which looks more and more like an amusement park every time they come).

Similarly, convenience and the customer interface can only have a binding effect if your company is seen by the customer as being price-competitive. As an Amazon Prime customer, I might not compare prices elsewhere for a book that only costs € 15.99, but I am certainly going to do it for a washing machine that costs € 500 or more. Nobody likes to pay too much.

There is no endless list of solutions to this problem. The first and most effective – but unfortunately also the most expensive – is to align your prices with those of your competitors. For example, the use of electronic shelf labels allows MediaMarkt to adjust its instore prices daily.

The second solution presents more of a challenge, but in the long term can lead to better financial results: make it impossible for customers to compare prices by only selling products that aren't sold anywhere else. In the previous chapter on verticalization, we saw how vertical collaboration between brand manufacturers and their dealers offers a way forward. Sixty percent of the products sold by Nike's strategic partners are exclusive.

Finally, it is also possible to guide customers towards products with the highest margin, even within the context of price matching. For example, you can give priority to brands where you know the brand manufacturer has the distribution chain under his complete control. Coolblue uses 'Coolblue's choice' as a way to negotiate extra-beneficial conditions with brand manufacturers, because both sides know that the products in question will be sold in large volumes. Sometimes the products are even specifically made for Coolblue with special article codes.

As long as a market has not achieved balance, differentiation strategies will always have their limitations. But even during the transition phase it is still possible to be successful as a multi-brand player. You want proof? Take a look at the example of Best Buy in the box below.

THE BEST BUY CASE

When I wrote my previous book, Best Buy – the MediaMarkt of the United States – had just begun its transformation. The previous years had been tough for the company. The rapid growth of e-commerce, with Amazon in the role of price-breaker, had pushed Best Buy to the brink of ruin. In an attempt to make showrooming impossible, at one point they even tried to block the signal of customers' smartphones in their stores, in order to prevent online comparison surfing. It succeeded, but only at the cost of driving down instore traffic and hence turnover.

Something else was needed and, since then, the company has dramatically changed course. The necessary condition to compete was the introduction of a price-matching guarantee: if the customer could find a product cheaper elsewhere, he could henceforth buy it for the same price at Best Buy. This soon put an end to showrooming: price was no longer a reason for buying from one of the company's rivals! In the Best Buy stores, product experience and advice were made a higher priority than had previously been the case. Customers were given the opportunity to test the latest products and technologies, whilst also getting useful and helpful information from Best Buy experts, where necessary.

Central to this transformation was the company's investment in its staff. By first listening to their concerns – which included poorly functioning systems and the scrapping of staff discounts – and then acting upon them, the commitment of the workforce was enhanced. In addition, the budget for training was significantly increased, with a focus on the newest technologies for which customers most frequently need advice.

Brands that were willing to pay – like Samsung, Microsoft and Apple – were allowed to set up shop-in-shops, either with their own personnel or with Best Buy personnel specially trained by the brand. Best Buy also recognized Amazon as a 'frenemy' – both friend and enemy. As a result, Amazon likewise has a shop-in-shop for its Echo loudspeakers. In reality, the brand manufacturers have little option but to agree to this kind of strategic collaboration: in the consumer electronics market in the United States, Best Buy is the only remaining player with a national coverage.

The improved levels of service were extended to beyond the stores. Before making their purchases, potential customers can now receive a free home visit from Best Buy advisers, who give tips about the most appropriate technologies for their particular house, apartment, etc. The Geek Squad later takes care of installation and any other after-sales queries and problems that may arise.

Of course, a significant part of Best Buy's turnover now comes from its webshop. Based on a strong omnichannel vision, the company uses its network of thousands of stores to bring its products closer to its online customers. For home delivery, its logistics system checks how the products can be got to the right address in the fastest possible manner: from a distribution center or from a store. The stores are now involved in some 40% of the online sales, either as a dispatch or collection point.

Last but not least, the company has dramatically cut its costs. Loss-making stores have been closed and fewer people are now employed by Best Buy than in the past. But this was achieved without the need for large-scale (and high-publicity) forced redundancies, since the company wished to avoid creating the impression that it was in a negative spiral. And with success. Improved financial results soon followed, so that Best Buy is now once again an attractive proposition for investors on the stock market.[172]

Finally, it is also worth noting that money can be earned simply by positioning yourself as a low price player in a particular market. The American company Wish was originally set up as an app on which you could keep your wish list and share it with your friends. It soon became clear to the company's founders that many of the products appearing regularly in people's lists were relatively cheap. The next step in their development was therefore to invite vendors to offer those articles for sale via the Wish website. Today, Wish is a marketplace where retailers and brand manufacturers can sell their end-of-series products and overstock with significant reductions, even for well-known brands. With more than 300 million users worldwide, the Wish app is now the most downloaded shopping app in 42 countries, including the US – which means that it is even more frequently downloaded than the Amazon app.

Another good example is AliExpress, a subsidiary of Alibaba. Chinese producers use this marketplace to sell their goods directly to European consumers. In the long-run, this represents a threat to store retailers who want to sell the same products as their store brand or fancy brand. Why would you buy a battery charger or no-name cover for your smartphone from Action or Aldi, if you can buy a comparable (or even identical) product direct from the manufacturer at a much cheaper price?

CHOICE

Thanks to their marketplaces, the dominant e-commerce companies like Amazon and Zalando have changed the competitive boundaries for many sectors. Their user-friendly customer interfaces and subscription formulas have allowed them to develop an important competitive advantage. It is utopian to think that you can simply copy this business model, because a marketplace can only operate successfully if you have a huge number of customers, who all have the perception that you are the place where they can find everything – literally everything. If Carrefour or Blokker set up a marketplace, it might make a profit, because it will increase their opportunities for sales. But it will never become a competitive advantage, because their offer will always remain smaller than the offer of the dominant players, which means that there is no real incentive for the majority of customers to switch to Carrefour or Blokker.

A good example of a marketplace that typifies the second wave of e-commerce is Houzz. Their website is an online community based around home design, decorating and remodeling ideas. A first part of the website shows photographs of completed projects for different kinds of rooms, which can be selected using the relevant filters. This is intended to give people inspiration for ways to renovate their homes. The second part of the website is a pure marketplace, where you can find all the renovation products you will need. And the third part is a directory of local professionals who can help you to turn your renovation dreams into reality. No other website offers more inspiration or a bigger assortment in the domestic decoration segment than Houzz.[173]

But having the largest choice is not the only way to differentiate yourself from your competitors. Coolblue has a sufficiently large range to be credible as a specialist (condition to compete) and has consciously opted not to become a marketplace. It prefers instead to make a difference (competitive advantage) with its high level of service, achieved in part through control of its own deliveries. Inviting others to sell via their webshop would loosen this control – and so they don't do it.

Specialization and discovering your own niche in the market is also another way to develop a competitive advantage. The Antwerp-based Moose in the

City sells a wide variety of products, whose only connection is that they all come from Scandinavia. It is a wonderful store to just rummage through and see what you can find – and this is the foundation of its success. In the sneakers market there are numerous specialist stores that seek to stand out from the crowd by offering a limited series of top brands that aren't available everywhere. Perhaps the most remarkable of these stores is Kith in New York. The competitive strength of Kith resides in the fact that the owner can sense exactly what people regard as 'cool'. For example, in 2017 the store organized its first fashion show in Samsung 837, the experience world of the Korean electronics giant. The show was also a huge party, with hundreds of young people queuing up to get in.

Both these examples illustrate that even as a small entrepreneur you can still create a competitive advantage – if you have the right assortment.

COMPETITIVE STRENGTH AND THE VALUE PROPOSITION

1. **Consider each of the six dimensions of the value proposition (convenience, experience, service, trust, inexpensive and choice) and ask yourself the following questions:**

   a. What are the competitive conditions for your target market and to what extent do you satisfy them?
   b. What competitive advantages currently exist in the market? How important are they for your target market?
   c. What are your competitive advantages?

2. **Look at the six dimensions again, but this time from a more dynamic perspective:**

   a. By which date do you expect which competitive advantage to be downgraded to a condition to compete? What is the situation with your current competitive advantages?
   b. What new competitive advantages will be created in the future? How important will these be for your target market?
   c. What competitive advantages will you have in three and five years' time?

3. **Depending on your answers to the above questions:**

    a. Which new initiatives are relevant for your target group?
    b. What will this cost?
    c. Based on a cost-benefit analysis, what priorities should you set, bearing in mind the ideal customer journey you want to develop in the long term?

UNTIL DEBT
TEAR US APART

CHAPTER 12

HOW TO CREATE VALUE?

'Unfortunately, people define risk

as something you avoid,

rather than something you take.'

Ann Mulcahy (former chairperson and CEO of Xerox)

Now that we have examined both the customer and the competition, the time has come to put our strategic choices into practice – and make money. This means that we now need to look at the value chain and the financial perspective.

THE 50% RULE

During my keynote speeches, I have recently started to ask my audiences what they would do differently in their companies if 50% of their turnover came from online purchases. It is a question that most of them have never stopped to think about. For the majority – and certainly for those who currently earn less than 10% online – it still sounds like something a long way off.

In particular, this is something that retailers don't like to think about, because it would present them with a huge and potentially impossible challenge. From their perspective, the key issue is to what extent the 50% of online turnover would be achieved by a decline in store sales or by the rapid growth of their webshop. In the worst case scenario, the store network would need to be drastically reduced, so that the resultant social liabilities alone might be sufficient to bring the company to its knees. It is only in the second instance that retailers move on to consider the possible impact on the logistic chain.

Manufacturers are generally more sanguine in this respect. Unless they have a large store network of their own, so that they need to reason like a retailer, they are more immediately concerned with the implications for distribution. Not that these are huge. Selling more to Amazon or Zalando and less to MediaMarkt or Footlocker: it makes very little difference to them. Companies like Toys"R"Us and Free Record Shop disappear from the market? Sad, but not really their problem. True, the transition may perhaps result in more channel conflicts. And the balance between direct and indirect sales can also be drastically altered. But apart from that...?

Next, I confront my audiences with the case of John Lewis. By the middle of 2018, this British department store, was already generating 39% of its turnover online.[174] If you extrapolate on the basis of the current rate of growth, this figure will reach 50% by 2020. What's more, this is not just a scenario: it is their strategic objective!

In fact, this was a theoretical exercise they conducted quite some time ago. In chapter 9, we looked at their most recent store in London, which now implements the ideal customer journey they have been developing over the past number of years. Because they were quick to anticipate the impact of digital innovation, they have been able to adjust without the need to close down stores. To put it cynically: they have left that to their competitors. In 2017, their store income even rose by 0.4%. But the real growth has come via the webshop.

John Lewis also focuses heavily on its own ptivate brands, and with success: their ladies fashion brand is growing three times faster than the category. The aim is ultimately that their assortment will consist of 50% store brands or exclusive third party branded products. Of course, this all goes hand in hand with major investment in new technology, but the most visionary aspect of the entire John Lewis approach – at least in my opinion – is the way in which they have redesigned the supply chain.

SELL ON, PICK ONE

In many sectors and categories 'colli picking' is now the norm. This means that you package a number of consumer units in an outer packing (for example, a number of t-shirts in a cardboard box), which is then sent first to a distribution center and then on to a shop, where it is opened, unpacked and the products put on the shelf. However, this doesn't work for e-commerce: unlike stores, consumers order a single t-shirt and not twelve in a large box. This means that for an online order you need to open the box of twelve and take out just one t-shirt. The result is that many companies now keep the 'order picking' for e-commerce and the stores separate from each other. Sometimes they are even physically kept at separate locations.

A second point that needs to be borne in mind is that different goods need different kinds of storage. In distribution centers some products are stacked on pallets, others are hung from racks and others are placed in cages on shelves.

For reasons of efficiency, all goods of a similar type are generally stored at the same location. For larger organizations, this often means at different centers, which, for historical reasons, are often situated in other towns or regions. When a single consumer order contains products that are stored in different places, this means he will be sent a number of different packages. This is not good for the customer (and the environment) and costs more for the company. In short: lose-lose. To overcome this, John Lewis took a visionary decision: 'Our discussion around the board table went: "We can't predict how the split between store and online will go, so we have to make it irrelevant".'[175]:

» All the John Lewis distribution centers have been brought together at a single location: one for large items (like televisions and furniture), one for hanging items (like clothes) and one for traditionally smaller items. The last two DCs are linked by a conveyor belt, so that if a customer orders products kept in both centers they can easily be amalgamated in a single package. In contrast, orders for the retail stores are packaged and transported per DC.
» The entire picking process is conducted in accordance with a philosophy that products are transported as and when they are sold. This means that for all orders – both for shops and consumers – it is a number of items that are picked, and not whole boxes. If a store wants to order a bulk supply of a particular item for a particular season, like Christmas, it now orders a specific number of that item, which are individually picked. Of course, this means more transactions and potentially a much higher cost, but John Lewis attempts to minimize this through a high degree of automation, which is viable because of the large scale of its DCs.
» The capacity of the DC's is determined in relation to moments of peak demand. The busiest day of the year is Black Friday. This is primarily a day for consumer orders. Shop orders have different peak periods, such as the start of each new fashion season. This spreading of peaks makes an important contribution to the efficiency of the system.
» Finally, this new approach is also beneficial for the stores. The fact that they can now order products in smaller quantities leads to an improvement in stock rotation!

The total investment in this system amounted to £ 150 million (roughly € 170 million). For the consumer this is hardly noticeable, but it means a huge step forward in the customer-oriented focus that John Lewis wishes to maintain.

WHICH 50% RULE?

After looking at the John Lewis case with my keynote audiences, I open up the floor for discussion. Suddenly, the idea of an online turnover of 50% seems less unrealistic! The transformation achieved by John Lewis should force everyone to look at their own approach more critically. Some companies, like Nike, are already on the right track. So, too, is FNG, the owner of (amongst others) Miss Etam, CKS and Expresso, which has a fully automated distribution center for clothing in Zoetermeer in the Netherlands. Many other companies, however, currently have such a small online turnover that they still prepare their e-commerce orders by hand. Of course, this is wholly unsustainable in the long run.

The following questions take us to the heart of the discussion:

» What percentage of online turnover do we need to achieve before we redesign the value chain?
» When are we likely to reach that point?
» In view of the above answers, when do we need to start the redesign process?

Self-evidently, this does not just mean the supply chain, but also the store network, staff profiles (also in company headquarters!), packaging procedures, etc. In short, the whole shooting match.

As brand manufacturers, we have key account managers, but do we also have them for Amazon? Do we have people in our set-up who focus exclusively on sales via the marketplaces? This is an area where many retailers are also lagging behind: they usually only have a procurement team, but no account managers of any kind.

The necessary adjustments to the value chain must be based on your value proposition and your ideal customer journey, and must also take into account your entire distribution strategy:

» As retailers, are we going to sell via marketplaces?
» As manufacturers, are we going to sell directly to consumers?

CASH IS KING

Many retailers have a number of difficult years behind them: the economy was struggling, online price transparency eroded margins, restructuring the store network cost a small fortune... At the same time, there was also a need to make heavy investments in new technology in general and in a webshop in particular. This combination forced many retailers out of business, while for many others the water is now up to their lips.

Many of you reading in this book about the huge changes that lie ahead are probably asking the same question: how on earth are we going to pay for it all?

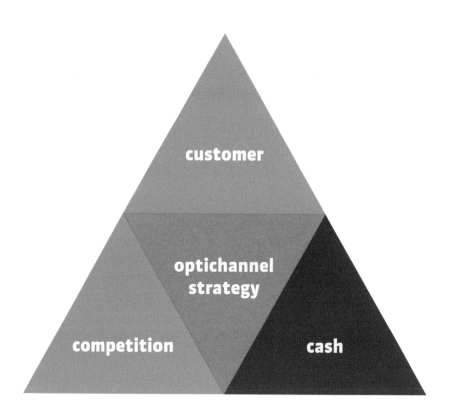

Things have been much less dramatic for the brand manufacturers. In recent years, they have experienced far fewer bankruptcies and their financial reserves have been less seriously depleted. Even so, in the years ahead they are faced with potentially an even bigger investment requirement than the retailers, since the shift towards fewer indirect and more direct sales will also make massive additional demands on their available resources. Their working capital will shoot through the roof as soon as the manufacturers need to start financing their own stocks (instead of passing this on to their retail customers) and the need to develop a store network is also hugely capital intensive.

What's more, the sheer speed of change, which seems likely to persist in the years ahead, leaves companies with very little breathing space. You need to keep moving forward and you need to do it immediately. And for this you need cash. Lots of cash. And therein lies the origin of the oft-heard claim that profit is highly overrated.

DOUBLE STANDARDS?

How is it possible that digital companies are so highly valued when they continue to make huge losses? Are double standards being applied? Or is something else going on?

The truth is that our accounting methods and rules need to be thrown onto the scrap heap. They are not suitable for reporting on the realities of the digital economy.[176] On the balance sheet of a traditional company you will primarily find details of tangible assets, such as buildings, machines, stocks of goods, etc., which the company uses to generate income. The application of depreciations allows the fixed assets to have an impact on the financial results, as totaled in the profit and loss account. In this way the final profit gives a more realistic picture of the company's performance and is a good basis for calculating its overall value.

However, this logic does not work with digital companies. To start with, they are 'asset light': they have few fixed assets. Even though they are relatively young companies, the average turnover of Zalando and ASOS is 6.9 times bigger than their fixed assets, whereas for H&M and Inditex, the mother company of Zara and Massimo Dutti, it is just 3.1 times bigger. As a result, the depreciations of the webshops only amount to 1.8% of their turnover, against 4.1% for H&M and Inditex. Consequently, the difference between the EBIT and the EBITDA is relatively small for the web players.[177]

What's more, they mainly invest in intangible fixed assets: at Zalando and ASOS some 39% of their capital expenditure is devoted to assets of this kind, in comparison with a mere 15.2% at H&M and Inditex. In real commercial terms this percentage is probably higher, but the prudence principle applied in accountancy regulations means that they are not able to capitalize all their technology expenditure. Zalando, for example, has some 2,000 people working in its technology department, but a significant number of them are working on projects that cannot be viewed in accountancy terms as investments. Consequently, their salaries are booked as operating costs, which cannot be capitalized and therefore have a heavy negative impact in the short term on the overall company results.[178]

Likewise, the depreciation principles of accountancy fail to reflect the commercial reality of the digital players. If you use a machine or building, it does indeed depreciate in value. But in the 'winner takes all' model, the opposite is true. The more customers I have, the more other companies are interested in selling in my marketplace. And the more sellers I have, the more additional new customers I can attract. In other words, a reverse effect is generated: instead of becoming less valuable with time, my portfolio of customers and vendors becomes more valuable. In this way, an increasing return to scale on intangible investments is created.

And it doesn't stop there. Accountancy rules make it difficult to appraise the value of ecosystems. Each additional Alexa skill increases the value of Alexa, but because Amazon is not the owner of those skills it cannot include that value in its balance sheet.

Of course, the prudence principle in accountancy is deliberately designed to be conservative when applying value to intangible assets. After all, it is true that the future value of a customer portfolio is inherently uncertain, but this does little to alter the fact that this value often accrues over time.

This explains why investors only pay limited attention to the annual balance sheet when setting their own value on digital companies. And rightly so. Statistics show that the earnings of companies founded after 2000 only account for 2.4% of stock returns! Or as the digital gurus put it: 'Profit is highly overrated'. Which is where we came in...

SHOW ME THE MONEY

The sources for companies to cobble together the financial resources they need are not limitless. Without wishing to give a lecture on corporate finance, the following options are some of the alternatives open to them.

» **Financing from within your existing operations.** Today's markets are typified by winners and losers, with nothing much in between. If you appear weak from the start, you are never going to be able to keep up with the big players. Just like you need to repair your roof when the weather is good, so you need to start your digital transformation when your finances are healthy. This will increase your chances of success exponentially.

» **New external financing.** Here again, the winners have an advantage. Companies that are performing well will find it easier to persuade banks and venture capitalists to agree to a new round of funding. In just over a decade, FNG has been able to grow into a fashion group with a turnover of half a billion euros, simply because investors were willing to finance their takeovers, expansion plans and transformations.

» **Sales of assets.** Many companies can create extra resources for investment by selling off some of their assets. For example, many retailers own significant amounts of real estate. The Spanish Mango fashion chain was able to raise € 150 million through the sale of its head office building and a logistics center.[179] An even more drastic measure is selling off or terminating part of your business activities, in the manner that the Blokker Holding has done by returning to focus on its original shop formula. In much the same way, you can also pull out of a particular geographic region to save money for investment elsewhere. But if you are going to do any of these things, the same golden rule applies: do it while the going is good. That way, you will get a better price. When Macintosh decided in 2008 to concentrate on its fashion activities (primarily in shoes), it hoped to raise the resources for its new growth from the sale of (amongst others) Bel Company, Halfords and Kwantum. Sadly, market sentiment shifted against them and the yield from the sales was not even enough to bring the group's level of debt down to manageable proportions. The outcome was inevitable...

» **Reducing the financing needs.** By cutting back the scale of your plans or activities, you can immediately reduce the level of resources you need to invest. By closing five of its stores, De Bijenkorf was only obliged to invest in the transformation of the remaining seven. In this process, anticipation is highly important. By closing the five stores when the company's results were still reasonably good, De Bijenkorf was able to avoid a cash drain. This underlines the importance of closing stores quickly, if it is clear they are no longer viable. Many important players have got into difficulties through trying to hold on to the past for too long.

» **Search for partnerships, alliances and collaborations.** In the network economy, with its various ecosystems, it is not always necessary to make all your investments yourself. You can hitch your wagon to the star of others; for example, by selling on a marketplace. There are even good opportunities for visionary independent entrepreneurs. Farfetch, founded in 2008, is a marketplace for 540 fashion boutiques all around the world, who all operate in the luxury segment and do not compete on price. Instead of all creating their own webshops, they host their products on this worldwide platform. In this way, they have the best of both worlds and their online presence is every bit as good as the customer experience in their physical stores. In this context, the 'make or buy' decision is more crucial than ever (see further).

» **Sell or merge.** Nowadays, having a minimum scale is a condition to compete. Some perfectly viable, healthy and well-run companies generate insufficient free cash flow to be able to push through their own transformation. If this is the case, be realistic and opt to be a successful part of a larger whole, rather than stubbornly trying to make it on your own. You won't succeed.

MAKE OR BUY IN THE DIGITAL ERA

During the 1990s, a lot of ink was spilt on the subject of what companies should do themselves and what they should outsource to others. The theories and rules that were developed then remain applicable, even in our new digital age. That being said, there is certainly a greater tendency nowadays for the outsourcing option.

When making this decision, there are three key factors that need to be considered:

1. How strategic is the activity?
2. What are the risks attached to outsourcing the activity?
3. What is the effect on our operations and costs?

In essence, companies develop three kinds of activities:

1. With **strategic activities** companies can really make the difference. These are the activities that allow you to differentiate and achieve a com-

petitive advantage. World-class is not good enough; in these activities you need to be the best of the best. For this reason, you also need to keep them under your own control at all times. If you can't do these things better than others, you are in the wrong business.

2. **Mission-critical activities** are essential for your ability to compete. You don't have to be better than the competition in these tasks, but just 'good' is not good enough. You need to be world-class – like your major rivals.

3. The **remaining activities** are necessary for your operations but have no decisive impact on your competitive strength. For these tasks, good is good enough. Typical examples include the running of your company restaurant or the cleaning of your office premises.

In particular, it is for the mission-critical activities that a great deal of thought is given to the potential risks of the 'make or buy' decisions. Obviously, this is closely related to the nature and reputation of the third party to whom you are thinking of farming out the activity. Will your partner be reliable? Will he remain loyal to you? Will he still be in business in three or five years' time? What will you do if his factory burns down?

These matters are all linked to your level of dependence on your partner. If the collaboration fails for whatever reason, do you have a plan B? How watertight are your contractual conditions? Can you easily switch somewhere else if things start to go wrong? What if your partner suddenly increases his prices? Of course, taking these risks can also yield benefits. Outsourcing can provide additional flexibility to your operations. Do you know in which direction technology in your sector is likely to evolve? If you buy or develop the technology, how do you know you are making the right choices? Is it not safer to outsource and then change partners, if it becomes clear you have backed the wrong horse?

Finally, it needs to be remembered that farming out activities has a major impact on both your operations and your costs. The 'make or buy' discussion began when companies first began to think about their focus. The argument was that a company can devote more attention to its strategic activities if it doesn't need to share that attention with non-strategic activities. In other words, attention must be primarily given to the development of competitive advantages. At the same time, outsourcing should also lead to lower costs. For things that are not of strategic importance, it is probable that others can do them better and cheaper. From a financial perspective, the purchase of your assets is an investment and therefore an additional capital requirement in the short term, while outsourcing results in periodic operating expenditure that is much lower in that same short term.

To carry out your activities, you need competencies and resources. You can outsource both, either or neither. You can hire in the resource of AI software as a service and at the same time develop AI analysis competencies in-house by having your own AI analysts on your payroll. Alternatively, you can farm out all your AI requirements by asking a bureau to do the analyses for you. This means that they then, of course, must have the necessary AI competence and resources.

It is essentially a matter of weighing up the pros and cons, before deciding what is best for you. In our AI example, developing your own AI is not usually the wisest choice: you don't have sufficient resources to do it better than the other players in the market. Recruiting your own AI analysts seems like a justified option in the eyes of many companies, but it is often difficult to achieve in practice, since the number of available talents in the labor market is small. How can you persuade the best of the best to come and work for you? In circumstances of this kind, employer branding becomes increasingly mission-critical!

In the digital world, more and more companies are opting to outsource. The first reason for this decision is the speed of technological change. This makes it harder to keep up with new developments independently. Consequently, outsourcing is often the only viable option, if you want to achieve the desired world-class level for mission-critical activities.

Moreover, this speed of change also leads to uncertainty. Smart outsourcing allows companies to maximize their operational flexibility and their room for maneuver.

A third reason for outsourcing in the digital era is the need to conserve finan-cial resources to push through your transformation process. The more you outsource, the less you need to invest.

Bearing all these choices in mind, making the correct 'make or buy' decision becomes a mission-critical competence in its own right.

MAKE OR BUY: COMPARING E-COMMERCE PURE PLAYERS WITH TRADITIONAL RETAILERS

The analysis of the 'make or buy' decisions of the large and dom-inant e-commerce pure players reveals some interesting insights into the activities they regard as strategically important. There is a clear pattern.

Firstly, they evolve as technological companies. The major inter-national players opt for the development of their own platforms and technologies, seeing this as a means of differentiation.

For example, the prospectus for the IPO or Initial Public Offering of Zalando in September 2008 makes clear that the company views itself first and foremost as a digital company. The found-ers were driven by their passion for the internet, not for fashion. They only picked on fashion as their core business because they saw a hole in the market in that segment at a European level.

This is reflected in the people employed by Zalando. Of its 15,000 personnel, no fewer than 2,000 work in the technology depart-ment.[180] That is roughly 600 more than the entire headquarters staff of bol.com, the largest e-commerce company in the Nether-lands![181] Zalando is very clear about the reasons for this: *'Proprie-tary technology solutions form the backbone of Zalando and drive all workflows from purchasing to ordering processes and fulfill-*

ment. (...) Our focus is on expanding our technology talent pool by providing an attractive and innovative work environment.[182]

This massive investment in technology more or less forces smaller players – traditional retailers and brand manufacturers, as well as national e-commerce pure players – to outsource their own mission-critical technology. This immediately explains the success of Amazon Web Services: as a retailer or brand manufacturer, it gives you on-demand access to state-of-the-art software, which Amazon developed in the first instance for its own activities.

The major players also invest in technology in the form of acquisitions. When Amazon realized the true added value of the Kiva robots it uses in its distribution centers, it decided to make a 775-million-dollar take-over bid for the company behind the robots. At that time, Kiva was also working for other companies, but that was not to the liking of Amazon.

All existing contracts were terminated and no new ones were made. Amazon wanted exclusivity.

This provides traditional companies with a dilemma. Common sense says that for your mission-critical technology it is smarter to opt for outsourcing. But what can you do if one of the big boys then buys up your outsourcing supplier?

Consider, for example, software like VirtuSize, which is used to provide tailor-made advice for the online sale of fashion articles, so that the likelihood of returns is kept to a minimum. As a fashion company, why should you make a serious investment to develop your own version of this kind of plug-in? You can't make anything better than what already exists. But what are you going to do if Zalando suddenly decides to take over VirtuSize? Scenarios like this make clear why it is important not to be reliant on a single supplier for your outsourcing. The ability to switch to an alternative is more important than ever before.

A second noteworthy similarity between the dominant players, even at local level, is that they invest heavily in their own distribution centers. These are nearly always under their full and direct control. For them, this is a strategic activity, for which they think their level of specialization and scale will allow them to perform better than their competitors.

The distribution strategies of the traditional players are more diffuse: some do their own distribution; others farm it out. This is the case for both online and offline distribution. That being said, there are exceptions. In particular, it is noticeable that companies with an omnichannel strategy make fundamentally different choices than the e-commerce pure players. This is clear from some of the examples we looked at earlier. Best Buy uses its dense store network to deliver products quickly. John Lewis has built a hybrid distribution center, suitable for dealing with both store and consumer orders.

Finally, it is worth noting that most of the e-commerce pure players outsource the actual delivery of their products. This is an area where cost is more important than the ability to differentiate: logistical service providers can transport more packages than individual companies, so that they can make more drops per kilometer, which increases efficiency and reduces costs. Once again, however, there are exceptions. We have already seen how Coolblue, most supermarkets and Hello Fresh prefer to make their own deliveries.

But there are also exceptions in this respect among the major e-commerce pure players. Amazon now owns a fleet of 40 freight aircraft, supported by several ships and countless lorries, and is currently conducting delivery trials on behalf of the vendors on its marketplace at prices that are potentially lower than UPS and FedEx.[183]

LIVING WITHIN YOUR MEANS

Companies that are unable to find adequate financial resources to fund their transformation will probably go under. A shame, but that is the harsh reality. The only alternative is to cut your commercial coat according to your cloth. This means giving up your ideas of a digital future and getting back to affordable basics.

After all, Action and Primark are doing very nicely without a webshop, aren't they? Yes, they are, but both are dangerous as a benchmark. They have the scale and the resources to pursue a resolute omnichannel strategy, but have consciously chosen to move in a different direction. On the one hand, they are able to achieve sufficient growth from their physical stores. On the other hand, their cheap mass-produced products are less suitable for viable online sale. It also needs to be remembered that they both invest heavily in digital applications – just not in a webshop!

That being said, they do at least serve as a benchmark to show that an analogue sales strategy can still work. It is clear, for example, that many independent entrepreneurs do not have the resources or the competencies to develop a well-functioning webshop that they can turn into a success through clever digital marketing. Consequently, it would be foolish for them to start a battle they know they can't win. But in my opinion they can still win the battle to differentiate, if only we can step away from the delusional idea that omnichannel is the only way forward in this day and age.

The famous STORY in New York is a perfect example of how you can turn a physical space into a unique shopping experience. As their website puts it: *'Point of view of a Magazine. Changes like a Gallery. Sells like a Store.'* Every few weeks, Story introduces a new theme, builds a story around it and renews its entire assortment and shop display. In this way, STORY gives inquisitive shoppers a reason to come back. The concept was so successful that STORY has since been bought up by the Macy's chain of department stores, which immediately appointed STORY founder Rachel Shechtman as their Brand Experience Officer.[184]

We all know of shops of this kind, with a unique assortment, friendly staff and a pleasing atmosphere, where you like to return time after time. Given the right location, this traditional form of retail can still survive and thrive. But only if your shop stands out from the crowd and is not thirteen-to-a-dozen in every high street. You still need to be different – somehow!

THE END OF AMAZON?

When I let it be known on social media that I was writing a new book about retail, someone replied that his retail slide show consists of just a single slide: 'Amazon'. And it is undeniable that the mega-company has been cast in the role of bogeyman for the retail sector in recent years. Nevertheless, I hope that the previous pages have already made clear that there is life for retailers and brand manufacturers alongside Amazon.

In fact, I think they can even look forward to a life AFTER Amazon. Because bold though it sounds, I believe that Amazon will no longer exist in five years' time, at least not in its present form.

Don't misunderstand me: Amazon is an outstanding company and its founder-CEO is a shining example of visionary entrepreneurship. Yet at the same time, Amazon is starting to reach the boundaries of what I consider to be fair competition.

For this reason, I predict that government authorities will step in and present a number of the technologically over-dominant players with a series of stark choices. And it won't just be Amazon in the firing line.

Booking.com is one of the first platform companies that has already been obliged to change its rules. In its standard agreement, it demanded that hotels give a guaranteed lowest online price. But have you ever searched for a hotel on Booking.com and then phoned up that hotel direct? If you have, you will probably have been offered a lower price than on Booking.com, because the hotel no longer needs to pay commission. So wouldn't it just be easier if hotels could immediately display their best prices to begin with? This is now possible in several countries, after German hoteliers (under pressure from the *Bundeskartellamt* or Federal Cartel Office) set up their own website to advertise their rooms at cheaper rates than Booking.com.[185] The underlying problem is that Booking.com has too many of the characteristics of a search engine, but actually applies the revenue model of a marketplace. A fixed fee, either for presence on Booking.com or per reservation, or a combination of both, would lead to a much fairer distribution of the added value than the present commission system.

In the Netherlands, it is now the turn of Takeaway.com to come under the regulatory spotlight. Having first established their dominance in the meal home delivery market, they unilaterally increased the level of their commission from 12% to 13%. Like Booking.com, Takeaway.com also insists on a parity clause that commits the participating restaurants to not advertise their meals at lower prices on their own website. It is this clause that is now under pressure, not just in the Netherlands but in similar instances in several other countries.[186]

The trend to allow the tech giants less freedom of action was also evident in the recent privacy problems of Facebook and the European condemnation of Google for infringing the free competition regulations. This is a problem inherent in the 'winner takes all' model: if a single company becomes so supremely dominant that it has a *de facto* monopoly, the only way to ensure the survival of free competition is to subject that company to stricter rules.

Viewed in these terms, why should Amazon be allowed to get away with some of its more doubtful practices? In its field, the company has also become so powerful that it is almost impossible to compete against it. The biggest complaint against Amazon is that it is a actually a cloud company that pretends to be a retailer, whereas in fact it uses the billions it earns from Amazon Web Services to subsidize the losses of its retail activities.

The company pursues this policy to fairly extreme lengths, even to the extent of sometimes financing discounts on products sold by third-party vendors on its marketplace. During the end of year period, it was possible to find numerous toys at a reduced price with a *'discount provided by Amazon'*.[187] The vendors in question were not even informed beforehand, although they were given the choice to accept or refuse the discount later on. This was very clearly a case of dumping, with an equally clear objective: the elimination of the competition. It is strange that this should be accepted, while in various European countries deliberately selling at a loss is prohibited by law, and in general voices are being increasingly heard to tighten regulation still further.

Unless something is done, free competition will be ever harder to achieve in the future, thanks to the combination of Amazon's increasingly wide assortment (assuming gigantic proportions), the Prime model that is now embedded in the homes of 50% of American families and the continuing deliberate sale of products at a loss.

It can't go on like this. My prediction is that Amazon will one day soon be forced to make a choice. It will no longer be permitted to carry out all its current activities and will be obliged to hive off a number of its current divisions. The first steps in this direction (like the GDPR) will be taken in Europe, precisely because the Americans , for the time being at least, are afraid of weakening their companies against their unregulated Chinese competitors. Even so, in the long run the American anti-trust authorities will have no option but to follow.

HOW TO CREATE VALUE?

1. **Answer the following questions, bearing in mind your ideal customer journey:**

   a. How much of your turnover will shift to online and when? How do you see the share of turnover being distributed between your own webshop, sales on marketplaces and indirect online sales?

   b. What is the role of your physical stores? What formats should they have? How will turnover be shared between direct and indirect sales?

   c. What competitive advantages are you seeking to achieve?

2. **What are the consequences of the above for your value chain?**

   a. Supply chain?

   b. People and organization (store staff, customer service, digital competencies, account management, etc.)?

   c. The assortment?

   d. The store network?

   e. Marketing and customer interaction?

   f. ICT?

   g. The organizational structure?

3. **What resources do you need to develop this new value chain?**

   a. What are the most important investment costs?
   b. Which priorities will you set and what investments will they require?

4. **Where will you find the financial resources to fund these investments?**

   a. How much cash can you generate from your own operations?
   b. Can you sell assets?
   c. How much external financing can you find?
   d. Are collaborative ventures an option?
   e. Are you taking the right 'make or buy' decisions?

5. **Decision-making**

   a. Given the financial requirements and your level of available resources, can you implement or even accelerate your plans?
   b. Do you have sufficient scale and/or resources to stand alone or would you be better off as part of a greater whole?

PART 4

IMPLEMENTATON

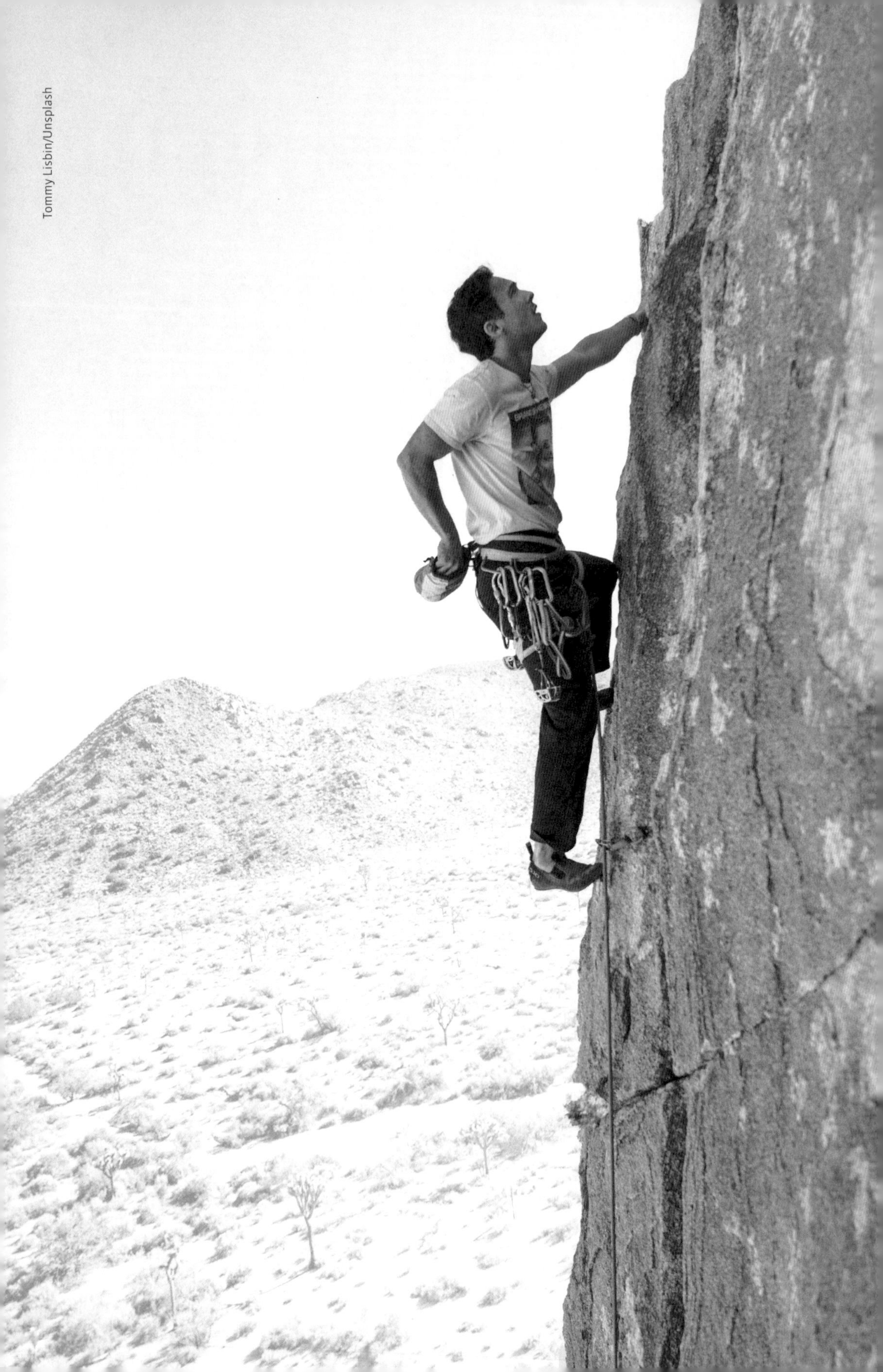

Tommy Lisbin/Unsplash

CHAPTER 13
THE ORGANIZATION

'Great ideas don't coincide with budget cycles.'

Anonymous

Imagine that you are climbing a mountain that rises steeply out of the ocean. Your whole body hurts from the effort you are making. Above you, still a long way away, the summit is shimmering in the sun. Sadly, there is not enough room for everyone on the summit, so you need to get a move on, if you want to beat the other climbers. Climbing back down is no longer an option, because the crashing waves would swallow you up and pull you down into the deep…

With this brilliant analogy, Frans Colruyt, director of the retail group of the same name, cleverly sketches the challenge faced by many of today's retailers.[188] In this fourth and last section, we will see how you can best tackle this difficult climb and reach the summit.

THE SLOWEST DAY OF THE REST OF YOUR LIFE

Change happens at all times and in all places. In 1964, Bob Dylan sang that 'the times, they are a-changin'. He also prophetically predicted that 'the first one now will later be last'. However, there is one major difference between the 1960s and today: with technology as the catalyst, change is now taking place at an exponential speed that Dylan could never have imagined. Hence the oft-made claim that, in terms of change at least, today will be the slowest day of the rest of your life. But what makes this speed of change so different? And what are its consequences?

Because in the past innovations came in waves, companies had time between the waves to adjust to them. This made it more difficult for newcomers to topple the existing market leaders from their throne. But that is no longer the case. Innovations now follow each other in rapid succession.

Many of you will be familiar with the clichéd statistics about the advancing speed of technological adoption. Electricity and telephones needed 30 and 25 years respectively before they reached 10% of households. After just five years, tablets had a penetration level of 50%.[189]

What's more, the accelerating pace of change goes beyond purely technological innovations. Consider, for example, the relative slowness with which
H&M conquered the international fashion world with their 'fast fashion' business model. Until 1975, the company was only active in Scandinavia. It then
took them another 28 years to extend their geographical coverage from four
to fifteen countries. In other words, their rivals had plenty of time to adjust to
the new H&M business model.

Compare this with Zalando, which just five years after its foundation was
already active in fifteen European countries.

Because change now moves so quickly, everything is more uncertain than it
used to be. In the technological field, we are constantly bombarded with new
innovations that we are told 'will change the world'. Of course, time eventually shows that most of these predictions were untrue. Most, but not all. So how
can you distinguish the game-changing trends from the spurious hypes?

For example, some of the digital gurus predicted that the 3D-printer would
disrupt the entire manufacturing cycle and the logistical chain. In the most
extreme scenarios, consumers would buy products online that they would
then print off in their own homes. No more factories, distribution centres,
stocks and couriers! So far, much of this has failed to materialize. 3D-printing
is certainly relevant, but to date it remains confined to custom-made solutions (like prosthetics for the medical sector), the production of goods for
which there is only a limited demand (like outdated spare parts), and gadgets
designed by consumers themselves (like fantasy jewelry in synthetics). But a
technological breakthrough? Not yet. Will it ever come? Who knows? Maybe
it will and maybe it won't. This uncertainty represents an additional challenge.

At the same time, complexity has also increased exponentially. Whereas
competition used to take place between broadly comparable and well established companies, nowadays we regularly see newcomers take the market by
storm. These so-called 'green field' players not only use a different and often
revolutionary business model, but are also unburdened by the weight of the
past. Their ICT systems are state of the art and have been designed specifically
with the digital age in mind. Their business culture exudes 'the spirit of the

valley' – the valley in question being Silicon Valley – a spirit that traditional companies only sniff briefly during their 'inspiration visits' to California and elsewhere. Their personnel are imbued with a different work ethic and no longer think in terms of 'acquired rights'.

This complexity is also reflected in a blurring of the lines between the different sectors. Is Amazon an online retailer, a B2B provider of cloud services or a brand manufacturer of consumer electronics, such as e-readers and intelligent loudspeakers?

NOTCO: THE END OF THE TRADITIONAL FOOD CHAIN?

I admit it: I am a true carnivore and can really enjoy a good piece of meat. As a result, the knowledge that cattle farming is harmful to the environment hardly fills me with great joy...

With people like me in mind, the Chilean start-up NotCo has come on the market with a business idea that has some interesting possibilities. Using an AI-driven algorithm, the company develops vegan alternatives for existing foodstuffs. The algorithm takes account of the nutritional value of the products and the needs/wishes of the consumer in terms of taste, texture and color, as well as the potential impact on the environment.

The most important input for the AI is a dataset containing the chemical, molecular and nutritional values of more than a thousand different vegetable proteins. On this basis, the algorithm suggests alternative vegan recipes for products that currently contain ingredients of animal origin.

The first product that NotCo has launched on the market is Not Mayo, a 100% vegan substitute for mayonnaise. The first attempt made use of beetroot, which tasted great but was purple in color. Similar green and red versions were also tested and rejected. Back to the drawing board.

But the final Not Mayo looks and tastes exactly like the real thing. It has been launched in 220 stores in Chile and is currently the third best-selling brand in these stores.

The company has already announced its intention to further release Not Yogurt, Not Cheese and Not Milk. In a pre-production taste test, their chocolate mousse was also a big hit with their sample public![190]

NotCo is a classic example of a company that has the potential to dislocate an entire sector. It is not just livestock farming and milk production that are under threat, but also the traditional manner of conducting research and development in the food industry.

Personally, I am convinced that sooner or later these tasty vegetable substitutes will find their way onto all our plates. But it remains to be seen whether NotCo can win the competitive battle with an established heavyweight like Nestlé!

THE ORGANIZATIONAL FIELD OF TENSION

The traditional way of running a company is not really suited to dealing with rapid change.

In a stable environment, it is sensible to opt for a rigid strategic plan for the medium and long term. Companies excel at consistently following a clearly defined path that allows them to develop a competitive advantage.

For example, the luxury lingerie company Van de Velde, owner of the lingerie brands Marie Jo, Prima Donna and Andrés Sarda, as well as the Rigby & Peller,

Intimacy and Lincherie store chains, achieved its prominence by focusing on the production of high-quality bras with a stylish contemporary design and a perfect fit for maximum comfort. The fitting room was a key element in the implementation of their business model: that was the place where the highly trained shop assistants needed to give the right advice about size and style, bearing in mind the specificity and variability of the female form. By hitting that particular nail on the head decade after decade, the company was able to grow into a successful market player. But once customers began to order lingerie via the internet, the importance of the sales assistant and the fitting room quickly began to decline. Even so, the company decided to maintain the same strategic direction and put a break on online sales. As a result, Van de Velde lost precious time in adapting to the digital revolution.

This immediately brings us to the second limitation of the traditional style of business management. The strategy is determined at the top of the company and then imposed downwards throughout the organization, where the personnel on the work floor are expected to implement it. The structure to make this possible is highly mechanistic. Each member of staff has a specific function and works in a specific department, reporting to a specific superior officer. Tasks are clearly defined, which makes it possible for the superiors to assess how well or not they are being performed. This performance assessment is then used to make any necessary adjustments. All the departments fit together as part of a coherent whole in a predetermined system with clear hierarchical lines and equally clear objectives and plans. Everything functions with machine-like precision.

In essence, this functional structure encourages silo thinking, since everyone is assessed by their own managers within their own departments. This runs contrary to the growing need in the digital era for more cross-functional collaboration as the best way to reach meaningful solutions. It also makes too little use of the bottom-up potential for remaining in touch with key developments in the market. As a result, opportunities, threats and possible solutions are identified too late, often with dire consequences. What's more, if you want to amend the organigram within this kind of structure, it soon becomes evident that the process is too time-consuming in our rapidly changing world.

In a dynamic environment, it is necessary to be able to react much more rapidly. In these circumstances, we speak of an adaptive strategy. The underlying assumption is that the traditional competitive advantages will become increasingly less sustainable. In the future, you will not win because you do something better than your competitors, but because you are capable of doing something new or something different more quickly than your competitors.[191]

Paula Nickolds, managing director at John Lewis, puts it as follows: *'The days of imagining it is possible to have a fixed five-year strategy, all neatly tied up in a bow, are unrealistic at best, and a recipe for disaster at worst.'*[192]

An adaptive strategy requires four competencies:

1. **The ability to quickly receive the right signals.** Almost 400 million people live close to an active and therefore dangerous volcano. For these people, predicting the likely eruptions of the volcano is a matter of life and death. To make such predictions possible, vulcanologists make use of all the information available to them: the analysis of ground vibrations, the composition of the gases emitted and subtle changes in the shape of the cone, identified with radar imagery.

    In much the same way, companies need to be able to pick up the signals of impending change. When did you first hear something about AI or voice search? How do you know if your customers are going to change their behavior as a result?

2. **The ability to experiment.** If the vulcanologists sound false alarms too often, their credibility will soon be called into question. Perhaps their next warning might be ignored...

    As a company, you need to be able to filter what is genuinely relevant. How are customers using a new technology? Does the evolution in consumer behavior resulting from voice search match what the experts predicted? Does an intelligent mirror in a changing room really add anything to the shopping experience? Does it increase turnover? Do the colors of stars in ratings actually make a difference? Small-scale tests into matters of this kind can often help to reveal new insights in the short term. And in a digital context, this can often be done with the use of only modest resources. If this is the case, it is pointless to waste time discussing what might or might not work best: just test it! The old adage 'fail fast, learn fast' is applicable for all companies.

3. **The ability to mobilize.** All the work of the vulcanologists will have been for nothing, if there is no evacuation plan in place to move people to safety once the likelihood of an eruption becomes almost certain.

   For companies, it is also essential to be able to translate the relevant signals into concrete action. If a test reveals a new insight and if the signals from the exterior world also suggest that a change in approach is required, make sure you do something about it – and do it quickly! If we decide it is useful, do we have a plan to install intelligent mirrors? If we don't have sufficient budget, do we have a process to quickly set key priorities? Altering the color of stars in ratings is technically quite straightforward, but what if the marketing director feels that the stars need to be kept in your house color? Are we simply going to let the hierarchy dictate? This final question brings us to the biggest challenge of all: what if we need to change our organizational structure? In the old analogue world, the organizational structure tended to flow naturally from your strategic choices. But in the new digital world, there is a growing tendency to decentralize decision-making, as a result of which people organize themselves differently, because they think it is preferable. In other words, organization now runs ahead of strategy.

4. **The ability to work together with other companies in complex systems.** Vulcanologists are just one link in the chain. If they give the signal to evacuate, a dozen other services move into action.

   As Peter Hinssen puts it: 'The network always wins.'[193] Collaborating with others instead of trying to do everything yourself, even with regard to your important core activities, is indispensible. It automatically gives you more flexibility and speed, since it is impossible to be good in every aspect of your operations. Marketplaces are a good example of this kind of network. Strategic partnerships go even further. Do you remember Nike and the way they opened up Nike Direct for a select group of strategic partners in indirect sales? This demands openness and mutual trust. Mirroring the success of Apple, many companies are anxious to build their own ecosystem. As we saw in the previous chapter, strategic partnerships and ecosystems transcend 'make or buy' decisions.

THE GRASS IS ALWAYS GREENER ON THE OTHER SIDE OF THE HILL

Large companies like to mirror themselves on start-ups and their entrepreneurial spirit. The beginners are more agile and can act much faster. They are less restricted, both in terms of material and mindset.

Starters have no legacy IT systems that have been developed over the years and are no longer suited to the needs of today. Their workforce is very young and dynamic. You seldom hear things like: 'But that's the way we've always done it' or 'We've tried that and it doesn't work'. There is no resistance to change.

For them, 'work hard, play hard' are more than just empty words. Also in a literal sense: ping-pong and pool tables are used during office hours, although these people don't really have office hours...

At the same time, it needs to be realized that start-ups face other challenges. They may not need to waste effort on bureaucracy and office politics, but instead they have an almost non-stop and time-consuming battle to find funding. Because they have literally started from nothing, they also spend a lot of time and resources on reinventing the wheel. Their sometimes chaotic way of working leads to inefficiency and a constantly shifting focus. In other words, their agility comes with a number of built-in disadvantages. The grass is not always greener on the other side of the hill.

For this reason, it is important to find a healthy balance between the stability of an established company and the dynamism of a starter.[194]

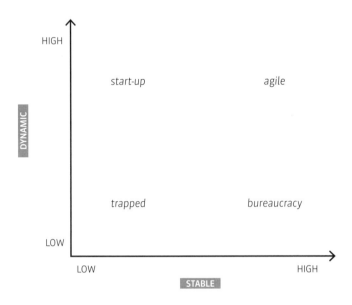

This right balance is not the same for every company. It is dependent on the answers to two questions:

1. **Is the threat you face imminent or latent?**

   While the worlds of music and books were given a drastic shake-up during the first decade of the new century, e-commerce in the fashion sector only really took off after 2010. In most western countries, the majority of supermarkets have been spared from a serious loss of business to online alternatives: with the exception of the United Kingdom and France, in Europe and North-America online turnover for grocery shopping is still less than 5%.

   The faster we are able to assess the nature of a threat, the more time we have to react to it.

A second closely related factor is the nature of your competition. As a traditional company, are you competing in agility against other traditional companies or are you up against e-commerce pure players? In the book sector, for example, the digital players dominate the market and are therefore the most important benchmark. By contrast, in the world of supermarkets – certainly in Europe – it is the traditional companies that still lead the way. Newcomers like Ocado in the United Kingdom and Picnic in the Netherlands respectively have a much lower online market share than Tesco and Sainsbury's, and Albert Heijn and Jumbo. In the fashion branch, the balance is somewhere in the middle. Because the market is highly fragmented, many traditional players earn an important part of their turnover from their own webshop, notwithstanding the market leadership of Zalando and ASOS.

You often see that not all companies in the same sector react with the same degree of alertness. While the French Darty and its Belgian subsidiary Vanden Borre were quick to commit to e-commerce and omnichannel, MediaMarkt hesitated for much longer. As a result, Darty and Vanden Borre had more time to react to changing circumstances, while for MediaMarkt the threat suddenly became very acute!

2. Does this threat impact on the totality of your organization and its activities or just on part of them?

Viewed worldwide, only 3% of the turnover in the builders' merchant and DIY market has shifted online. But for specific product categories within the market the picture can sometimes be very different. For example, the online turnover for power tools has followed much the same evolution as consumer electronics: more than 30% of sales are now made via the internet. Similarly, the online impact in the supermarket sector varies from product to product. In the United States, some 30% of beauty products, disposable diapers and foodstuffs are now purchased through digital channels, while as little as 2% of dairy products, deep-freeze items and alcoholic drinks are purchased in the same manner. A special situation arises when new product groups are developed that are capable of cannibalizing existing turnover. The advent and rapid growth of meal boxes, like Hello Fresh, may not dislocate the sector entirely, but will certainly cost it turnover.

Like product groups, the impact of threat can also vary significantly from target group to target group. Large industrial companies purchase their maintenance products and spare parts (the so-called MRO or Maintenance, Repair and Operations) in a different way than consumers and self-employed entrepreneurs. The larger companies take account of the total cost of ownership, instead of focusing exclusively on the lowest price. Consequently, they prefer to use suppliers who can help to think about solutions that will minimize lost production time. As a result, Amazon is not well-suited to serve this segment. It is a different story with small independent businesses, which still tend to buy their products and parts in the spirit of the first wave of e-commerce: 'I know what I need and I want it as cheaply as possible'.

Last but not least, the indirect effects of threat must also be considered. Retailers not only need to think about the level of their turnover that can move online, but also about the future role of their physical stores. Brand manufacturers need to think about their entire distribution chain, in the hope of reestablishing control over it. Factors of this kind mean that the impact of a threat can be much wider than the simple shift of sales to online channels.

The object of all this thinking is to find the right balance between stability and dynamism. Does the entire organization need to become more agile or only certain parts and functions? To what extent can this agility be introduced in phases? In practice, we see that large organizations generally adopt one of three models:

1. the speedboat
2. the tugboat
3. the patrol boat

THE SPEEDBOAT

Imagine for a moment that we can turn back time. Let us return briefly to the final years of the 20th century. You are a leading bookstore, like Barnes & Noble in the United States, Fnac in France or Waterstone's in the United Kingdom. You understand how the online sale of books has the potential to disrupt your entire business model. As a visionary leader, you don't want to take the risk that new start-ups will undermine your market supremacy and so you persuade your shareholders to set up your own webshop. My colleague Professor Marion Debruyne refers to this as 'creating your own worst nightmare'. If your webshop is a success, you will wreak havoc in your own store network. But at least this is better than the alternative, which is that someone else creates a successful webshop that decimates your sales.Then you will lose your market leadership and even risk going out of business altogether. Either way, of course, the result is a bloodbath.

What can you do to maximize your webshop's chances of success? Vijay Govindarajan and Chris Trimble[195] have provided us with a clear methodology for dealing with this situation. On the one hand, you need to free yourself from your existing business model (autonomy). On the other hand, you must use a key advantage that you have and the start-ups don't: the ability to create synergies with your existing company. In other words, you need to ask what you want to 'forget' about your mother company and what you want to 'borrow' from it.

To begin with, your plans will often come into conflict with the existing bureaucratic culture of your organization and the profile of your current workforce. Everyone in the company is attached to the idea of physical stores. What's more, many of them love books and are highly skeptical about the prospects for a successful online bookshop. For this reason, you need to forget this culture entirely and recruit a completely new digital team, based at a separate and preferably trendier location. Otherwise, you may find it difficult to get sufficient digital talent on board: they won't want to work in an environment that is dominated by the bookworms and their old way of thinking. Of course, you will also be faced by people's usual resistance to change: 'You are ruining the book industry we love!' This will initially put a brake on the growth of your webshop.

At the same time, you should also be searching for synergies. Why should you create a new purchasing department for the webshop, if you can make use of the stores' purchasing department? This will allow you both to bulk purchase books at highly competitive terms. It also makes sense to use the brand name of the stores, since this will avoid the need to invest in brand awareness. And who knows: if the book industry had done things this way, we might never have heard of Amazon...

The main advantage of the speedboat method is that you can make rapid progress, because you are not held back by the past. The main disadvantage is that the synergy benefits do not work both ways. The method of 'forgetting' and 'borrowing' may indeed maximize the chances of success for the online start-up, but it does little to find a good solution for the mother company. In the example above, the physical stores are sacrificed on the altar of the web-shop more than is strictly speaking necessary. At the same time, the digital learning effect for the mother company is very limited, so that there is little likelihood that staff in the stores will become ambassadors for the webshop.

In essence, the speedboat method results *de facto* in a multichannel rather than an omnichannel approach. For this reason, it is recommended when speed is important and/or when the mother company needs no synergy ben-efits from the start-up. Attempting to integrate the speedboat into the mother company at a later stage is not without risk. The staff in the speedboat are unlikely to react positively to this, so that integrations of this kind inevita-bly take time. In other words, the time that you gain in the short term is lost again in the long term.

NEXTAIL: THE SPEEDBOAT OF BLOKKER HOLDING

For a long time, Blokker Holding – in origin a Dutch company but with activities throughout the Benelux, France and Germany – was slow to respond to digital developments. In its domestic market, the retail group operated in three sectors. The first to be badly hit was toys, a segment in which bol.com was increasingly active online after 2009. Next to get into difficulties was the household segment, again following a move by bol.com in 2011 to profile itself as a general online store, a move which soon persuaded more and more consumers to buy their pedal bins and vacuum cleaner bags via the internet. It was only in the home and lifestyle segment, with Leen Bakker as the jewel in the crown, that the group was not seriously affected by online competition. At that time, Blokker Holding earned less than 2% of its turnover from e-commerce. Only half of their fourteen different store formulas had a webshop.[196]

In other words, it was already five to twelve before the company finally decided to commit to a digital acceleration. In 2014, Nextail was set up as 'the online innovation branch' of the company. Based in separate premises in Amsterdam, Antoine Brouwer, who had previously been VP Marketing & Multichannel at Media-Markt in the Netherlands, was given the green light to launch a start-up that was backed to the hilt by a financially strong mother company. 'In terms of knowledge and experience, it's a great place to work. When you enter, you immediately find yourself among a group of like-minded people. This is what we hear from those who have joined us from the operating companies: there, they were just experts in their respective head offices; here, they are part of a team. This means that we can all learn a lot from each other and there is plenty of horizontal communication between us. That creates a kind of infectious enthusiasm.'[197]

Nextail ran the webshops of all the group's different store formulas. It also took care of the digital marketing and was responsible for omnichannel innovations on the shop floor, such as kiosks, automated price-setting and CRM.

Following the sale of many of its chains, Blokker Holding has now effectively been dismantled, so that in 2018 Nextail ceased to exist as an independent entity and was absorbed into the mother company. At the present time, online sales generate roughly 15% of total turnover, with an annual growth of 25%.[198]

An alternative to the speedboat method is to take over one or more e-commerce pure players, but this still presents the same problems of synergy and integration. The Media Saturn Holding, the former mother company of MediaMarkt, decided in 2011 to buy up the German-based webshop redcoon, which had been founded back in 2002 by an ex-manager of MediaMarkt.[199] MediaMarkt itself had missed the digital train and at the time of the takeover had no webshop of its own. However, once its own webshops eventually began to take off, the company withdrew the redcoon webshop from several European countries. Today, the holding is taking steps to try and have the initial takeover nullified on legal grounds.[200]

For the Albert Heijn supermarket chain, the acquisition of bol.com was a venture into a new market – namely, non-food. This makes it more logical that bol.com should continue as a stand-alone operation. In the US, synergies are being sought through knowledge exchange within an Ahold Delhaize digital centre of excellence.

In a similar vein, following its takeover of the Jet.com e-commerce platform, Walmart appointed Jet's CEO as its new e-commerce director. Since then, a whole plethora of new acquisitions has been made.[201]

THE TUGBOAT

The difference between a speedboat and a tanker could hardly be greater: small versus big, fast versus slow, agile versus cumbersome. Even so, many large organizations have more in common with a tanker than a speedboat...

Fortunately, it is possible to nudge these big, slow and cumbersome tankers in the right direction with the assistance of a tugboat. Like a speedboat, a tug is relatively small and has plenty of power in relation to its size. However, this power is not used to generate speed, but to create strength that will allow it to take the tanker in tow. In this way, progress – innovations and change – is made more slowly, but at least everyone is on board. As a result, a tug is more suited than a speedboat for implementing an omnichannel strategy – on condition, of course, that the threat is not so acute that speed of action is of the essence.

In practice, your tug is a relatively small team that is responsible for promoting your digital transformation. This team must possess the same creative, 'can-do' mentality of a start-up. But there is a crucial difference. This time, the team does not steer its own course, but serves the needs of the bigger picture. This means that the focus and ultimate objectives are set in relation to the strategic direction that the wider organization as a whole wishes to follow. The team itself is still agile and is capable of quickly switching from one priority to another. But those priorities are now chosen less impulsively.

To make this possible, the tug needs to be in direct contact with the captain of the tanker. This serves a double purpose. On the one hand, this system of direct reporting ensures a shorter and therefore faster decision-making chain, which allows hierarchical restrictions to be bypassed by the – often young – members of the transformation team, safe in the knowledge that senior management will back them in the event of any disputes. On the other hand, this communication works in both directions, so that the tug's focus can be set by senior management. In this sense, the autonomy of the tugboat is less far-reaching than the autonomy of the speedboat.

A tug is also highly visible. In fact, that is its explicit purpose. The whole organization must be able to see the initiatives that the digital team is developing. Lack of visibility will only lead to greater resistance later on. Of course, being visible to all is not the same as involving all your stakeholders in your projects. Traditional decision-making processes – broad consultation with the aim of securing universal buy-in – are left to one side in favor of the ability to act more quickly.

Visibility may at first generate suspicion and mistrust. But once the first results of the transformation are noticeable, skepticism will evolve into curiosity, interest and, eventually, commitment.

To increase the likelihood of obtaining relevant results and buy-in, it is a good idea to include an experienced manager from the traditional wing of the organization as a member of the digital team. For example, the French-based

Boulanger, a player in the consumer electronics market with links to the Auchan group, insists that at least one member of the digital team must come from the store network. He is given the title of 'omnichannel manager' and his task is to represent – with an open mind – the voice of the physical stores in the team. In this way, it is possible for the team to develop sufficient empathy for the worries and concerns of people on the shop floor, but without the drawbacks of tunnel vision and/or unnecessary delays.

A typical consequence of this approach is that more and more people within the organization want to make use of the services of the digital team. Unfortunately for them, projects are not started at the request of specific users. The team remains focused at all times on the long-term objectives of the organization in its entirety. This is yet another reason why it is important for the tugboat to have a direct line to the boardroom.

The use of this method brought about considerable movement and significant changes within the Belgian Colruyt Group.[202] This company is an icon of consistency. It was made great on the basis of its culture of internal consultation and decision-making, with maximum involvement of the staff. At the same time, however, this often led to slowness, which did not mesh well with the dynamic environment in which Colruyt operates. Its tugboat allows the group to link the stability of the organization to a highly focused dynamism of action. The ultimate objective is not simply to initiate and successfully complete projects, but also to develop agile processes. This agility is targeted at the right priorities, so that its effects are contagious. In this way, the agility of the organization as a whole can gradually be increased.

THE PATROL BOAT

A patrol boat is also relatively small and powerful. In contrast to a speedboat, it does not set its own course, but monitors and explores the area around its flagship. In contrast to the tugboat, this means that it operates beyond the vision of the flagship.

The patrol boat is once again a small team that works in comparative isolation from the rest of the organization. Its objectives are less closely related to bringing about short-term change and are focused instead on keeping in touch with the latest developments in the field of technology. It is a test laboratory, where the company can experiment to the full.

These experiments can be organized in different ways:

» **The incubator.** Large companies often set themselves up as an incubator for start-ups. For example, the John Lewis Partnership has founded JLAB,[203] which invites starters to pitch their ideas, not necessarily on themes suggested by John Lewis. The winners are able to make free use of office space in the company's headquarters and also receive coaching from senior managers. More importantly, they have the opportunity to test out their ideas in practice, by being given access to the stores, webshop and customers of both John Lewis and its sister company Waitrose. The Partnership also has a fund that it uses to participate financially in some of these start-ups.

» **The laboratory.** Many companies also set up laboratories (not necessarily linked to an incubator), which conduct research and carry out tests relevant to the organization's long-term plan. It was with this in mind that Walmart created Store No. 8 in 2017. Based in three separate units, teams explore new ideas that have a time horizon of at least five and often more than ten years. As their website puts it: *'We are a multi-disciplinary team of ex-entrepreneurs, next-generation retail specialists, strategists, business leaders, operators and audacious thinkers interested in not only imagining the future of retail, but creating it.'*[204] Store No. 8 has also been made responsible for the company's digital acquisitions. For example, Walmart recently took over Spatial, an up-and-coming name in the world of virtual reality.

Of course, the time horizon can sometimes be shorter than Walmart's. Within the John Lewis Partnership, John Vary fulfils the role of futurologist. He leads a team that develops initiatives such as those that can now be seen in the most recent JL store in London, which we discussed in chapter 9. From their base in Room Y (an old washing machine testing area) of the John Lewis headquarters building, they also assess how consumers will be likely to react to new innovations. A brilliant example of one of their experiments is the way they were able to translate the 'any shape, any fabric' concept to the shop floor (see the box below).

» **Lead user and low impact tests.** Even without an incubator, it is still possible for a company to set itself up as a lead user for new applications, the main objective of which is to learn.

As an alternative to lead usership, other companies prefer to organize their own test projects. For example, the creation of an Alexa skill that has no direct business purpose, can still be extremely informative in terms of assessing customer action and reaction. Tests of this kind help to keep the company's finger on the pulse of new technologies.

ANY SHAPE, ANY FABRIC

The 'any shape, any fabric' concept makes it possible for customers to get various models of armchairs and sofas in many different fabrics and colors. Perhaps this sounds like nothing special, but it is presented on the John Lewis website in a highly imaginative way. All the models are shown in a neutral grey, so that the choice of model is not influenced by the color depicted. After that, with just a single click of your mouse you can see the model of your choice in a range of different materials and tints.[205] It all looks very similar to the approach of a recent British start-up...[206]

The challenge facing John Lewis was how to present a concept of this kind in an attractive manner on the shop floor. To answer this problem, the Lewis laboratory set up a test display that cost less than £ 1,000. Scale models of the armchair and sofa designs were made with a 3D-printer, with samples of the different fabrics placed alongside. All the elements are fitted with an RFID code.[207] If you put the model and fabric of your choice on a special presentation table, the 'finished' armchair or sofa is projected onto an adjacent computer screen. It's a neat and cheap idea.

> In a period of just ten weeks, no fewer than 65,000 customers used this test display in the John Lewis flagship store in London's Oxford Street. Many of the users were not even adults, but children who thought it was a great toy...![208]

WHICH IS BEST FOR YOU?

Each of the three models has a different function, although they can be used to complement each other. A supermarket might use a speedboat to launch a meal box onto the market, while it might prefer a tugboat to initiate a transformation process and a patrol boat to keep in touch with the latest technological innovations.

The following table offers a summary of the most important points:

	SPEEDBOAT	TUGBOAT	PATROL BOAT
OBJECTIVE	new business	transformation	learning
TIME HORIZON	short term	medium term	long term
SPEED OF IMPACT	high	average	low
SYNERGY	low	high	low
AUTONOMY	high	directed by senior management	high
SCOPE	broad or narrow	broad	ad hoc

A final important condition is that the company must have minimum scale to make it feasible to maintain permanent and independent teams to kick-start their transformation process. Even the development of a skill for Alexa can mean a relatively large investment for a smaller company. On the plus side, smaller companies do not need a tugboat to help them to change course.

In fact, they have all the necessary potential to operate as a speedboat. The biggest difference is that they have no option but to sharpen their priorities with fewer insights, because their more limited resources already puts an automatic cap on the number of paths they can follow.

THE ORGANIZATION

1. **To what extent do you possess the competencies to develop an adaptive strategy?**

   a. Do you have the ability to pick up signals quickly and correctly?
   b. Do you have the ability to experiment?
   c. Do you have the ability to mobilize for action?
   d. Do you have the ability to collaborate with other companies in complex systems?

2. **To what extent do you place an emphasis on stability rather than dynamism?**

   a. Is the threat imminent or latent?
      · How fast is the market changing? How much time do you have to react?
      · Are you competing with similar companies to your own or with greenfield players, and, in particular, with digital players?
   b. Does the threat to your organization and activities affect all or just part of your organization?
      · Are all your products threatened or just some of them?
      · Are all your target groups equally sensitive to your competitor's new offer?

3. **Which method is most suitable for increasing your agility?**

   a. The speedboat?
   b. The tugboat?
   c. The patrol boat?

CHAPTER 14
GETTING STARTED...

'Toute action est un empiétement sur l'avenir.'[*]

Henri-Louis Bergson (French author and philosopher)

---

[*] 'Every action is an encroachment on the future.'

'Before you start, you need to be fully aware that the digital age will be a golden time for companies that excel , but a nightmare for those that don't. As a result, retail is destined to become a sector of winners and losers. So make sure you go for gold! Discover the positive power of daring to think big. This is the only way that your company can become the new Messi in the retail landscape. And even if you don't reach the giddy heights of the Barcelona wunderkind, you can still significantly increase your chances of enjoying a successful career as a pro footballer. Sometimes in life (and in business) we have to settle for the bronze medal – and that is no mean achievement. But make sure you at least get to the finals and don't get knocked out in the qualification rounds!'

If you think you have read these words before... You have! They were the closing words to the introduction of this book. Now you have reached the final chapter. The time for action has arrived. Everything starts with learning how to think bigger, but in the end it is only concrete action that can win you that gold medal. *'Action expresses priorities'*, as Mahatma Gandhi so tellingly put it. In this last chapter, we will summarize all the key steps that will lead you to success.

1   CHOOSE YOUR TARGET MARKET AND BRING IT TO LIFE

Describe with sufficient clarity the target market in which you want to be the best:

» Target group: define the target segment and describe who your core customers are. Create a persona for each different type that will allow you to bring a specific segment to life. You must develop your competitive advantage with these core customers clearly in mind.
» Product categories: choose the categories where you can really make a difference. These are the categories where your core customers must opt to buy from you because you are much better than your competitors.
» Context: decide in which buying occasions you wish to excel.

Your strategic choice to focus on a particular target market also implies a choice about which markets you will not compete in. In your target market,

you must be the best; it is as simple as that. In other markets, you can be no
more than competitive.

The biggest potential pitfall is that your choice makes you blind to potential future developments. Guard against making snap judgments like: 'Our customers
are less digitally minded, so we don't need to do anything for the time being'.

2 SKETCH YOUR IDEAL CUSTOMER JOURNEY
FOR THE FUTURE

How would your core customers most like to purchase (and later use) your
strategic product categories during your most important buying occasions?

» Free yourself from all practical considerations. Think out of the box and
  take no account of the present situation and potential problems.
» Sketch the customer journey from end to end. Do not simply limit yourself
  to the path to purchase.
» Be aware that your ideal customer cannot sketch this journey for you. It is
  something you have to do yourself.

The ideal customer journey will give shape and form to your optichannel
strategy. It will set your direction of march. You can amend this at a later
stage, which will almost certainly be necessary. But your final destination will
always remain the same. It is possible that in your case there is no single ideal
customer journey; if so, sketch more than one. Customers are all different, so
they may need to be viewed in terms of a different product category and/or
context.

The biggest pitfall is that of getting lost in the detail. You can't have ten ideal
customer journeys. If this is the case, you haven't defined your target market
with sufficient clarity. You don't need to delineate each phase of the journey
right down to the finest operational detail. The aim is to identify and define
where you want to make a real difference in the future. This brings us to a
second common pitfall: you must be able to think out of the box, without any
reference to the current situation.

3 CONDUCT A SCAN OF YOUR ORGANIZATION AND ITS ENVIRONMENT

You need to set the right priorities in your strategic planning. To make this possible, you first need to analyze the current situation and assess likely developments in the short and medium term.

» Carry out a technology scan. Which technologies will be available today, tomorrow and the day after tomorrow? How can they contribute towards your ideal customer journey? Do you need to adjust that journey to take account of the impact of these technologies?

» Carry out a competitor analysis. Who are your most important competitors today, tomorrow and the day after tomorrow? Make a distinction between companies comparable to your own and the new digital players. Take account of the increased blurring of sectoral boundaries. Is the threat posed by the rise of new competitors imminent or latent? Will these competitors have an impact on your company as a whole or only on specific target groups and/or product categories?

» Assess your financial strength. How large is your free cash flow? What additional sources of financing can you free up? Is external financing via shares or loans a possibility? Can you sell off assets or even part of your operations? Do you have options for outsourcing and/or strategic partnerships? Can you participate in a network or ecosystem?

The situation analysis is the most important input for transforming your vision of the ideal customer journey into concrete plans.

The biggest pitfall is the danger of overestimating the impact of new technologies in the short term and underestimating their impact in the long term. As a consequence, there is a risk that the threats posed by new competitors will not be taken seriously, so that your cash flow eventually runs dry. It is, of course, perverse that a healthy operating cash flow is a condition for securing external financing. In short, you need to repair your roof while the weather is still fine!

4 DETERMINE YOUR PLANNING FOR MOVING TOWARDS YOUR IDEAL CUSTOMER JOURNEY

'Vision without action is a daydream. Action without vision is a nightmare.' Or so says an old Japanese saying. This step must launch your implementation phase:

» On the basis of your competitor analysis and the current state of technological progress, you must determine what the conditions are to compete in your target market, both today and tomorrow. How are you going to achieve the Olympic minimum? How much will this cost?

» Bearing in mind your available financial resources and the evolution of technology, which actions will you take today and tomorrow to move you closer towards your ideal customer journey? What competitive advantages will you have today and tomorrow? How much will this cost?

» Will your cash flow allow you to take these actions? If not, how can you solve this problem? Can you sharpen your focus by selling assets and terminating certain activities? Can you collaborate with others?

» In particular, you must pay close attention to your data strategy for today. What data do you need in which phases of the customer journey? How can you obtain this data? How can you transform the data into useable information?

The answers to these questions should make possible the compilation of a concrete action plan for the short and medium term. Who will do what and by which date? What performance indicators will be used?

The biggest pitfall is that you attempt to implement this plan too rigidly. The longer the time horizon, the greater the likelihood that developments in the future will make adjustments necessary. In other words, you need an adaptive strategy. A second possible pitfall is that you pull the wool over your own eyes by ignoring the realities of the situation. That you underestimate the challenge and overestimate your resources and resilience.

5 BUILDING THE RIGHT LEVEL OF AGILITY INTO YOUR ORGANIZATION

The analysis in step 3 also helps you to determine the level of agility you need in your organization:

» To what extent do you need to act quickly, because the digital threat is imminent rather than latent? To what extent does the threat affect all of the organization or just part of it?
» In your organization and context, what is the ideal balance between stability and agility?
» How can you increase your organizational agility? Will you opt for a speedboat, a tugboat, a patrol boat or a combination of all three? Or is your company sufficiently small to be directed from the top of the organization? The key question is to what extent you require either synergy or independence between the old and new way of doing things.

It is difficult to see an increase in agility as an element in a step-by-step plan. As a process, it is probably the most critical success factor of all for building the right kind of organization for your circumstances.

The biggest pitfall is your commitment to agility being more in word than in deed. Senior management must be in agreement on this matter and make their vision clear throughout all levels of the organization. Teams that are responsible for implementing the transformation must be fully supported from the top.

6 CHOOSE AN APPROPRIATE STRATEGY

The first three steps are based on assumptions and estimates. You make hypotheses about the requirements of your target market, the ideal customer journey, the development of technology, the strengths of the competition and of your own organization. Sadly, in our complex and rapidly changing world the future remains highly unpredictable. As a result, you need to question and reassess your assumptions almost continuously, so that you can adapt your vision, strategy and planning.

- » Do you have the ability to pick up signals quickly and correctly?
- » Do you have the ability to experiment?
- » Do you have the ability to mobilize for action?
- » Do you have the ability to work together with other companies in complex systems?

The manner in which you deal with these matters is inextricably linked with the level of agility in your organization. The more dynamic your organization becomes, the more frequently you will need to adapt your strategy. In particular, you will need to constantly re-attune the right balance between dynamism and stability.

This is where the biggest pitfall lies. If you adapt more quickly than is necessary, you will suffer from the same cultural disadvantages as a start-up: chaos, the reinvention of the wheel and, ultimately, a lack of efficiency and strategic direction. At the other end of the spectrum, if you adapt too slowly, you will lose your grip on the rapidly changing circumstances, which risks sending you into a negative spiral.

7   INITIATING THE RIGHT FOLLOW-UP

In a traditional organization with a classic strategy, we link hard performance benchmarks (KPIs) to quantifiable objectives with a clear time line. Where do you want to be in a years' time and how can you measure it?

In an agile organization that works with an adaptive strategy, it is necessary to have two different sets of performance indicators:

- » For projects and processes in which stability takes precedence over dynamism, it is possible to use traditional indicators, including the detailed level of planning and the frequency of evaluation.

» For the projects and processes in which dynamism takes precedence over stability, it is necessary to work less with strict planning, but to increase the frequency of evaluation and follow-up. In this case, the evaluation must place a greater emphasis on the learning effect than on the realization of concrete objectives.

In this way, the evaluation process is in keeping with the desired balance between stability and dynamism.

The biggest pitfall is that the evaluation will attempt to weigh the stable and dynamic projects against each other. This must be avoided, since it creates negative energy. Those who are evaluated under traditional KPIs think it is unfair that they are subject to stricter objectives, for which failure is not an option. Those who work on the more dynamic projects feel that they are always standing in the shadow of traditional activities, when it comes to size of budget, size of team and overall impact on the organization (see box below).

KPIS IN A 'FAIL FAST, LEARN FAST' WORLD?

Would you invest in something if your chance of success was only 10%? But what if that success would bring you a hundred-fold return? Amazon wouldn't hesitate. Their answer is: 'Do it!'[209]

This betrays an attitude you simply won't find in traditional companies – even though taking risks, experimenting and failing is the quickest way to gain new insights. In agile companies, space is deliberately created to make this possible. Jeff Bezos writes with justifiable pride: 'I believe we are the best place in the world to fail (we have plenty of practice!).'[210] Just like Facebook, whose office walls are covered with posters bearing slogans such as 'Move fast & break things.'[211]

This kind of culture requires a special kind of evaluation process. Otherwise, which manager would ever be prepared to initiate a

project with only a 10% chance of success, if he knew he would
be evaluated on the basis of its success or failure?

With this in mind, let's compare the traditional and new methods of working. First, the traditional way. Let's imagine that
we want to test a product presentation in a brick-and-mortar
store network. First, we take a lot of time to judiciously choose
the right test design. Then we carefully select the right stores
in which to carry out the test and the control stores that will
be used to compare the results. The most senior (and usually
oldest) manager will have the final word about how the test will
actually be carried out.

Now, the new way. Let's imagine we want to amend a product
presentation in a webshop. If we have an interesting idea, we
test it immediately. We don't discuss in advance whether or not
it will work. Instead, we just show a percentage of customers
a variant: the so-called A/B test. Within 24 hours, we will know
whether the alternative presentation produces better results.
If it doesn't, at least we have learnt something (and all we have
lost is a little bit of turnover). If it does, we make the necessary
adjustments and are ready to move on to the next test. The
manager doesn't need to be involved. The data will make the
decision.

Sadly, A/B tests only work well for operational experiments. For
these kinds of experiments you would be mad not to use them,
especially as they are also extremely low-cost. But what about
more strategic projects? They tend to require greater resources
and more people, as a result of which they are followed up more
closely by senior management. In a speedboat approach, we
might even set up a separate company to do it. With a patrol
boat approach, we would work via projects. But in both cases
the innovative nature of what is involved makes it very difficult
to correctly predict the outcome. Consequently, we are working
in great uncertainty. This explains why for innovative projects

less time is spent in detailed planning and more time is spent on frequent evaluation.

It also explains why Govindarajan and Trimble propose the learning effect as the ultimate performance indicator.[212] At the start of the project, estimates about the eventual outcome are no more than a wild guess. Given the high degree of uncertainty and the innovative nature of the undertaking, you can't really blame the project team for this. But as the project progresses, the wild guess first becomes an educated guess and, eventually, a relatively reliable prediction. This increasing ability to more accurately predict the outcome is a sign that the team is gaining more control over what is happening. In other words, the learning effect is significant. You could falsely interpret this to mean that the setting of objectives and the measuring of results is not important at the beginning of the project. But the opposite is actually true: it is only by predicting and measuring outcome from the beginning that you can see if the predictions are becoming increasingly more accurate.

Because tolerance of failure is not in keeping with the tradition- al way of working, it is very important to separate the evaluation of dynamic environments from the evaluation of stable ones. In a traditional organization, 99% of the personnel work in a stable environment. Since this is the environment where 99% of the turnover is earned and strict planning is in place to make this possible, failure is indeed not an option!

The 1% of staff who work on innovation projects contribute very little to the company's business results in the short term. On the contrary, they cost the company a bucketful of money.

What's more, they are allowed – according to popular perception – to assess the likely outcome of this expenditure with what is effectively a 'wet finger' approach. And they are not even repri- manded when things go wrong (as they often do).

When you are preparing your budget cycle, you are asking for trouble if you let the innovative teams and the traditional teams make their pitches on the same day. Not only can it heighten the unhealthy rivalry (even envy) between the teams, but it makes things difficult for senior management, who find it hard to switch back and forth between the different kinds of evaluation that both teams require.

8 ENSURE THAT THE ENTIRE APPROACH IS PERIODICALLY UPDATED

In a complex and rapidly changing world, five-year plans are doomed to failure. The further you look ahead, the more you talk about your vision of the future and the less you make concrete strategic plans.

But this does not relieve you from the obligation of redoing your 'homework' periodically. You may spend less time on making plans, but you need to spend more time on re-evaluating the plans you do have. You must make sure that you are still on the right track. It is not necessary to have a fixed timetable for these re-evaluations, since this goes against the concept of an agile organization. Instead, your ability to pick up signals quickly and correctly will allow you to discover organically when you need to adapt. That being said, it would be unwise to take the risk that you might miss certain signals or that they do not penetrate sufficiently within your organizational structure. For this reason, it is always advisable to have a minimum frequency of reappraisal. Doing it annually is sensible, but there is no harm in doing it more often, if you feel there is a need.

To finish this section, I would like to paraphrase Anne Mulcahy, the former CEO of Xerox: *'Strategies have a shelf life. Timeliness trumps perfection.'*[213] Or to put it differently: the quickest way to success is to devise an imperfect plan quickly and then evaluate it regularly to make sure you are still moving in the right direction – and amend it if you are not.

A BEAUTIFUL SPRING DAY IN 2030...

'The best thing about the future is

that it comes one day at a time.'

Abraham Lincoln (American president)

A BEAUTIFUL SPRING DAY IN 2030 ACCORDING TO THE GOSPEL OF THE DIGITAL GURU

It looks like being a beautiful day. For the first time this year, the temperature is set to nudge above the 20°C mark. In short, ideal weather for doing something outdoors!

It's amazing how much easier life is than it used to be, certainly now that we've got an iButler in our home! I hesitated before having the chip implanted in my head, but now I'm really glad I did it. It means I don't even need to talk to James – that's the name we've given him. The chip sends my brainwaves directly to him via the wireless network.

Yesterday, I asked James to order a new lawnmower, because the old robot one was badly in need of replacement. From now on, James will mow the grass. That's why we bought a hand-operated mower this time. I even let him choose the mower that best suited him. It's being delivered this afternoon, but of course that doesn't mean we have to stay at home. We've been using a smart lock to let the courier into the garage for years. So James will be able to get on with mowing the grass straight away!

I ask him to reserve a car. It will come and pick us up at 11 o'clock. It's a shame, but there are no longer any convertibles available. Still, I suppose that was to be expected on the first nice day of spring. Everyone wants to feel the sun on their skin again. I console myself with the thought that Corine and myself will soon be enjoying a leisurely aperitif without the need to worry about whether we have drunk too much to drive.

Twenty years ago, we seldom left the house before lunchtime, because there was always so much we had to do. Shopping, for example. I always hated shopping for groceries on Saturday morning. But what a difference now with James! He keeps a check on exactly what we've got in our fridge and cupboards, and can look into our agendas to see when we will be eating at home and when not. And the menus he suggests for the coming week are really great. To top it all, thanks to UsChat he even knows what we ordered at the pizzeria last Sunday, so he also knows he doesn't need to suggest insalata Caprese for a while!

This evening, the children are coming to visit. James is well aware that wraps is what they love to eat the most, just like when they were living at home. Because he can listen in when the kids phone us, he doesn't need to ask whether all three of them are coming and whether they are bringing anyone with them. He adjusts his shopping list automatically. It's also handy that he can clean the vegetables and prepare the guacamole. It's much better than what I used to make and it means we don't need to get home early this afternoon to slave away in the kitchen. What a luxury!

The groceries will be delivered at around 4 o'clock. James will receive them and put them away. He knows exactly where everything needs to go in the fridge, freezer and cupboards.

So, time to set off for our day out. Now where the hell did I put my walking shoes? Corine reminds me that I left them at the coast last time we were there. No problem. I really need a new pair anyway. James downloads the same model and size for me and prints them off on the 3D-printer.

Okay, I think we're ready to go. I wonder where that car is? It should have been here by now. I hope we don't get a Skoda again…

A BEAUTIFUL SPRING DAY IN 2030: BEYOND THE DIGITAL HYSTERIA

It looks like being a beautiful day. For the first time, this year the temperature is set to nudge above the 20°C mark. In short, ideal weather for doing something outdoors!

It's amazing how much easier life is than it used to be, even though that old idea about a single robot taking over all our household tasks is still just a pipe dream. Of course, we can't complain. In addition to a robot lawn mower and vacuum cleaner, we recently got a kitchen robot as well, to help with the cooking. You wouldn't believe the time it saves!

The children are coming to visit this evening. Now that Soccer Analytica, the AI start-up of our youngest son, William, has FC Barcelona as one of its main customers, he is seldom in the country. We'll be eating wraps, just like we used to when they lived at home, but we'll be using that delicious Not Chicken from NotCo. I never imagined that I would one day become a vegetarian! The kitchen robot can clean the vegetables, but I'll be making the guacamole: it's still the best in town! Last time, we left it to the robot, but it wasn't good: far too much pepper!

Last Christmas, I was given an iButler as a present. I have called him James. He's not much more than a toy, really – certainly if you see how much he costs. He's a kind of Siri on wheels. The neighbors have one as well and use him to mow their grass, but you need to buy a special hand-operated mower. For me, my old robot mower is more than good enough – and does the job just as good.

The only really useful thing about James is that I can send him alone to the baker's on the corner to buy a loaf of bread. Or at least I could. I don't do it anymore, because all you read about in the papers is the increasing number of iButlers being stolen on the street. Last week, the police rolled up a network of these butler-nabbers, but I still don't trust it. Apparently, it's a piece of cake to re-boot an iButler, so that it is no longer traceable.

Luckily, I remembered to add bread to the list of groceries that are being delivered this morning. I always prefer to be at home when that happens.

Then I can put everything away where I know I can find it again! Besides, I am one of those people – and there are lots of us – who still thinks there's something a bit creepy about deliveries with smart locks. That's something else I don't trust…

'What's that you said, James? Okay, thanks.' 'Corine, James has just got a message that the groceries will be delivered between twenty past ten and twenty to eleven. Shall we leave straight away after that?'

It's really useful that the supermarket can predict our shopping list with reasonable accuracy. And it's amazing that nowadays they can even take account of special promotions. They know I would rather buy in an extra bottle of laundry detergent when there is a special offer, rather than wait until our last bottle has run out. Since the consumer association proved that you pay more if you let Alexa compile and order your list, lots of people have started making their own lists again…

So, time to set off for our day out. Now where the hell did I put my walking shoes? Corine reminds me that I left them at the coast last time we were there. No problem, I'll just buy a new pair. James finds a cool looking model that's available in my size and in stock in a shoe shop not too far from here. Within half an hour, they are delivered by a SprintBot. It's just as well we don't live near the canal, where the couriers refuse to use their robots anymore. If they don't get stolen, they get vandalized. Last week, they pulled out fifty or so that had been pushed into the water…

Now that the kids have moved out, I have bought myself a convertible again! It's great! Okay, it's now a self-driving model, but at least it's mine! Call me old fashioned, but I have never really liked that idea of car-sharing. In theory, you can select your size and model – like hiring a car in the old days – and they tempt you with a flashy photo of a Volkswagen. But when you open your front door, you usually find a Skoda waiting for you! And if the last user left it in a mess, that's just your bad luck.

That's why a lot of people are giving up the idea of car-sharing. The analogy with the transition from horse to car just doesn't wash anymore. They used to tell us that at the start of the 20th century you exchanged your horse for a car, but could keep a horse as a hobby, if you still wanted to ride one. And they suggested it was the same with a self-owned car at the start of the 21st century. What nonsense! We were expected to exchange our own property for shared property, but that's not the same thing at all. As a result, self-owned cars are back in fashion – to the extent that the socialist party is now pleading for a luxury tax on private car ownership.

Before we go, I think I've just got time to watch the news in the garden. A few months ago, the Chinese president for life was forced to resign under popular pressure against the Social Credit system. And now the first free elections have been won by Duan Zi and his Freedom Party. Super! In his victory speech, he repeats his promise to give back the Chinese their privacy and to abolish all systems that allow the government to rate individual citizens. The first step will be the dismantling of WeChat. It seems that the supremacy of Tencent, Alibaba and JD.com is over...

Ah, the SprintBot is here already. Thanks to the 3D-scan of my feet, the new walking shoes fit perfectly. And look, the groceries have just arrived as well! We'll put them away quickly and then we can leave. I'm really looking forward to that aperitif, and perhaps a glass or two of wine with lunch. They're wonderful things, those self-driving cars!

A WORD OF THANKS

The last couple of months, I spent nearly every school holiday and long week-end shut off from the outside world. Writing is indeed a lonely activity. So this book was penned in more or less complete isolation, but at least I had a nice view of the sea. For me, this was a highly inspirational and productive period. For my partner, however, it was a very busy period, during which the task of caring for the children fell entirely on her shoulders. Thank you Corine, for giving me the space I needed. And an even bigger thank you for being who you are, so that together we can be what we are!

The ideas in this book have ripened through collaboration with companies and in many fascinating discussions with entrepreneurs and managers. This is the only way to keep in touch with the real challenges and the solutions that work. For this reason, my heartfelt thanks also go to my many clients – big and small, retailers and manufacturers – who each in their own sector wrestle with these challenges and solutions every day.

In particular, I would like to express my gratitude to the companies with whom I have a deeper relationship. The growth path of the FNG fashion house, where I am one of the board members, has served – and continues to serve – as a kind of non-stop laboratory to develop my ideas around optichannel. On the advisory board at Tribu, we have discovered together how it is possible in the digital era to put high-end garden furniture in the worldwide market spotlight. At the Trade Marketing Association we explore the crucial interaction between brand manufacturers and retailers in a rapidly changing world. It was a privilege to have witnessed these developments from the very front row.

In addition to my company connections, I am also delighted to be a part of a number of super-interesting ecosystems. At Vlerick Business School, I have the pleasure of interacting with brilliant people, both colleagues and participants, who together create an innovative culture in which you realize that the world is so much more than just retail.

RetailDetail gives me access to one of the most trend-setting hubs for the retail sector on the European continent. At the same time, it is also a window on the world – and one to which I am happy to make a contribution. Thanks, Jorg & co.!

Every author owes a debt to those critical readers who are willing to read his draft texts. They always add something extra! So thank you to Jan Huysmans, who let loose his e-commerce expertise on my manuscript. And thank you to Marc Buelens, whose many expertly crafted assists only needed tapping into the goal by me.

Last but not least, I am convinced that even in our digital age a good publisher will remain as relevant as ever. The title, the theme, the lay-out, the editing, the marketing... No author can do it all by himself. These are mission-critical tasks that I was certainly happy to outsource! Thank you for all your hard work, Hilde, Niels, Lotte and everyone behind the scenes.

Gino Van Ossel

END NOTES

1   Source: Yahoo Finance – consulted on 11 February 2018.

2   Walmart, Costco, Home Depot, Walgreens Boots Alliance and Kroger.

3   See amongst others https://en.wikipedia.org/wiki/Greater_fool_theory

4   Over a longer period, technology shares do record a higher share price to earnings ratio. During the past five years, this amounted to an average of 31.72 for the Nasdaq against 21.80 for the S&P 500 general share index. Sources: Ycharts.com (Nasdaq) and multpl.com (S&P500) – consulted on 11 February 2018.

5   https://pando.com/2013/01/30/andreessen-predicts-the-death-of-traditional-retail-yes-absolute-death/ – consulted on 15 February 2013.

6   Fully in line with his column of two years earlier in *The Wall Street Journal*: M. Andreessen (11 August 2011). 'Why software is eating the world', *The Wall Street Journal*.

7   https://en.wikipedia.org/wiki/Marc_Andreessen – consulted on 9 February 2018.

8   https://www.theguardian.com/us-news/2017/jul/22/mall-of-america-minnesota-retail-anniversary – consulted on 31 August 2017.

9   See amongst others http://www.wnd.com/2015/05/retail-apocalypse-6000-chains-closing-stores/ – consulted on 15 January 2018.

10   See also https://www.forbes.com/sites/gregmaloney/2017/10/23/retail-apocalypse-yawn/#39805b65df2e – consulted on 31 October 2017.

11   https://www.mingtiandi.com/real-estate/china-retail-real-estate-news/jd-com-says-it-will-open-1000-convenience-stores-every-day/ – consulted on 22 April 2018.

12   https://news.sky.com/story/house-of-fraser-lenders-call-ey-for-help-amid-high-street-crisis-11301591 – consulted on 31 March 2018.

13   https://www.bloomberg.com/graphics/2017-retail-debt/ – consulted on 13 February 2018.

14   Zalando started in the Netherlands in 2010.

15   S. Van Belleghem (2017). *Customers the day after tomorrow. Hoe trek je klanten aan in een wereld van AI, bots en automatisering?* Leuven: LannooCampus.

16   J. Snoeck & P. Neerman (2017). *The Future of Shopping. Waar iedereen retailer is.* Leuven: LannooCampus.

17   https://www.nrc.nl/nieuws/2018/03/02/wie-wil-blijven-moet-veranderen-a1594262 – consulted on 2 April 2018.

18   These figures relate to 2016 and may have risen in the meantime. Even so, e-groceries still score lower than other sectors. https://www.kantarworldpanel.com/en/PR/UK-online-grocery-sales-reach-73-market-share – consulted on 15 September 2017.

19   The figures for this paragraph were obtained from a presentation given by Valérie Vander Haeghen, Shopper Based Design Leads Europe, P&G at the Vlerick Business School (January 2018).

20   See, for example, the Twinkle100 for the Netherlands in 2016.

21   In 2016, the largest 18 were responsible for 44% of worldwide turnover (source: Internet Retailer's Ranking of the World's Top 1000 e-Retailers 2017). In view of the rapid rate of consolidation, I estimate that by now this figure has risen to around 50%.

22   https://www.digitalcommerce360.com/article/us-ecommerce-sales/ – consulted on 17 February 2018.

23   https://www.forbes.com/sites/mikalbelicove/2013/09/18/how-many-u-s-based-online-retail-stores-are-on-the-internet/#334fed4837a4 – consulted on 13 February 2018.

24   Details for the company in 2017, for Belgium and the Netherlands combined.

25   https://www.nrc.nl/nieuws/2018/02/02/de-donkere-wolk-boven-bolcom-a1590816 – consulted on 13 February 2018.

26   https://twinklemagazine.nl/2017/09/twinkle100-2017/index.xml – consulted on 13 February 2018.

27   ASOS turnover growth for 2017, as reported in https://www.asosplc.com/~/media/Files/A/Asos-V2/reports-and-presentations/quarterly-trading-statement-2018.pdf – consulted on 15 March 2018.

28   Zalando turnover growth for 2017, as reported in https://corporate.zalando.com/en/ investor-relations/en/press-releases/zalando-advances-growth-course – consulted on 15 March 2018.

29   https://en.wikipedia.org/wiki/1-Click – consulted on 14 February 2018.

30 https://www.shortyawards.com/9th/zero-click-ordering – consulted on 14 February 2018.

31 https://www.time.com/4283913/dominos-zero-click-ordering-app/ – consulted on 14 February 2018.

32 https://www.campaignlive.co.uk/article/case-study-dominos-crispin-porter-bogusky-transformed-pizza-chain-tech-company/1422647 – consulted on 14 February 2018.

33 M. Schaeffer (2017). *Het geheim van bol.com*. Amsterdam: Atlas Contact.

34 https://www.statista.com/statistics/623555/distribution-of-amazon-traffic-by-source/ – consulted on 14 February 2018.

35 See, for example: https://www.wolfgangdigital.com/uploads/general/eComK-PI2016-Public2.pdf – consulted on 13 February 2018.

36 http://uk.businessinsider.com/amazon-market-share-china-alibaba-jd-chart-2017-2?r=US&IR=T – consulted on 13 February 2018.

37 https://www.twinkle.be/nieuws/169545/10-grootste-webshops-belgie-volgens-twinkle100/ – consulted on 13 February 2018.

38 Presentation given by Giovanni Colauto, CEO of De Bijenkorf, Captains of Benelux, Vianen (September 2014).

39 These and the following figures are based on: *The State of Omnichannel* (2017). Bristol: Brightpearl.

40 International research has yielded many similar insights, but do not always use the same definitions. In '*CEO Viewpoint 2017: the Transformation of Retail* (January2017) JDA/PWC is 10% omnichannel/profitable, 12% omnichannel/unprofitable and 38% cross-channel. In *The State of Omnichannel* study by Brightpearl (2017) 91% of retailers stated that they had an omnichannel strategy, but only 8% that they were 'mastering omnichannel'.

41 Particpants in the Vlerick Retail Platform, October 2017 (n=84).

42 Amazon (2017). *Annual Report*.

43 https://www.asosplc.com/investors/our-strategy#our-opportunity – consulted on 15 March 2018.

44 Based on V. Mayer-Schönberger & K. Cuckier (2013). *Big Data. A Revolution That Will Transform How We Live, Work and Think. Introduction to chapter 4*. London: John Murray.

45 https://www.digitalcommerce360.com/2017/10/02/nike-signals-shift-away-who-lesale-channel/ – consulted on 15 October 2017.

46 http://s1.q4cdn.com/806093406/files/doc_financials/2017/Q2/FY18-Q2-Com-bined-NIKE-Press-Release-Schedules.pdf – consulted on 15 March 2018.

47 https://www.statista.com/statistics/268451/distribution-of-esprit-sales-by-distri-bution-channel/ – consulted on 15 March 2018.

48 https://www.userlike.com/en/blog/multichannel-vs-omnichannel – consulted on 3 April 2018.

49 https://www.business2community.com/digital-marketing/sms-versus-email-marketing-0957139#!bth7SG – consulted on 3 April 2018.

50 https://www.forbes.com/sites/jasonbloomberg/2016/12/23/how-dbs-bank-be-came-the-best-digital-bank-in-the-world-by-becoming-invisible/#45b844d13061 – consulted on 3 April 2018.

51 https://www.astutesolutions.com/blog/articles/beyond-the-buzzword-opti-chan-nel-engagement – consulted on 3 April 2018.

52 https://www.proximus.be/support/nl/id_sfaqr_device_return_dcd/particulieren/welkom-bij-support/televisie/tv-een-probleem-oplossen/andere-oplossingen/een-toestel-omruilen-of-terugsturen.html – consulted on 7 June 2018.

53 https://www.sec.gov/Archives/edgar/data/1018724/000119312517120198/d373368dex991.htm – consulted on 4 April 2018.

54 https://www.sec.gov/Archives/edgar/data/1018724/000119312517120198/d373368dex991.htm – consulted on 4 April 2018.

55 https://www.sec.gov/Archives/edgar/data/1018724/000119312517120198/d373368dex991.htm – consulted on 4 April 2018.

56 https://www.corporatefinanceinstitute.com/resources/knowledge/finance/hockey- stick-effect/ – consulted on 4 June 2018.

57 https://www.foodpersonality.nl/klantenkring-ah-vs-jumbo-p04-2016/ – consulted on 5 April 2018.

58 MRO stands for Maintenance, Repair and Operations. The term relates to spare parts, maintenace products and tools that are used in production companies.

59 https://www.asosplc.com/investors/our-strategy#our-opportunity – consulted on 5 May 2018.

60 M. Schaeffer (2017). *Het geheim van bol.com*. Amsterdam: Atlas Contact, p. 144 and following.

61 https://www.sec.gov/Archives/edgar/data/1018724/000119312517120198/d373368dex991.htm – consulted on 4 April 2018.

62 https://edition.cnn.com/travel/article/most-popular-cities-international-travel-2017-mastercard/index.html – consulted on 4 April 2018.

63 Hamleys is now part of the French Ludendo Group, one of the largest toy retailers in Europe, with stores in France, Belgium and Spain.

64 https://www.sec.gov/Archives/edgar/data/ 1018724/000119312517120198/d373368dex991.htm – consulted on 4 April 2018.

65 ComScore via https://www.emerce.nl/research/reizigers-geen-voorkeur-bestem-ming-vakantie – consulted on 6 June 2018.

66 ComScore via https://www.emerce.nl/research/reizigers-geen-voorkeur-bestem-ming-vakantie – consulted on 6 June 2018.

67 http://www.kiddotravel.be/ – consulted on 6 June 2018.

68 https://srprs.me/nl – consulted on 6 June 2018.

69 https://www.pockies.nl/shop/heren-boxershorts/ – consulted on 4 April 2018.

70 https://www.forbes.com/sites/forbesagencycouncil/2018/01/29/the-continued-rise-of-voice-search-and-how-your-business-can-leverage-it/#7af4074f301c – consulted on 4 April 2018.

71 For the most recent updates, see Wikipedia: https://en.wikipedia.org/wiki/Amazon_Echo

72 https://www.techcrunch.com/2018/01/12/39-million-americans-now-own-a-smart- speaker-report-claims/ – consulted on 5 April 2018.

73 https://www.forbes.com/sites/johnkoetsier/2018/05/25/massive-rever-sal-google-home-sales-explode-483-to-beat-amazon-for-smart-speaker-crown/2/#77dbff6f7643 – consulted on 3 June 2018.

74 https://www.Juneperresearch.com/researchstore/innovation-disruption/digital-voice-assistants/platforms-revenues-opportunities – consulted on 5 April 2018.

75 *Amazon Intelligence: Voice, excerpt* (June 2017). Gartner L2.

76 https://searchenginewatch.com/2016/09/27/more-online-product-searches-start-on-amazon-than-google/ – consulted on 30 September 2016.

77 https://www.nytimes.com/2017/08/30/technology/amazon-alexa-microsoft-cortana.html – consulted on 5 April 2018.

78 https://www.gva.be/cnt/dmf20171220_03253954/antwerpse-pakjesbezorger-parci-fy-overgenomen-door-bpost – consulted on 5 June 2018.

79 http://www.transportmedia.be/parcify-test-slimme-sloten-voor-pakjeslevering-in-huis/ – consulted on 4 May 2018.

80 https://www.techcrunch.com/2017/09/21/walmart-partners-with-smart-lock-maker- august-to-test-in-home-delivery-of-packages-and-groceries/ – consulted on 25 September 2017.

81 http://waitrose.pressarea.com/pressrelease/details/78/NEWS_13/10145 – consulted on 17 October 2018.

82 https://www.cnbc.com/2017/06/22/amazon-echo-show-gets-smart-doorbell-support.html – consulted on 25 September 2017.

83 https://www.venturebeat.com/2018/03/02/ai-weekly-amazons-ring-acquisition-is- about-letting-a-giant-through-your-front-door/ – consulted on 5 April 2018.

84 https://www.techcrunch.com/2016/09/15/amazon-echo-owners-spend-more-on-ama- zon-says-npd/ – consulted on 20 September 2018.

85 D. Murph (4 October 2011). 'iPhone4S hands-on!' *Engadget*.

86 http://uk.businessinsider.com/98-of-iphone-users-have-tried-siri-but-most-dont-use-it-regularly-2016-6?r=US&IR=T – consulted on 5 April 2017.

87 https://www.prnewswire.com/news-releases/teens-use-voice-search-most-even-in-bathroom-googles-mobile-voice-study-finds-279106351.html – consulted on 5 April 2018.

88 https://www.thinkwithgoogle.com/consumer-insights/voice-assistance-consumer-experience/ – consulted on 5 April 2018.

89 https://www.forbes.com/sites/jaysondemers/2018/01/09/why-you-need-to-prepare-for-a-voice-search-revolution/#18cdd70c34af – consulted on 5 April 2018.

90 https://www.searchengineland.com/voice-search-explosion-will-change-local-search-251776 – consulted on 5 April 2018.

91 https://www.thinkwithgoogle.com/data-gallery/detail/voice-assistance-natural-language/ – consulted on 5 April 2018.

92 https://www.adage.com/article/digital/hey-alexa-voice-strategy-brands/310893/ – consulted on 5 April 2018.

93 https://www.ocadotechnology.com/blog/alexa-ask-ocado-to-add-tea-to-my-basket/ – consulted on 5 April 2018.

94 https://www.nieuws.ah.nl/met-siri-je-boodschappenlijstje-maken-in-de-appie-app/ – consulted on 5 May 2018.

95 https://www.dutchcowboys.nl/technology/amazon-echo-is-officieel-te-krijgen-in-nederland-maar – consulted on 5 April 2018.

96 https://www.developer.amazon.com/docs/custom-skills/develop-skills-in-multiple- languages.html – consulted on 3 June 2018.

97 https://www.techcrunch.com/2018/02/23/google-assistant-will-support-over-30-lan- guages-by-year-end-become-multilingual/ – consulted on 12 April 2018.

98 https://www.amazon.com/P-G-Productions-Tide-Remover/dp/B01M9B7ZTB – consulted on 12 April 2018.

99 https://www.amazon.com/s/ref=nb_sb_ss_i_1_4?url=search-alias%3Dalexa-skills&field-keywords=campbells+kitchen&sprefix=camp%2Calexa-skills%2C218&crid=28NOO39657JS7 – consulted on 12 April 2018.

100 https://www.cnet.com/news/all-the-new-alexa-announcements-from-ifa-2017/ – consulted on 12 April 2018.

101 https://www.l2inc.com/daily-insights/how-alexa-transforms-brand-visibility-on-amazon – consulted on 12 April 2018.

102 https://www.amazon.com/One-Future-Don-Peppers/dp/0385485662 – consulted on 6 April 2018.

103 https://howtospendit.ft.com/womens-style/202881-inside-the-shops-of-the-future – consulted on 6 April 2018.

104 M. Duggan & S.D. Levitt. 'Winning Isn't Everything: Corruption in Sumo Wrestling'. American Economic Review, 92. December 2002, pp. 1594-1605.

105 T. Brants & A. Franz (2006). *Web 1T5-Gram Version1*. Linguistic Data Consortium.

106 https://bits.blogs.nytimes.com/2012/03/28/bizarre-insights-from-big-data/ – consulted on 6 April 2018.

107 https://blogs.scientificamerican.com/guest-blog/9-bizarre-and-surprising-insights-from-data-science/ – consulted on 7 April 2018.

108 https://patents.google.com/patent/US6266649 – consulted on 7 April 2018.

109 https://www.hbr.org/2018/02/the-most-successful-brands-focus-on-users-not-buyers – consulted on 7 April 2018.

110 https://www.walgreens.com/steps/brhc-loggedout.jsp – consulted on 7 April 2018.

111 http://www.mobihealthnews.com/44291/more-than-70-percent-of-walgreens-rewards-tracking-members-were-still-active-after-a-year – consulted on 7 April 2018.

112 http://www.mobihealthnews.com/content/walgreens-pill-reminder-activity-tracking-both-improved-medication-adherence-study – consulted on 7 April 2018.

113 https://www.walgreens.com/images/adaptive/si/pdf/Immunizations_ARM_BRHC_Flu_Poster_Final.pdf – consulted on 7 April 2018.

114 http://www.pearsoned.co.uk/bookshop/detail.asp?item=100000000128831 – consulted on 8 April 2018.

115 https://www.lincherie.nl/LS_experience_center.html – consulted on 8 April 2018.

116 https://www.mckinsey.com/industries/retail/our-insights/the-need-for-speed-capturing-todays-fashion-consumer – consulted on 5 May 2018.

117 https://www.parool.nl/amsterdam/heineken-stapt-met-beerwulf-in-online-bierhandel~a4474630/ – consulted on 5 May 2018.

118 https://www.tijd.be/ondernemen/voeding-drank/De-niet-te-stillen-datahonger-van-Carlos-Brito/9979564 – consulted on 5 May 2018.

119 http://www.weissbeerger.com/ – consulted on 5 May 2018.

120 https://www.coolblue.nl/klantenservice/23/informatie-over/bescherming-persoonsgegevens.html – consulted on 7 April 2018.

121 https://techcrunch.com/2016/06/01/it-might-be-time-to-stop-looking-for-the-wechat-of-the-west/ – consulted on 15 June 2016.

122 https://www.wired.co.uk/article/chinese-government-social-credit-score-privacy-invasion – consulted on 7 April 2018.

123 https://www.adidasknitforyou.com/#home – consulted on 8 April 2018.

124 https://www.designboom.com/technology/adidas-knit-for-you-03-22-2017/ – consulted on 8 April 2018.

125 https://www.cnbc.com/2016/09/15/netflix-and-kill-is-streaming-hurting-movie-theaters.html – consulted on 8 April 2018.

126 https://www.across-magazine.com/revolution-film-projection/ – consulted on 5 May 2018.

127 *Retail Richting 2030* (2018). In Retail.

128 The train station in London where the Eurostar arrives and departs.

129 https://www.tageos.com/case-studies/decathlon/ – consulted on 5 May 2018.

130 https://www.gondola.be/nl/news/non-food/saturn-test-kassaloze-winkel-oosten-rijk – consulted on 5 May 2018.

131 https://www.tijd.be/ondernemen/retail/Spar-opent-kassaloze-winkel/9985260 – consulted on 5 May 2018.

132 https://www.buurtsuper.be/nl/actueel/nieuws/d/detail/spar-university-skipt-de-kassa – consulted on 5 May 2018.

133 https://fd.nl/ondernemen/1247643/in-kassaloze-supermarkt-loop-je-meteen-door-naar-buiten – consulted on 5 May 2018.

134 *Research Summit* (15 February 2018). Eindhoven: NRW.

135 P.-L. Caylar & A. Ménard. How telecom companies can win in the digital revolution [Online]. October 2016 [Consulted on 8 April 2018; via https://www.mckinsey.com/business-functions/digital-mckinsey/our-insights/how-telecom-companies-can-win-in-the-digital-revolution

136 S. Van Belleghem (2017). *Customers the day after tomorrow. Hoe trek je klanten aan in een wereld van AI, bots en automatisering?* Leuven: LannooCampus, p.99 and following.

137 https://www.retaildive.com/news/lowes-testing-holoroom-how-to-virtual-reality-helper-for-diy-projects/437610/ – consulted on 5 May 2018.

138 https://www.transfermarkt.nl/eredivisie/besucherzahlenentwicklung/wettbe-werb/NL1 – consulted on 1 May 2018.

139 https://www.vint23ovx3c3jzp43dw4xvd-wpengine.netdna-ssl.com/wp-content/up- loads/2015/09/Redevco-Market-Attractiveness-4-luik-b834xh210mm_LR-FINAL. pdf – consulted on 1 May 2018.

140 https://www.stores.org/2017/03/15/stay-and-play-2/ – consulted on 1 May 2018.

141 https://www.retaildive.com/news/sephora-opens-nyc-beauty-tip-workshop-con-cept-stores-debuts-tap-and-try/439533/ – consulted on 1 May 2018.

142 https://www.johnlewispartnership.co.uk/media/press/y2018/press-release-19-march-2018-the-modern-department-store-is-a-place-to-shop-do-and-learn- says-john-lewis-managing-director-paula-nickolds.htm – consulted on 19 March 2018.

143 https://www.psfk.com/2017/12/friday-afternoon-super-glue-pop-up-lets-shop-pers-test-the-strength-of-the-product.html – consulted on 30 December 2017.

144 https://www.across-magazine.com/boschs-first-monolabel-store-europe-opened/ – consulted on 15 May 2018.

145 https://www.fortune.com/2017/10/10/ikea-third-party-websites-selling/ – consulted on 15 October 2017.

146 John Lewis Partnership. *Annual Report 2017*, p.21.

147 ASOS (2017). *Annual Report and Accounts*, p.20.

148 Esprit (2016/2017). *Annual Report*, p.24.

149 https://www.tijd.be/nieuws/archief/Shoe-Discount-opvolger-Bristol-mag-niet-langer-Nike-verkopen/9903602 – consulted on 1 May 2018.

150 http://s1.q4cdn.com/806093406/files/doc_events/2017/10/updtd/NIKE-Inc.-2017-Investor-Day-Transcript-With-Q-A-FINAL.pdf – consulted on 31 October 2017.

151 https://www.brandservices.amazon.co.uk/ – consulted on 15 May 2018.

152 Question from Purdue_Pete in December 2017 – see: https://sellercentral.amazon.com/ forums/t/restrictions-on-microsoft-products/338232 – consulted on 15 May 2018.

153 Answer from MAV-DAK to the above question – same URL

154 Answer from MAV-DAK to the above question – same URL

155 https://www.ft.com/content/23d071ca-381c-11e8-8b98-2f31af407cc8 – consulted on 15 May 2018.

156 https://www.emerce.nl/nieuws/coolblue-lanceert-eigen-app-ios – consulted on 5 May 2018.

157 https://www.parool.nl/amsterdam/albert-heijn-bezorgt-binnen-een-kwartier-bij-de-zuidas~a4538339/ – consulted on 14 May 2018.

158 http://www.alizila.com/hema-to-open-30-new-stores-in-beijing/ – consulted on 14 May 2018.

159 https://www.techcrunch.com/2018/03/26/amazon-partners-with-french-retailer-monoprix-to-launch-prime-now-grocery-deliveries-in-paris/ – consulted on 1 April 2018.

160 https://corporate.zalando.com/en/newsroom/en/stories/zalando-plus-makes-returns-pick-available-throughout-germany – consulted on15 April 2018.

161 Amazon (2017). *Annual Report, Jeff Bezos' letter to the shareholders*.

162 https://www.supermarktenruimte.nl/picnic-verstevigt-marktpositie-in-amers-foort/ – consulted on 15 April 2018.

163 https://www.twinklemagazine.nl/2018/05/niels-agatz-last-mile-delivery/ – consulted on 3 June 2018.

164 https://www.ecommercenews.nl/idee-geen-haast-bestelbutton-in-webwinkel/ – consulted on 3 June 2018.

165 http://uk.businessinsider.com/walmarts-pickup-towers-are-coming-to-zara-2017-12?r=US&IR=T – consulted on 5 January 2018.

166 http://www.vogue.co.uk/article/gucci-garden-alessandro-michele-florence – consulted on 5 May 2018.

167 https://www.forbes.com/sites/nicolafumo/2018/01/09/gucci-garden-florence/#56557a0a6417 – consulted on 1 February 2018.

168 https://www.campaignlive.com/article/inside-jack-daniels-150th-anniversary-pop-up-general-store/1409512 – consulted on 11 April 2018.

169 https://www.techcrunch.com/2016/09/28/b8ta-a-physical-store-for-tech-gadgets-raisers-15-million-series-a-round/ – consulted on 11 April 2018.

170 https://b8ta.com/sell – consulted on 11 April 2018.

171 https://www.google.be/search?q=hoe+in+een+tegel+boren&oq=hoe+in+een+tegel+boren&aqs=chrome..69i57j0l2.6927j1j8&sourceid=chrome&ie=UTF-8 – consulted on 4 June 2018.

172 https://www.nytimes.com/2017/09/18/business/best-buy-amazon.html – consulted on 20 September 2017.

173 https://en.wikipedia.org/wiki/Houzz – consulted on 11 April 2018.

174 John Lewis Partnership (2018). *Interim report 2018.*

175 https://www.drapersonline.com/business-operations/supply-chain/inside-john-lewiss-150m-magna-park/7011898.article – consulted on 2 May 2018.

176 https://hbr.org/2018/02/why-financial-statements-dont-work-for-digital-companies? – consulted on 1 April 2018.

177 These are my own calculations, based on the annual reports for the 2017 financial year for these four companies. In each case, the figures are mathematical averages, either for Zalando and ASOS, or for H&M and Inditex.

178 A. Srivastava. 'Why have measures of earnings quality changed over time?' *Journal of Accounting and Economics*, 57, 2–3, April-May 2014, pp. 196-217.

179 https://www.retailtrends.nl/item/51866/dit-is-er-aan-de-hand-met-mango – consulted on 2 May 2018.

180 Zalando (2017). *Annual Report*, p.4.

181 https://www.pers.bol.com/over-bolcom/ – consulted on 4 June 2018.

182 Zalando (2017). *Annual Report*, pp. 84-85.

183 https://www.wsj.com/articles/amazon-to-launch-delivery-service-that-would-vie-with-fedex-ups-1518175920 – consulted on 1 April 2018.

184 https://www.cnbc.com/amp/2018/05/02/macys-acquires-ny-based-concept-store-story.html – consulted on 5 March 2018.

185 https://twinklemagazine.nl/2015/12/duitse-hotels-af-van-laagsteprijsgarantie-booking.com/index.xml – consulted on 9 April 2018.

186 https://www.nieuws.nl/economie/20171031/horeca-boos-over-tarieven-thuisbezorgd- nl/ – consulted on 9 April 2018.

187 https://www.reuters.com/article/us-amazon-discounts/amazon-discounts-other-sellers-products-as-retail-competition-stiffens-idUSKBN1D512G – consulted on 14 February 2018.

188 *The future of food retail*, presentation by Frans Colruyt during the RetailDetail Congress (26 April 2018).

189 https://hbr.org/2013/11/the-pace-of-technology-adoption-is-speeding-up – consulted on 8 April 2018.

190 http://uk.businessinsider.com/eggless-mayo-startup-out-to-beat-hampton-creek-taste-test-2017-9?r=US&IR=T – consulted on 9 April 2018.

191 M. Reeves & M. Deimler (2011). 'Adaptability: The New Competitive Advantage'. Harvard Business Review, July-August 2011.

192 https://www.telegraph.co.uk/business/2018/04/28/great-high-street-experiment-online-pressures-forcing-retailers/ – consulted on 2 May 2018.

193 P. Hinssen (2014). *The Network Always Wins*. Leuven: LannooCampus.

194 This graphic is an manded version of: W. Aghina, A. DeSmet & K. Weerda. 'Agility: it rhymes with stability'. *McKinsey Quarterly*, December 2015.

195 V. Govindarajan & C. Trimble. 'Building Breakthrough Businesses within Established Organisations'. *Harvard Business Review*, May 2015.

196 T. van der Heijden & B. Rijlaarsdam (2018). *Blokker: Hoe het imperium de familie ontglipt*. Amsterdam: Ambo/Anthos.

197 https://www.marketingfacts.nl/berichten/antoine-brouwer-nextail-wij-zijn-een-startup-met-een-kapitaal-en-daadkracht – consulted on 2 May 2018.

198 https://www.ecommercenews.nl/blokker-stopt-alweer-nextail/ – consulted on 2 May 2018.

199 https://de.wikipedia.org/wiki/Redcoon – consulted on 2 May 2018.

200 https://www.retaildetail.eu/en/news/m-tail/media-saturn-wants-turn-back-red-coon-acquisition – consulted on 2 May 2018.

201 https://www.cbinsights.com/research/walmart-acquisition-targets/ – consulted on 2 May 2018.

202 I have borrowed the tugboat analogy from a presentation given by Jessie Maras, Head of Strategic Marketing at Colruyt, during the Vlerick Retail Platform (September 2017).

203 https://jlab.co.uk/ – consulted on 2 May 2018.

204 https://www.storeno8.com/culture – consulted on 2 May 2018.

205 https://www.johnlewis.com/browse/furniture-lights/sofas-armchairs/any-shape-any-fabric/armchairs/_/N-5qiuZ1z1407q – consulted on 2 May 2018.

206 https://www.sofa.com/gb – consulted on 2 May 2018.

207 https://www.rfidjournal.com/articles/view?12283 – consulted on 2 May 2018.

208 https://www.telegraph.co.uk/business/2018/04/28/great-high-street-experiment-online-pressures-forcing-retailers/ – consulted on 2 May 2018.

209 *Jeff Bezos' first letter to the shareholders*, 1997.

210 Amazon (2016). *Annual Report, Jeff Bezos' letter to the shareholders*.

211 Core findings, Shopping 2020 (August 2014).

212 V. Govindarajan & C. Trimble. 'Building Breakthrough Businesses within Established Organisations'. *Harvard Business Review*, May 2015.

213 R. Komisar. 'How we do it: three executives reflect on strategic decision making'. *McKinsey Quarterly*, March 2010. The original quote is: *'Decisions have a shelf life.'*